THE LEGAL CODE

OF ÆLFRED THE GREAT

EDITED

WITH AN INTRODUCTION

BY

MILTON HAIGHT TURK, Ph. D.

WHITE PROFESSOR OF ENGLISH IN HOBART COLLEGE

The Lawbook Exchange, Ltd.
Clark, New Jersey

ISBN 978-1-58477-392-4

Lawbook Exchange edition 2004, 2026

The quality of this reprint is equivalent to the quality of the original work.

THE LAWBOOK EXCHANGE, LTD.
33 Terminal Avenue
Clark, New Jersey 07066-1321

Please see our website for a selection of our other publications
and fine facsimile reprints of classic works of legal history:
www.lawbookexchange.com

Library of Congress Cataloging-in-Publication Data

The legal code of Ælfred the Great / edited with an introduction by Milton Haight
   Turk.
      p. cm.
   Originally published: Boston: Published by Ginn and Co., 1893.
   Includes bibliographical references.
   ISBN 1-58477-392-8 (cloth: alk. paper)
      1. Law, Anglo-Saxon. 2. Law—England—History—To 1500. 3. Alfred, King of
   England, 849-899. I. Alfred, King of England, 849-899. II. Turk, Milton
   Haight, 1866-1949.

KD543.T852003
349.42—dc21   2003056437

Printed in the United States of America on acid-free paper

THE LEGAL CODE

OF ÆLFRED THE GREAT

EDITED

WITH AN INTRODUCTION

BY

MILTON HAIGHT TURK, Ph. D.

WHITE PROFESSOR OF ENGLISH IN HOBART COLLEGE

HALLE.

MAX NIEMEYER

1893

TO MY FATHER.

PREFACE.

The preparation of a separate edition of Ælfred's Legal Code is due to the conviction that the nature of this work rendered desirable its consideration from a literary point of view. Philologically also its existence in one very old manuscript gives it among Anglo-Saxon Law-Books a peculiar value. But its chief claim to special consideration rests upon its author's great significance in Anglo-Saxon Literature. King Ælfred's literary tastes and occupations strongly colour this work; indeed in the Introduction the lawgiver is plainly supplanted by the man of letters, who, even in the actual laws, often presses close to the view. To prepare this monument for a place among Ælfred's literary works is the object of the present edition.

The last edition from the Mss. (Thorpe's, 1840) gave E rather inaccurately. We print from our own copies E, B, and the fragments Ot and Bu. The parts of the Vulgate used by Æ. in his introduction are given parallel to Ms. E. Besides the Bibliography and description and examination of the Manuscripts, with a discussion of the sources of Lambarde's text, an attempt is made to elucidate the literary characteristics of the work, to define the position of the laws called Ine's in it, and, as well as may be, to ascertain the probable date of its publication.

Although our citations are, with few exceptions, independent, yet the Bibliography owes a considerable debt to Professor Wülker's "Grundriss zur Geschichte der Angelsächsischen Litteratur", as must every work of this kind in the department of Anglo-Saxon. Furthermore, the consideration of the order of Æ.'s works in the "Grundriss", Schmidt's excellent treatise on the Beda, and the paper "Zu den Gesetzen der Angelsachsen", by Dr. F. Liebermann, have all been of much use. For personal favours in connection with this work the editor is further indebted to Prof. Wülker and to Dr. Liebermann. The Rev. Samuel S. Lewis., M. A., F. S. A., Fellow and Librarian of Corpus Christi College, Cambridge, has laid him under obligations by many kind acts, including securing for his use from the Rev. F. J. A. Hort., D. D., LL. D., Professor in Cambridge, opinions on important points in Ælfred's use of Biblical sources. To these gentlemen and to the Rev. T. K. Cheyne, D. D., Canon of Rochester Cathedral, for placing the Textus Roffensis at his disposal, the editor wishes in this place to return hearty thanks.

Leipsic, July 1889.

Contents.

Preface   V

Part First — Introduction.

I. Bibliography.
A. Manuscripts of Ælfred's Code   3
B. Editions of the Code   3
C. Extracts from the Code   5
D. Translations of the Code   7
E. Writings concerning the Code   8
F. Other Works of Importance   8

II. The Manuscripts.
A. History and Description of each Ms.   10
B. Relation of the Mss. one to another   19
   1. Readings of the Mss.   19
   2. Phonological Complexion of the Mss.   25

III. Literary Observations.
Chapter I. The Composition of Ælfred's Code   30
   1. General Remarks   30
   2. The Original Parts of the Historical Introduction: Its
      Construction; Comments   31
   3. Comparison of Ælfred's Translations with the Vulgate:
      The Decalogue; The Rest of the Mosaic Law, with Lists
      of Omissions, Alterations, Augmentations; The Apostolic
      Letter; Summary   33
   4. The Sources of the Laws as given in the Introduction
      Proper. Divisions of the Laws. II—XXXIX: The Mis-
      cellaneous Laws   38
   5. XL—XLIII: Ælfreds Revision of Æðelbirht's Code con-
      cerning Bodily Injuries   41
   6. XLIV—CXX: The Laws called Ine's: Their Relation to
      the Code: Ms. Evidence; Views of Schmid; The Com-
      pendious Character of this Work; Right of Ine's Laws to
      be considered an Intrinsic Part of it; These Laws not
      revised by Ælfred, but interpolated by his Predecessors   42

7. Conclusion: Construction of the Code as a Whole; The
   Chapter Headings; Critical Comments   47
Chapter II. The Date of the Code   48

Part Second — Text.

Ms. E. (Left-hand pages) . . . . 58—134
Ms. B. (Right-hand pages) . . . . 59—67, 85—101, 103—135
Vulgate Extracts (Right-hand pages) . . . . 69—81
Ms. H. (Right-hand pages) . . . . 81—85, 101—103
Appendix A. Ms. Ot 136
    „   B. Ms. Bu 142
    „   C. Texts of Treaty between Ælfred
and Guthrum 146

General Note.

The selection and arrangement of texts and variant readings are explained on pp. 24—5. In the Anglo-Saxon texts the use of italics indicates the completing of the ordinary abbreviations, or an insertion from some other text, the only kind of emendation that the ed. has permitted himself. In the Vulgate text italics designate words not translated.

In the variant readings every accented word is included, though the basic text may have an accent as well. On the other hand, the want of an accent found in the basic text does not constitute a variant reading. Furthermore, in making up the lists of variants no regard has been paid to such unmeaning differences as those between þ and ð, an abbreviated and a complete word, or a large and a small letter. A number of words together in the variants indicates generally a deviation in their order, rarely a word added or substituted. 'Vac' indicates a word wanting, a hyphen often designates an erasure within or at the end of a word, 'above' or 'ab'. points to an insertion above the line.

PART FIRST.

INTRODUCTION.

I. BIBLIOGRAPHY.

A. Manuscripts of Ælfred's Code.

925—50. **E.** Ms. of Corpus Christi College, Cambridge, No. 173. P. 65—104, Code complete.

1000—25. **Ot.** Ms. of British Museum Cottoniana Otho B XI. Three burned leaves, reset as 49, 50 and 52—3. First leaf of Code, XXXVI (40) to XXXIX (43), and last leaf.

1025—50. **Bu.** Ms. of British Museum Burney 277. A double leaf: XLIV (Ine Introd.) to LXVII (Ine 23).

1075—1100. **G.** Ms. of British Museum Cottoniana Nero A I. Fol. 45 a— 48 a and 51 a— 57 b, Code to Introd. 49, 5.

1100—25. **H.** Ms. of Rochester Cathedral called Textus Roffensis. Fol. 9 a— 31 b, Code complete.

1125—50. **B.** Ms. of Corpus Christi College, Cambridge, No. 383. P. 13—42, Code incomplete, beginning to IV (3) and XXXVII (41) to XXXIX (43) being wanting. — Also p. 6, the shorter and p. 83—4, the longer, text of Peace between Æ. and Guthrum, Appendix C.

B. Editions of the Code.

1568. Lambarde. *APXAIONOMIA*, sive de priscis anglorum legibus libri, sermone Anglico, vetustate antiquissimo, aliquot abhinc seculis conscripti, atque nunc demum, magno iurisperitorum & amantium antiquitatis omnium commodo, è tenebris in lucem vocati. Gulielmo Lambardo interprete. Londini, ex officina Joannis Daij. An. 1568. (4 to).

Fol. 0 b— 44 a Code with a free Latin translation by Lamb. (0 b Ines æ, Leges Inæ Regis; 18 b Præfatio in leges Aluredi regis; 26 b Ælfredes æ, Leges Aluredi Regis.) Text from unknown sources. Cf. p. 17 and p. 23. — Fol. 44 b— 46 a gives longer text of Peace betw. Æ and Guth., slightly different from B.

1644. Whelock. (2nd edition of Lambarde.) *Aρχαιονομία*, etc., as above. Gulielmo Lambardo interprete. Sexcentis in locis a libro ipsius castigata, quo pro exemplari utimur; cum multis aliis additionibus. Accessere in hac nostra ultima editione leges Henrici primi, nunc primum

1*

4

editæ, ex manuscripto in fisco regis habito: Una cum Glossario earum antiquo ex manuscripto codice olim S. Augustini Doroboriensis. Canta-brigiæ: ex officina Rogeri Daniel, celeberrimæ Academiæ typographi. MDCXLIIII. Prostant Londini apud Cornelium Bee, sub Insignibus rega-libus in vico vulgo vocato Little Britain. (Folio.)

P. 1—35 Code with transl. (1 Ines æ etc.; 15 Præfatio etc.; 22 Ælf. æ.) Translation only revised. — Ælf.-Guth. follows Code.

1721. WILKINS. Leges Anglo-Saxonicæ Ecclesiasticæ & Civiles. Accedunt Leges Edvardi Latinæ, Guilielmi Conquestoris Gallo-Normannicæ, et Henrici I. Latinæ. Subjungitur Domini Henr. Spelmanni Codex Legum Veterum Statutorum Regni Angliæ, quæ ab ingressu Gui-lielmi I. usque ad 'annum nonum Henr. III. edita sunt. Toti Operi præ-mittitur Dissertatio Epistolaris admodum Reverendi Domini Guilielmi Nicolsoni Episcopi Derrensis De Jure Feudali Veterum Saxonum. — Cum Codd. MSS. contulit, Notas, Versionem & Glossarium adjecit David Wilkins, S. T. P. Canonicus Cantuariensis, Reverendissimo in Christo Patri ac Domino Domino Guilielmo Divina Providentia Archiepiscopo Cantuariensi, &c. &c. a Sacris Domesticis & Biblioth. Londini, Typis Guil. Bowyer, impensis Rob. Gosling ad Portam Medii Templi Bibliopolæ. MDCCXXI. (Folio.)

P. 14—46 Code. (P. 14 Leges Inæ; p. 28 Leges Ælfredi.) Text on inside, transl. on outside columns, with variant readings and copious historico-legal notes below. Text is substantially Lamb. Mss. E and H are used in variants and occas. in text. — P. 47 Foedus Ælfredi & Guthrumi Regum. L.'s text with Lat. transl. and foot-notes.

Proposals concerning this edition appeared some time before. Hickes as Præfatio shows, desired it made, and Wm. Elstob worked upon it. Wilkins began his work in 1716. He reprints Lamb.'s and Whelock's prefaces and their foot-notes.

1832. SCHMID. Die Gesetze der Angelsachsen. In der Ur-sprache mit Uebersetzung und Erläuterungen herausgegeben von Dr. Rein-hold Schmid, Professor der Rechte zu Jena. Erster Theil, den Text nebst Uebersetzung enthaltend. Leipzig, F. A. Brockhaus, 1832.

P. 14—57 Code (P. 14 Ine's Gesetze; P. 32 Ælfred's Gesetze), text and German translation parallel. The Introd. is here divided into chap-ters, substantially as now, but termed: Mosaische Gesetze. The Text is Wilkins's. — A second part was not published; Thorpe brought so much new material that a second edition of the whole was made, which super-seded this and is always meant by the citation 'Schmid'.

1840. THORPE. Ancient Laws and Institutes of England; comprising Laws enacted under the Anglo-Saxon Kings from Æthelbirht to Cnut, with an English Translation of the Saxon; The Laws called Edward the Confessor's; The Laws of William the Conqueror, and those ascribed to Henry the First; also Monumenta Ecclesiastica Anglicana, from the seventh to the tenth century; and the Ancient Latin Version of the Anglo-Saxon Laws. with a compendious Glossary, &c. Printed by command of His late Majesty King William IV under the direction of the Commissioners on the Public Records of the Kingdom. MDCCCXL. (Volume the First; containing the Secular Laws.)

P. 44—151 Code in proper Ms. order und Engl. Transl. on opposite pages. Text (not very accurate) of E with variants from B, G, and H. — Ælf.-Guth. is given p. 152—7 accdg. to B (both texts) with transl. To Vol. I is prefixed a list of Mss. where the designations are assigned that have been retained and augmented since. The Introd. is short.

This edition was begun by R. Price and our Code was of the part already in press at his death. Th. retains Price's work upon it.

1858. Schmid. Die Gesetze der Angelsachsen. In der Ursprache mit Uebersetzung, Erläuterungen und einem antiquarischen Glossar herausgegeben von Dr. Reinhold Schmid, Professor der Rechte zu Bern. Zweite, völlig umgearbeitete und vermehrte Auflage. Leipzig: F. A. Brockhaus. 1858.

P. 20—105 Code, text on left, German and ancient Latin transl. on right hand pages. (Latin of Introd. 1—48 wanting. P. 20 Ine's Gesetze; p. 58 Ælfred's Gesetze, Einleitung; p. 68 Ælfred's Gesetze.) Text and variants are Thorpe's, but old misplacement of Ine's Laws retained from Schmid I, and many of B.'s chapter headings are given. — Ælf. Guth. P. 106—9 accdg. to Thorpe and Lamb. with transl. From Wanley's Catalogue, chiefly, Ed. has compiled the first detailed account of Mss. containing A.-S. Laws; he gives also a useful introduction and a learned Antiquarian Glossary.

This, the best edition of A.-S. Laws, is still very lacking, especially from a philological point of view. A new edition is therefore in preparation for the 'Savigny Stiftung'. From its editor has already appeared, as a valuable addition to Schmid's information concerning Mss.:

1884. F. Liebermann. Zu den Gesetzen der Angelsachsen. Zeitschrift der Savigny Stiftung für Rechtsgeschichte. Fünfter Band. Germanistische Abtheilung. S. 198—226.

Here Bu is mentioned for the first time and the first two leaves of Ot. The relation of the Mss. is discussed and mistakes of Th.-Sch. corrected. For the ancient Latin Version much is done.

C. Extracts from the Code.

1566—7. A Testimonie of Antiquitie, shewing the auncient fayth in the Church of England touching the sacrament . . . ., aboue 600 yeares agoe . . . . Imprinted at London by John Day . . . .

The first A.-S. publication. At the end Decalogue according to Ms. E (10 wanting). Reprint: 1849 and 1875. Ʒodcunde Lar 7 þeowdom. Others under original title.

1610. M. Freher. Decalogi, orationis, symboli Saxonica versio vetustissima. Anno MDCX. Place not given. Decal. reprinted from above.

1623. W. L'Isle. A Saxon Treatise concerning the Old

and New Testament, ... a second edition of A Testimonie of Antiquitie, etc. .... London, printed by John Haviland ....

1639. H. Spelmann. Concilia, decreta, leges, constitutiones, in
re ecclesiarum orbis Brittanici, ... opera et scrutinio Henrici Spelmann.
Primus tomus .... Londini .... (Folio).

P. 354—364 Præfatio, seu apparatus R. Alur. M. etc.; p. 364—375
Leges Eccles. Alur. M. R. Angl. etc.; p. 182—186 Leges Eccles. Inæ etc.
Lamb.'s text and transl.

1650. M. Z. Boxhornii Rudimenta Religionis Christianæ Antiquissima Saxonum & Alemannorum linguâ scripta. Lugdunensis Bata-
vorum.
Entire introd. accdg. to Lamb., exc. Decalogue, accdg. to Freher and
the Testimonie.

1713. J. G. Eccardi Monumenta Cathechetica Theotisca,
Hanoveræ. Decalogue reprinted from Freher.

1727. J. Schilteri .... Thesaurus Antiquitatum Teutonicarum,
Eccles., civil., literarium. Tomus Primus ... Ulmæ sumptibus Danielis
Bartholomæi.
Tomi Primi Pars Altera (third numbering). P. 76—7 Decal. Eccles.
Anglo-Saxonicæ sub Rege Aluredo; p. 89 Synod. Apost. Epistola ....
quæ in Concilio Hierosolymitano scripta .... Actor. XV. 23—29 ....
Text of Lamb.-Whelock, with many blunders.

1737. D. Wilkins. Concilia Magnæ Brittaniæ et Hiberniæ,
a Synodo Verolamiensi A. D. CCCCXLVI. ad Londinensem A. D. MDCCXVII.
.... a Davide Wilkins, ... collecta. Vol. I (446—765) Londini
sumptibus R. Gosling .... (Folio).
P. 186—191 Rex Saxon. Ælfred, Præfatio; p. 191—194 Leges eccles.
Ælf. M. regis Angl.; p. 58—59 Leges eccles. Inæ regis occid. Saxon.
Text substant. that of Wilkins's Leges. Mss. named are not used.

1798. J. Oelrichs. Angelsächsische Chrestomathie .....
Hamburg u. Bremen. P. 45 Die zehn Gebothe, ex Leg. A. Sax. Wilkins's
Text, with errors.

1838. H. Leo. Alt- u. Angels. Sprachproben. Halle. No. 8,
p. 39 –51, König Ina's Gesetze (complete). Text of Schmid I.

1847. F. W. Ebeling. Angels. Lesebuch. Leipzig. No. 2, Aus
den Gesetzen König Ine u. Ælfred.

1849. L. F. Klipstein. Analecta Anglo-Saxonica. New York,
Putnam. Vol. I, No. 24, From A.-S. Laws.

1850. L. Ettmüller. Engla and Seaxna Scopas and Boceras.
Quedlinburg und Leipzig. No. 10, Aus den Gesetzen der Ags. P. 56 Ine,
p. 57 Ælfred. Text of Wilkins.

c. 1855. T. Müller. Angels. Lesebuch (never publ. complete).
No. 10, p. 88—92, Gesetze König Ine's. No. 11, p. 92—6, Ges. König
Ælfred's.

1861. M. Rieger. Alt- u. Angels. Lesebuch. Giessen. P. 159,
Aus Ælfreds Gesetzen; P. 161, Aus Ine's Ges. Text of Thorpe emended.

1870. F. MARCH. Introduction to Anglo-Saxon. New York. P. 43, Laws of Alfred.

1880. A. S. COOK. Extracts from the Anglo-Saxon Laws. New York, Holt. P. 2—4 Ine; p. 4—6 Ælfred. Text of Thorpe emended.

1880. K. KÖRNER. Einleitung in das Studium des Angel-sächsischen. 2. Teil: Ags. Texte. Heilbronn. No. 14, p. 54—7, Einleitung zu Ælfred's Gesetzen. Text of Schmid emended.

1884. H. SWEET. Anglo-Saxon Reader. Fourth Edition (No Laws in previous editions). Oxford, Clar. Press. No. XI, p. 51—3, From the Laws (Ine's). Text of Ms. E.

1888. F. KLUGE. Angelsächsisches Lesebuch. Halle. No. VII, p. 33 —5. Aus den Gesetzen (Ine's). Text reprinted from Sweet.

D. Translations of the Code.

c. 1113—20. Vetus Versio (Ve.), an ancient Latin translation comprising, with most other codes, that of Æ., which is given first (Ine being in all old Mss. at the end of the code). The rendering was made as the first part of the Law-Book of Henry I by a cleric no longer altogether master of the A.-S. tongue. He probably belonged to East Middle England.[1]) This Code in this Version is found in a number of Mss.[2])

c. 1150. Hk. Holkham Ms. f. 34—53. Code complete.

c. 1175. Dm. Ms. Brit. Mus. Cott. Domit. VIII. f. 107—109 b. Beginning of code.

c. 1190. R. Ms. Brit. Mus. Reg. 11. B 2. f. 118—136. Code.

c. 1190. M. Macro Ms. Beginning lost. f. 46—49. End of code.

c. 1250. T. Ms. Brit. Mus. Cott. Tib. A 27. f. 104 b seqq. Code.

c. 1290. K₂. Ms. Brit. Mus. Cott. Claud. D 2. made under Eduard I. Makes use of f. 2—4 Ine, f. 5 seqq. Æ. from Intr. 49 on.

c. 1300 — 25. Co. Ms. C. C. C. C. No. 70. f. 2 Ine, f. 5 seqq. Æ. (wi. Intr.).

c. 1425. Br. Ms. C. C. C. C. No. 96; Br. Ti. Ms. Cott. Tib. E. XIII. Two Mss. of Bromton's Chronicle, written in the 14th century, which makes use of Ve. from Intr. 49 on, putting Ine first.

Ve. was published except Introd. 1 — 48 incl. by Thorpe[3]) from T compared with Br. Hk. and M., and by Schmid[4]), who adds variants from Bromton.

Of modern translations we have LAMBARDE[4]) a Latin paraphrase; WHELOCK[4]), Lamb. with corrections; WILKINS[4]), Latin, closer than Lamb., but with many blunders; SCHMID[4]), German, the best extant; THORPE[4]) a fair English translation; GILES in 'The Whole Works of King Alfred the Great. Jubilee Edition. London 1858.' Vol. III (bound with II), No. XXI, a bad English translation, not complete. The translator wishes to show by using a large number of non-existent words, how

---

[1]) cf. B., Liebermann, p. 199.   [2]) cf. same, p. 202—6.
[3]) cf. B., Vol. II, p. 447—472.   [4]) cf. B.

8

much Modern English resembles A.-S. He proves conclusively that it is very different. His translation is unintelligible to one not acquainted with Anglo-Saxon.

E. Writings concerning the Code.

1678. J. Spelmann. Ælfredi Magni. .... Vita. Oxonii (Folio). P. 62—67.

1831—2. F. Palgrave. The Rise and Progress of the English Commonwealth. Anglo-Saxon Period. . . London. Vol. I, p. 47—8.

1840. Thorpe. (cf. B) Vol. I, p. X.

1851. R. Pauli. König Ælfred und seine Stelle in der Geschichte Englands. Berlin. P. 164—176. Translation by Thorpe, R. Pauli's Life of Alfred the Great. London. (Bohn's Lib.) 1853. — An interesting and instructive account.

1858. Schmid. (cf. B.) P. XXXV—XXXVII and p. XXXIX—XLI.

1877. B. ten Brink. Geschichte der Englischen Litteratur. Bd. I, P. 89—90. Translation by Kennedy: Early English Literature. London (Bohn's Lib.). 1883. P. 71.

1885. R. Wülker. Grundriss zur Geschichte der Angelsächsischen Litteratur. III. § 454—459.

1887. G. Körting. Grundriss zur Gesch. der Englischen Litteratur. I. § 59.

The language of Thorpe's ed. of Ms. E of the Code finds phonological treatment in:

1883. O. Priese. Die Sprache der Gesetze Aelfred's des Grossen und König Ine's. Strassburg. (Dissertation.)

F. Other Works of Importance.[1]

1722. F. Wise. Annales Rerum gestarum Ælfredi Magni, auctore Asserio Menevensi. Oxonii.

1840. T. D. Hardy. Guilielmi Malmesburniensis Gesta regum Anglorum. Engl. Hist. Soc.

1851. Pauli. (cf. E.) P. 212—240. Transl. also.

1859. J. Bosworth. King Alfred's A.-S. Version of Orosius. London. Introd. P. VIII.

1871—2. H. Sweet. King Alfred's West-Saxon Version of Gregory's Pastoral Care. London. E. E. T. S. Introduction; p. XXXIX—XLII. — A.-S. Text here. Latin in Migne, Patrologiae Latinae Tomus 77. P. 14—127.

1876. R. Wülcker. Ueber die Quellen Laʒamons in Paul u. Braune's Beiträgen zur Gesch. der Deutschen Spr. u. Litt. Bd. III. P. 527—532, on Ælfred's Beda. — A.-S. Text in J. Smith. Historiæ Ecclesiasticæ Gentis Anglorum libri V . . . . auctore . . . Bæda. Cantabrigiæ, 1722. P. 471—649. Latin also; better in A. Holder. Bædæ Hist. Eccl. gent. Angl. Freiburg u. Tübingen, 1882. or G. Moberly. Oxford, 1881.

---

[1] Useful in determining the date of the code.

1877. TEN BRINK. (cf. E.) P. 94—103. Translation. P. 74—81.
1885. A. LEICHT. Zur Angelsächsischen Bearbeitung des Boetius, in Anglia Bd. VII, p. 187—202. — A.-S. Text in S. FOX. King Alf. A.-S. Version of Boethius de Cons. Phil. London (Bohn), 1864. Latin: R. PEIPER. A. M. S. Boetii Philos. Consolationis Libri V. Lipsiæ, 1871.

1885. WÜLKER. (cf. E.) III. § 438 — 486, espec. § 439 — 452. The starting-point of III, Chapter II, on the date. Accepted by all following.

1886. H. SCHILLING. König Ælfred's Ags. Bearb. der Weltgeschichte des Orosius. Halle. — A.-S. Text in H. SWEET. King Alfred's Orosius. Part I. London: E. E. T. S. 1883. Latin also; complete in ZANGEMEISTER. P. Orosii Hist. adversum paganos libri VII. Vindobonæ, 1882.

1887. A. EBERT. Allgemeine Gesch. der Literatur des Mittelalters im Abendlande. 3. Band. Leipzig. P. 239—248.

1887. KÖRTING. (cf. E.) I. § 53—60.

1889. J. WICHMANN. König Aelfred's Angels. Uebertragung der Psalmen I—LI. Leipzig (Diss.), also Anglia Bd. XI, p. 39—96. ·

1889. A. SCHMIDT. Untersuchungen über König Ælfred's Bedaüber-setzung. Berlin (Diss.) cf. sub 1876.

II. THE MANUSCRIPTS.

A. History and Description of each Ms.

1. Ms. E.

This manuscript is to be found in the Library of Corpus Christi College, Cambridge, as No. 173 (according to the old enumeration S. 11). Thither it came through the gift of Archbishop Matthew Parker, who, in collecting from various sources Mss. relating to Saxon antiquities, took this one from the Cathedral Library of Christ Church, Canterbury, where it had been since the beginning of the eleventh century. It seems to have been brought thither from Winchester, where it was written and attached (but not immediately) to the well-known Parker Chronicle, with which it is now bound in one volume. — Shortly after Parker found it, it was used for the text of the Decalogue found in the Testimonie[1]), which Joscelin, Parker's secretary, is believed to have edited at the latter's instance in 1566—7. Lambarde in 1568 must then have known it; whether he used it at all is doubtful. About this time E was used to gloss and complete the fragment G, probably by Joscelin. Wilkins in 1721 gave occasional variants and textual emendations from it, which Sch. I in 1832 followed. Thorpe in 1840 printed it in full, whom Sch. II in 1858 followed.

The volume is a small folio; it is of very heavy parchment and well preserved. The Ms. of the Chronicle in the beginning of the volume, written by different hands at different times, is the best extant. Itself beginning a layer, our code,

---

[1]) cf. 1 C.

complete and unaccompanied by any other laws, occupies pages 65—104. It is written throughout·in the same hand. The hand is very round and large, and equally fair and clear throughout. The text remains perfectly plain, except that in a few places it is rubbed somewhat dim, the parchment being so very hard and smooth that the ink did not take good hold, and a few pages are spotted as if splashed with water. There are, however, practically no doubtful readings whatever. Occasional holes in the parchment, a few pages of which are rough, with flaws, were avoided by the scribe. The scribe makes a wide margin, which he rarely oversteps, by means of scratched lines. In the same way he marks off the lines, twenty five on the page. He puts the numerals designating the chapters generally in the space left on the last line of the chapter preceding; if there be none, he either leaves a place at the end of the first line of the new chapter, or he puts the numeral in the middle of a line by itself. He never puts a numeral on the margin, nor at the left just before the beginning of a chapter, where we would naturally place it. The chapter headings occupy nearly five pages, the rest of the fifth and all the sixth page are then left blank. The text then begins with a number of capitals, of which the first, *D*, is merely marked out very large, probably to be made in red or illuminated, which was never done. Each chapter begins with a capital from $1^1/_2$ to 3 lines deep; some of these are quite ornate, but in black ink only. At the end of each chapter is a punctuation mark consisting of two dots with a comma just below them. Capitals smaller than those beginning the chapters, but not of uniform size, are used within the chapters to begin sentences and clauses. Here the capital *G* like the modern letter (only with square corners) is never used; the other, shaped like the small letter (*ʒ*) alone appears and being of all possible sizes is hardly to be distingnished in many cases from the small *ʒ*.[1]) The dot above the line is the only punctuation within the chapter. Such a dot appears also on each side the numerals and occasionally also between X and V.

---

[1]) On this account in printing we must be guided occas. by the sense.

12

Only once (*oððe æt his swister borenre* 42, 7) is anything of importance added . above the line and then the customary comma-like mark designates the place of insertion. It is worth notice that the first three *y*'s (*scyle, borᵹ bryce, cynᵹes*) are in the old form, with points toward the left, in imitation, no doubt, of the Ælfredian original. Besides the common A.-S. *s*, the long *s* is also found throughout the Ms. There are a considerable number of accents.

On palaeographical grounds this Ms. is to be assigned to the second quarter of the tenth century.

2. Ms. Ot.

This manuscript is in the British Museum catalogued as Cottoniana Otho B XI. The volume is now a collection of 53 badly burned leaves, carefully reset in pages of thick paper and beautifully bound. The Ms. came to the Museum with the Cotton collection after it was partially destroyed in the great fire of 1731 at Ashburnham House. Originally[1]) the Ms. contained the Chronicle to 1001 copied from the Parker Chronicle, Ælfred's Beda, our Code, and part of the Laws of Æðelstan. The Code is in the same hand with the Chronicle and was therefore probably made at Winchester, possibly at Canterbury.[2]) — No use seems to have been made by editors of this Ms. of the code. Lieb.[3]) gives some variants from the first two of the three leaves.

The Ms. was an octavo volume of good parchment. All that now remains of our code, are the charred fragments of three leaves, reset, wrong side first, as f. 49, 50 and 52—3 (the last leaf is set in two pieces, whose relation to each other escaped apparently the restorer). Fol. 49 contains the chapter headings to LIII, fol. 50 the Laws XXXVI (40) *hundniᵹontiᵹ* to XXXIX (43) *weorþunᵹe*, 52—3 contains CX (Ine 66) to end. The handwriting is exceedingly regular and ornate; in shape it is more elongated than that of E. There are 27 lines on the page. Enough can easily be deciphered to show that

---

[1]) Cf. Wanley's Catal., p. 219.

[2]) Cf. above, under Ms. E.

[3]) Cf. I B, p. 219—21. Before Lieb. it was not known that fragments of our code remained in this Ms.

in respect of capitalization, the placing of numerals, etc., Ot
is entirely similar to E. Occasionally a letter stands above
another (*i* above *y* in *ʒyf*, to imitate the original) and sometimes a letter is inserted above a word with the use of the
comma, as in E. Ot seems to have had no accents.

This Ms. is assigned to the first quarter of the eleventh
century. This date is sufficiently established by its being
together and in the same hand with the copy of the Chronicle
to 1001.

3. Ms. Bu.

This manuscript is to be found in the British Museum,
catalogued as Burney 277.[1]) It is one of a large number of
miscellaneous fragments, mostly Latin, that have been attached
to blank leaves in a large folio volume. It is a double octavo
parchment leaf, which was used as a book cover and is punc-
tured with holes made in sewing. On one side of it a great
part of the text is obliterated. It was the inside double leaf
of its layer and gives therefore a continuous text, extending
from XLIV (Ine Introd.) *æfter* to LXVII (Ine 23) *mæʒes*. —
The hand here is not a fair one; the letters are elongated
similar to Ot. It follows the same rules as to placing numerals, etc., as the other Mss. There are 25 lines on the page.
No accents are to be seen in the fragment.

This Ms. is to be placed in the second quarter of the
eleventh century.

4. Ms. G.

This manuscript also is in the British Museum, in the Cottoniana Nero A I. It is said to have come from the Cathedral
Church of Worcester. It may be one of the Mss. collected at
the instance of Archbishop Parker; to Joscelin, Parker's secretary, are ascribed the glossing and completing of this Ms.
accdg. to E. It then passed, like many copies etc. by Nowell,
Lambarde and others, into the collection of Sir Robert Cotton.
— Thorpe 1840 printed variants from it, which Schmid II
1858 followed.

This is an unhandy volume, very small, not more than

---

[1]) It was not known until Liebermann, cf. I B, p. 203.

14

duodecimo, and very thick. It is of heavy parchment. Many
layers throughout the volume, which is a collection of laws,
are wanting. What remains, however, is in an excellent state
of preservation.[1]) Leaves 45 a—48 a contain the chapter headings
of our code. Immediately upon these on the same page, 48 a,
follows, '*Romʒescot sỹ aʒifen on scs. petrus mæssedæʒ* etc.', then,
still on the same page, '*Ælc man þe riht demeð* etc.', which
extends to fol. 50 b. On the blank part of this page is written
a Latin version of Ælf. Introd. 49, 9, presumably by Joscelin
according to Bromton [2]). Leaves 51 a—57 b contain the text of
the code to Introd. 49, 5 ðæt, within two words of the end of
the Apostolic Letter. — The hand of Headings and Introduction
is unquestionably the same with that of the pieces separating
them. It is round and not especially beautiful. The scribe
leaves almost no margin and gets 19 lines on the small page.
Capitals are sparingly used. The *D* of *Drihten* (the first word)
is here altogether wanting. A number of careless mistakes are
made, E. g. *Be þan ðe mannes ʒestaliʒe* for *ʒeneat staliʒe* LXVI.
G has a large number of accents. The headings of this Ms.,
excepting I and XLIV (*Be ines domum*), are glossed in Latin,
by Joscelin according to Bromton, no doubt, who puts Ine's
Laws before the rest of the code and omits these two headings.
The text is glossed from Ms. E., some words being crossed because wanting in E., and then all the rest of the code is added
accdg. to E., except the chapter headings inserted over each
chapter, which are sometimes from G. All this is the work
of Joscelin. As no erasures were made, the Ms. is not injured,
and the additions may be simply disregarded.

This Ms. seems to belong to the last quarter of the eleventh
century.

5. Ms. H.

This manuscript is in the strong room of Rochester Cathedral,
where it has been for some seven centuries. It is commonly
called Textus Roffensis, also Chronicon Claustri Roffensis. It
was made in the reign of Henry I at the command of Bishop
Ernulf of Rochester, who died in 1124. That it was written,

[1]) Full contents Lieb. (I. B) p. 203.
[2]) Cf. I. D. Vetus Versio, last mentioned Mss.

15

however, in Canterbury rather than in Rochester concludes
Liebermann from the fact that the scribe, having copied down
Cnut's gift to Christ Church, Canterbury, then stops, leaving
the rest of fol. 58 blank. — Lambarde used this Ms. in 1576
in the 'Perambulation of Kent'[1]), p. 307—312, though evidently
not in the 'Archaionomia' 8 years before. Thos Hearne[2]) published
'Textus Roffensis, Oxonii, 1720' with the omission, however, of
all pieces that had already appeared in the two editions of the
Arch. (and were about to appear a third time in Wilkins's
Leges). Wilkins 1721 used H with E for variants and occasional emendations, Thorpe 1840 gave more variants from it.

The Ms. is a quarto on heavy parchment, a thick volume.
It alone contains the laws of Æðelbirht of Kent, as well as
the two codes ascribed to Hlothar and Eadric and to Wihtræd,
of Kent. Fol. 9 a to 31 b contain our code complete.[3]) It is
written in a very fair hand, but its neatness is marred by
many erasures and numberless instances of letters or even
words above the line, the customary comma being used as a
sign. Like the Ms., the corrections, apparently in the same
hand, are carelessly made and while they often bring the Ms.
into conformity with its original, must in many instances take
it farther from it. The Ms. is to be read as it stands, as the
corrections are old ones and, many erasures having taken
place, the original readings are undiscoverable. The margins
here are of considerable width and there are but 17 lines on
the page. The chapter headings are crowded into two columns
on the page. The numerals are in red here and throughout
the Ms., where as in other Mss. they are repeated at each
chapter. There is a greater profusion of capitals here than in
the before mentioned Mss. Occasionally the old y with the
points toward the left appears, copied presumably from the
original. H has very few accents.

This Ms. as already shown, belongs to the first quarter
of the twelfth century.

---

[1]) See Grundriss I § 9.
[2]) See Grundriss I § 37.
[3]) See Schmid, p. XXIII, for full contents.

16

6. Ms. B.

This manuscript is in the Library of Corpus Christi College, Cambridge, No. 383 (19, 2). It may have been used by Lambarde, but in later days its existence has been unknown until Thorpe. Liebermann has assigned it to Essex or that neighbourhood. — Th.-Sch. have variants from it.

This Ms. is a small octavo on parchment. In it our code originally stood complete p. 1—48 (in all probability), but before the pages were numbered the first layer was lost and the fourth, of 12 pages, was bound in its place; the sixth leaf of the second layer was also lost. What now remains stands therefore on 30 pp. numbered 13—42. These contain[1]) IV (3) *oðres bisceopes* to the end of XXXVI (40), and XXXIX (43) *daʒas to eastron* to end of the code. On the page numbered 6 is found the shorter, and on pp. 83—4 the longer text of the Treaty of Peace, Appendix C, both in the same hand. — The handwriting of B is neat and clear, but very compressed in every way; the scribe, keeping fair margins, gets 26 lines on the page. The numerals are left to be made in red; so is the first letter of every chapter, the first two lines beginning back from the margin to give space for it.

The numerals were never made, but the capitals were supplied much later by a very indifferent penman, who made in red ink awkward round capitals that never take up the space left for them. The same hand inserted also in red in a very slovenly manner in the space left of the last line of a chapter and on the right hand margin a set of chapter headings, — this continues throughout the volume, which is a collection of legal documents — introducing on the margin many new ones, where B, like all other Mss., makes no new chapter and requires no such heading.

Still another and much later hand has been at work on B, supplying in black ink on the margins omissions noted in the Ms., using a sign consisting of a circle with a dash through it, and occasionally adding a letter, or 7. These additions are altogether foreign to B and easily distinguishable from it, and can only be taken into the text, if taken at all, in italics, like

---

[1]) Full contents Lieb. (I. B), p. 202.

a reading from another Ms. New accents are also recognisable and are to be rejected always. — As to the chapter headings just mentioned, although they are cited as belonging to B, it must be borne in mind that the original set of headings that undoubtedly preceded B were like those of older Mss. and very different from these later additions.

This Ms., later additions aside, belongs probably to the second quarter of the twelfth century.

7. Lamb.

Lambarde's Archaionomia, 1568: To the information already given [1]) may be added the following from Lamb's preface:

Obtulit mihi superiori anno Laurentius Noelus diligentissimus inuestigator antiquitatis, mihique multa et iucunda consuetudine coniunctus, ac qui me (quicunque in hoc genere sim) effecit, priscas Anglorum leges, antiquissima Saxonum lingua et literis conscriptas, atque a me (quoniam ei tum erat trans mare eundum) ut latinas facerem ac peruulgarem vehementer flagitauit . . . . Jam vero ne quis domi nostræ has natas esse leges arbitretur, plane suscipio atque profiteor magna fide et religione ex vetustissimis (ut quæ ante quingentos annos, uti coniectura autumo, saxonicis depicta sunt literis) exemplaribus fuisse desumptas, quorum pleraque in Reuerend. in Christo patris, atque optime de Antiquitate meriti, D. Matthei Cantuariensis Archiepiscopi Bibliotheca, alia aliorum in librarijs visenda supersunt.

This is all the direct information at hand towards settling the interesting question as to the sources of Lamb's text, which Whelock, Wilkins and Schmid I practically reprinted. L. was born in Kent in 1536, admitted to the Society of Lincoln's Inn in 1556. He studied under L. Nowell and for professional purposes took up the study of Saxon customs and jurisprudence. The Arch. was the first fruit of both legal and Saxon studies.[2]) Considering the tremendous difficulties attendant upon the study of A.-S. at that time [3]), it is not likely that at his age L.'s knowledge of the language was very great, and we are led to suppose that his edition was prepared in the absence of his teacher Nowell.

---

[1]) Cf. I, B.
[2]) Cf. Bibliotheca Typographica Brittanica, Vol. I, p. 493—509.
[3]) Cf. Grundriss I, § 14, L'Isle's preface, over 50 years later.

As to the sources L. might have used, there is good ground for believing, independent of a comparison of his text, that he knew three of the four principal Mss. now in our possession. H Lamb. did not know at the time he edited the Arch. This is shown, according to Sch., by his comment on the text of Æðelbirht in that Ms., 'Harum autem exemplar haud scio an aliud usquam extet, ac propterea hunc librum magni facito quisquis es, qui eum nactus fueris. W. L. 1573 in gratiam antiquitatis'. Undoubtedly had Lamb. known of the existence of these Kentish Laws in 1568 he would have taken them up into his edition.[1]) L.'s remark in the preface points to E and B, the Corpus Mss., as Parker's Library for the most part went thither. B contains a number of pieces otherwise known only in Lamb.; other indications as to it are wanting. It does not contain all the laws in Lamb., though it has most of them and may well have had all when complete. There are some documents in it, however, that are not found in Lamb., which might have been expected if he knew B. E Lamb. undoubtedly was acquainted with, for Joscelin had used it a year or two before for his text of the Decalogue in the 'Testimonie', the only A.-S. print that L. could use as a pattern and whose publisher he also patronized. Joscelin's having glossed the G fragment of our code (from E) makes it likely that L. knew G also. That Lamb. used more than one Ms. is clearly indicated by the words above, 'ex vetustissimis exemplaribus fuisse desumptas'.

Furthermore, Lambarde undoubtedly was acquainted with Bromton's Chronicle[2]), containing the ancient Latin version excepting 1—48 of the Introd. Probably he knew the Ve. for this part also. Br. was used for glossing in G. There is still a Ms. of it and one of the complete Ve. in Corpus Christi College. There are also Mss. of both among the Cotton Mss. It is not possible to suppose he could have remained ignorant of the existence of this Latin version. That he should not mention it is natural, as it would take from him the chief credit of his editorship, viz: his translation. We do not believe, either,

---

[1]) Cf. Lamb.'s remarks at end of his preface, reprinted by Wilkins.
[2]) Cf. I., D and Lieb., I., B.

that L. could have made this translation from the A.-S. unaided, and it is worth notice that he gives a paraphrase so loose that it might as well have been made from the Latin as from the Anglo-Saxon text. — In considering Lamb.'s readings we shall treat this subject farther.

B. Relation of the Mss. one to another.

1. Readings of the Mss.

At the head of the Mss. just described stands E, both for its age and because it gives altogether the most correct text of the code, copied conscientiously at a time when Æ.'s Laws were still of vital importance from an Ælfredian Ms. in his capital city. Probably the scribe reproduced the original Ms. as to paragraphs and externals altogether, but, striving simply to copy syllable by syllable his original, he was not exempted from clerical errors. Such appear occasionally: E. g. 1. Skipping *wisan budan* in 7 *eow hefigran wisan budan to healdanne*, Int. 49, 3; probably as he wrote *an* of *hefigran* his eye rested on *an* of *budan* and he proceeded from there. 2. Skipping one line from *zelæstanne*, Ælf. 1, 2, to the same word in the line below. Similar mistakes occur in Ælf. 30 and 39, 2. Other errors are clerical ones of small account. The text was meant for a good copy and it is such.

The value as a copy of each of the other Mss. is in proportion, in general, to its agreement with E and that again seems about in proportion to the antiquity of each Ms. The scribe of E in the second quarter of the tenth century had an Ælfredian original which he respected; as time went on Æ.'s laws lost their importance and in the later collective Mss., G and especially H and B, the scribes grow careless and a considerable personal element is introduced into the work of each.

Nearest to E stands Ms. Ot. There are very few established variant readings in the fragments that are left. These are:

Headings XXVII *monnes wif* (*wifmonnes* E G H); Ælf. 40 *monnes* conjectured to be wanting because there seems to be no room for it on the line (*monnes* E H B Lamb.); 42, 2 *cyrican ponne* is conjectured st

2*

ðonne cyrican EH because an *e* is found where *n* ought to stand. Lamb.
has cyricean ðonne. The clause, oððe æt his swister borenre, 42, 7,
found in text of Ot., is above the line in E, yet certainly old. Further
Ine 70, 1 wilisces, as HB Lamb. st. E wilisc, and 76, 2 œtfealle as HB
Lamb. st. E œ fealle, the former certainly correct.

There are many points of resemblance between the two Mss.
Ot has in I *him mon* with E. against *man him* of GH, Ot
keeps in 42, 7 *sweoster borenre* of E against *sw. œnum borenre*
H Lamb., &c. As the Ms. of the Chronicle contained in the
same vol. and written by the same hand as Ot, is a copy of
the Chron. Text now found with E, one naturally considers
the possibility that E and the Parker Chron. were then together,
and that the copy of both texts was made shortly after 1001,
to which date the Ot Chron. extends, probably in Winchester,
possibly in Canterbury, where the entries in the Parker Chron.
after 1001 were made. The evidence just collected is not
sufficient to determine the question. The variations do not
absolutely establish, it seems to us, the independence of Ot,
still, considering how little of the Ms. remains, they must make
its dependence very doubtful. Ot is, however, certainly closely
allied to E, prob. copied from same Ms.

Bu also stands not very far from E. Its variants are:
Ine: 3, 2 vac. *his* before *hlafordes* (*his* EHBLamb); 5 ȝeœrne (ȝeierne
EHBLamb); 5, 1 vac. *he* bef. *cirican* (*he* EHBLamb); 6 *habbe* (aȝe EHB
Lamb); 6, 2 vac. *he* after ȝebete (*he* EHBLamb); 6, 3 *mon* (ðonne EHB
Lamb), *bure* (ȝebure EHBLamb); 6, 5 *bið on* ȝebeorscipe ȝeciden (*on*
ȝebeorscipe hie ȝeciden EHBLamb); 8 *hine* (*him* EHBLamb); *mid XXX*
(vac. *mid* EHBLamb); 12 *monna liese* (*mon aliese* EHBLamb); 13, 1 vac.
oð before *VII* (*oð* EHBLamb); 13, 1 with 14 makes LVIII (with H, against
EB); 14 *he* (*se* EHBLamb); 15, 2 with 16 makes LX (with H, against
EB); 16 *he* (*se* EHBLamb); 20 *lesanne* (*aliesanne* EHBLamb); 21
ðeofðe (ðeof EHBLamb); 21, 1 vac. ðonne before dirneð (ðonne EH
BLamb). •

It will be seen that these variations are, excepting perhaps the change in division of chapters, of very slight importance. Only two are shared by any other text and it is not
difficult to attribute all directly to the scribe of Bu and to
suppose for Bu an original very closely in agreement with E
and its original. Bu itself is to be regarded, like Ot, as a
younger representative of the group of which an Ælfredian
Ms. is the source and E the oldest member.

G is younger and departs more from E:

Headings I *man him* H (*him mon* E Ot), LIII *man rihtes* (*he him ryhtes* E, *hine man ryhtes* H), LXXIX *he þæt môte aðe* (*he mote aðe* E, *he mott þæt mid aðe* H), CVI *ceace* H (*ceape* E). Introd. 11,3 *habbe sylf* (*self hæbbe* E H Lamb), 11,6 *æt ðas temples dura* (*to ðære dura þæs temples* E H Lamb), 12,2 *hie faran freo* Lamb. (vac. *faran* E H), 13,1 *hyne ymbe ne sierede* Lamb (*hine ne ymbsyrede* E, *him ne syrwde ymbe* H), 17,1 *ʒyf ðonne he idæʒes sie dead* (*ʒif he ðonne sie idæʒes dead* E Lamb, *ʒif he þonne byþ idæʒes dead* H), 18 *ʒetæcan* Lamb (*ʒereccen* E H), 20,1 *sylfe* (*ilce* E H Lamb), 21,1 *twam daʒum oððe þrim êr* (*twam daʒum êr oððe ðrim* E H Lamb), *nyste ʒif he hit ðonne* inserted, the clause *se hlaford bið unscyldig* being taken to belong to this sentence, Lamb (vac., said clause belongs to preceding sentence E H), 21,2 *sy he þæs ylcan domes wyrðe* (*ðæs ilcan domes sie he wyrðe* E H Lamb), 21,3 *se oxa sie* Lamb. (vac. *sie* E, *sy se oxa* H), 28,1 *ʒâ ladiʒe* (*ʒeladiʒe* E H Lamb), 34 *sceaððan ʒe hie nahwer nê ne deriað* (*sceðða ʒe ne hie nawer deriað* E, *scyþþað 7 ne hy nawer deriað* H, *sceapæþ ʒe hi ne hi na hwær deriað* Lamb), 43 *swiðe rihte 7 swiðe emne* Lamb (*swiðe emne* E, *swiþe ryhtne dom* H), 49,3 *hefigran wisan budan* H Lamb (vac. *wisan budan* E), *ûs ða eallum ʒelicode* (*us eallum ʒelicode ða* E Lamb, *us eallum ða ʒelicode þa* H), 49,5 *þæt is* H (vac. *is* E Lamb). — Less important: Insertions: 15 *hym*, 23,1 *he*, 25,2 *he*, 28,1 *ôu* H, 28,2 *he* H, 41 *on* Lamb; Omissions: 15 *he* H, 15,1 *his*, 21,1 *inne*, 24 *wið*, 25 *na*, 28,2 *hit*, 34 *þa*, 35 *swa* H Lamb, 40 *þæs*, 49,2 *ðonne, to*; Substitutions: 12 *he* (*hio*), 19 *for* Lamb (*wið*), 31 *se* H Lamb (*he*), 33 *þâ* (*no*), 36 *oððe* H (*and*), 47 *ðone* (*hine*), 49,5 *is* (*wæs*); Slight Changes: VII *cyricena* (*-can*), XXXVIII *fæhðum* H (*-ðe*), LVI *þeofe* (*-fum*), CIII *cu* (*cuus*), CV *sceatum* H (*-te*), CXII *siðcundes* (*ʒes-*), 3,1 *ðone* (*þam*), 3,2 *sæ* H (*sæs*), 8 *ʒebete* (*bete*), 21,3 *ðeowne* H Lamb (*ðeowmennen*), 22 *delfe* (*ad-*), 30 *ʒaldorcræft* Lamb (*-tiʒan*), 35 *ʒesylle* Lamb (*selle*), 49,3 *rihton* (*ʒer-*); Mistakes: IV *burh* H (*borʒ*), CXVIII *þeofwealh* (*þeow-*), 49,3 *wyrcað* (*wyscað*); Blunders: LXVI *ʒestaliʒe* (*ʒeneat st.*), CI *mannes tale* (*stale*), 10 *wyce* (*wyrc*), 29,1 *witoman weotuman*, 32 *of* (*ofer*), 49,5 *ðeow* (*ðe eow*).

Of all these variations only that in 21,1 has any effect on the sense and it is easy to see how that might arise. The many agreements of Lamb with G probably indicate only the use of G by Lambarde. Only a few are supported by H. The variations are not sufficient to put G out of the class to which the beforementioned Mss. belong. The scribe of G had an original not much different, we should judge, from E. He was somewhat careless, writing rather fast, and introduced often words of his own, still oftener a new word-order.

The two remaining younger Mss., H and B, bear some

22

outward marks of having had a common original. H gives
as *CXXI* in the headings *Be blaserum* 7 *be mordslihtum* and
joins it, with this number, to the end of the code, leaving
then a space of two lines before proceeding to the next piece
in the collection. The chapter headings preceding B are lost
and it has no numbers, but this same piece follows immediately
the laws in B also. This would indicate that both H
and B were copied from a Ms. where this piece followed Æ.'s
code. As this could only be the result of chance, it could
hardly occur in many Mss., so that a common original for H
and B would be expected. There are, however, important
points of difference between these two Mss. H against EOtGB
puts XXIII (25) after the next three closely related chapters
as *XXVI*. This change is undoubtedly on account of the
related subject of the two chapters thus brought together.
Lamb. for the same reason brings up 26 and puts it after
XXIII (25); Thorpe-Schmid do the same by both XXVII and
XXVIII (26, 27, 28). This change is entirely in accord with
the spirit of the scribe of H towards the text, for we note
often deliberate changes in phraseology and word order,
whereas the sense of the whole is as a rule kept well in
mind. B's peculiarities are largely omissions through care-
lessness, less regard for the sense being shown. Such being
the case, this change in H, considerable as it is, may be, with
other lesser alterations[1]), laid to the account of the scribe of
H as well as to any predecessor. The change must have
been made deliberately by some scribe, the other is beyond
peradventure the original reading. B's principal differences
from H, being unsupported as a rule by any other Ms., may
be laid to the door of B's scribe. In this way a belief in a
common original for H and B is not impossible. At all events
these two Mss. stand somewhat apart from EOtBuG. Lists
of variants of these Mss. from E would be far too bulky to
be useful. The arrangement of the text furnishes every faci-
lity for making comparison. Important additions to our knowledge of the text are made by neither of these Mss. They

---

[1]) See under Bu two other changes in Ine 13, 1 and 15, 2. Often H
supports E against B, often however they agree against E.

correct occas. clerical errors in E, but serve on the whole only to show the excellence of that text.

The later chapter headings of B would require a separate consideration if they deserved any at all. They vary greatly from all other Mss. and are therefore given parallel to those of E. They are not valuable, however, except to show how far a late version may depart from the original form; they are clearly ʻthe result of the arbitrary will of the scribe.

The text of Lambarde is, as already indicated[1]), in all probability not from any one Ms. Lamb. and Vetus Versio have in common, however, certain variations from all Mss. that would at first sight indicate that he and the maker of Ve. had related and peculiar Mss. before them. Lamb-Ve. give two additions to the Decalogue, restoring parts in 3 (*ðu 7 ðin sunu 7 ðine dohter 7 ðin ðeowe 7 ðine wylne 7 ðin weorcnyten 7 se cuma þe biþ binnan ðinan durum* Lamb) and 8 (*wiþ ðinum nehstan* Lamb) according to the Vulgate. In Intr. 15 *7 hit onbestæled sie . . . . mæge* is omitted and in Intr. 49, 2 *þæt him belampe* substituted for *þæt him ne speow* to agree with the Vulg. Lamb-Ve. concur also in omitting the last three sections of XVI (18, 1; 18, 2; 18, 3), and Lamb with Bromton, the worst source of Ve. readings, puts a clause that belongs at the end of 18, 1 at the end of XI (10) against all Mss. The supposition that these agreements of Lamb and Ve. spring from a common A.-S. source is, nevertheless, to be definitely rejected. In the Ve. the variations in the Introduction are simply the result of adopting Vulgate readings instead of translating the A.-S., a course which the translator adopts very often where Lamb. does not agree with him. The omission in XVI is on account of the subject-matter of the parts omitted and is also to be ascribed to the translator. Lamb's additions and alteration present an interesting question. Ælfredian they could not possibly be. Æ. would not have translated *ancilla* by *wylne*, but by *þeow mennen, þeowenne* or *mennen,* nor *jumentum* by *weorcnyten,* but by *neat* or *nyten,* nor *advena* by *cuma,* but by *utancumene* or *elðeodiȝe. Þæt him belampe,* short as it is, is an unfortunate substitution for *þæt him ne speow,* as the conjunction

---

1) See p. 17.

is changed to a relative without any antecedent. It may be that these bits of Anglo-Saxon appeared as very late glosses on some A.-S. Ms. We are not however inclined to date them earlier than the third quarter of the 16 [th] century. Joscelin's Dictionary [1]), or his collections for it, seems to us their most probable source. The same wish to agree with the Vulgate and Ve. did not cause L. to translate any difficult passages. In agreement with Bromton, however, he made undoubtedly the other changes mentioned. Many other changes in headings are undoubtedly arbitrary alterations of Lamb. accdg. to his view of the requirements of each case. These variations aside, Lamb. follows, where G remains, that Ms. and E pretty closely. In the other parts his readings are generally those of E, though in certain places, as IX—XIII his text shows a remarkable resemblance to B. He has a number of its late glosses and many chapter headings like those found only in the late collection on the margins of B. Perhaps L. used G as it now stands, with the glosses and giving all that was to be found in E except its chapter headings. Whether he used B or not, it can hardly be doubted that he possessed some lost collective Ms. too, which he used more, perhaps, in other parts of his collection, where so many Mss. as exist of our code were not at hand. But his chief variations are probably of unworthy origin, his text is composite, and were the supposed lost Ms. found we could not expect from it any addition to our knowledge of the text of this Code.

Conclusion as to the Text. Our investigation gives the following scheme of Mss., from which Lamb and Ve. must be omitted:

In printing we accordingly give E and B, as most widely separated, in full, parallel to each other. Ot, B and G are given

---

[1]) See Grundriss I § 8.

as variants from E. H is given variant from B, where B exists; otherwise it is printed in full or — where the space is occupied by the Vulgate Extracts — given variant from E. How much of the text really remains in the mutilated fragments Ot and Bu, and the consequent value of their variants, will be seen by reference to Appendices A and B, where they appear in full, page for page and line for line, with the parts wanting supplied in italics from E. Peculiar readings of Lamb-Ve. are noted in the variants, also readings of Lamb are adduced where they agree with one Ms. against the others in some remarkable variation.

2. Phonological Complexion of the Mss.

Our principal Ms., E, has already received the grammatical treatment it so well deserves from Priese.[1]) He gives it detailed consideration and in reply to Schmid's statement that it was Mercian, shows it to be a West-Saxon monument. Though written two centuries later, the Mss. H and B each deserve a similar detailed consideration. As each is but part of a large collection, such a treatment should include many other monuments besides ours, and even were this not the case, the work is beyond the limits of our space. Both show, as will be seen, many late forms, but B seems to be more uniform in this respect, whereas H retains in many places the forms of its original, which in others it supplants with more modern forms. For the fragments Ot Bu G we have attempted a classification of the phonological variants from E, which, in view of the existence of Priese's work, will sufficiently illustrate the phonological peculiarities of each. In the case of the latest and longest of these, G, it must, however, be admitted that the results are rather cumbrous. This fragment, moreover, like H and B, is a part of a collection; indeed only Bu stands utterly alone.

The language of Ot is in general that of E. Very few of the variations possess great significance.[2]) They are:

---

[1]) See I E. Unfortunately the untrustworthy character of Thorpe's text detracts at times from the value of Priese's work.
[2]) In parenthesis are forms that occur elsewhere in E.

a for *œ*, *maȝum* 42, 1 end, cf. Priese 6.
o for *a* (*o*), *londes* Ine 67, cf. Pr. 14.
e for *œ* (*e, a*), *ofsleȝenum* X; *œ* for *e* (*œ*) *cwœðað* 42, 5.
eo for *i, sweoster* 42, 7, cf. Pr. 15.
io for *eo* (*io*), *hiora* XVII.
i for *y, twyhindum* XXIV.
y for *i, ȝyf* 42, 1, 3, 4; Ine 67; *forȝyfen* 42, 7; *forȝyfene* 43.
ŷ for *î, slyte* XXI.
y for *ie* (*i, y* I uml. of *eo*), *cyrlisces* XXXII. Pr. 18.
ŷ for *îe* (*ê* I uml. of *êa*), *tymþ* Ine 75, *lyfað* 42, 6.
   îe, î (I-uml. *êo*), *ȝestryndon* 41, *flys* Ine 69. Pr. 18.
Unaccented: *eo* for *e, o, bisceopes* 40, 41, *bisceopum* XV.
Doubled-Cons.: *ð*: *oððera* XLIII, *l*: *forstollenne* Ine 75.
Also *borh* (*borȝ*) IV, *cynınȝes* (*cynȝes*) VIII, *dumbra* (*dumbera*) XIV.

A similar examination of Bu's variants yields more of
interest. This Ms., in direct contradiction of G, shows the tendency to make *y* (umlaut of *u* as well as of *ea, eo*) give place
to *i* and very often to *e*. Still it displaces *i* with *y* a few
times. Perhaps we are to argue that *i* and *y* are not distinguished and the closed *e* and *i* had likewise become confused.
The tendency here shown is remarkably strong. The variations
are as follows (the numerals refer to Ine):

a for *œ, habbe* 5, 22, (also 6 for *aȝe*) optative.
œ for *a* (*œ*), *wrœce* 9. Priese 1, p. 7.
   e (*œ, a*), *ofslœgenan* 21 end.
ê for *â* (*ê̂*), *þœm* 1; 2; 21, 1 twice.
e, i for *y* (I uml. of *u*), *ofspereð* 17, *scildig* 4, 11, *kining* 23, *kininȝes* 6;
   15, 2; *unsinȝian* 21, 1. Pr. 18.
   y, ie (*i*, I uml. of *ea* br. of *a*), *ofslehð* (E *ofslihð*) 16, *ȝederneð* 17,
   dirneð 21, 1 (cf. below *nyhtum*).
   y, ie (*i*, I uml. of *eo* br. of *e*), *werce* 3, *forwerce* 5, 1, *sixtiȝ* 19,
   cirlisc 18.
e, i, y for *y, e, i* (after palatal), *ȝeld* (verb) 22, *anȝeldes* 22, *anȝelde*
   22. — *ȝafolȝildan* 6, 3. — *forȝylde* 9.
i for *ie, y* (*i*), *ȝeirne* 5, 1, *betiȝen* 15, (cf. *betwyȝen* 18).
ê for *ŷ* (I uml. of *û*) *ȝecepan* 16, *remeð* 21, 1 (cf. *ȝecyþan* 21).
î for *îe* (*î, ŷ*, I uml. of *êo*), *hrime* 20.
y for *i* (*y, ie*, pal. uml. of *ea*, br. of *a*?), *nyhtum* 2, 8. Pr. 19.
ŷ for *î* (old), *swycne* 15, 2. Pr. 8.
eo for *ie* (I uml. of *eo*), *þeofðe* 7, 2, *weorðe* 8.
ie for *eo* (I uml. to *ie*), *wierðeð* 21, 1.
ie for *î, sien* 4.
o for *eo, forcund* 20; *eo* for *o, ȝefeohtan* 6, 4.
eo for *io* (*eo*), *freoh* 3.

èo for *ìo* (*êo*), *beon* 7, 2.
ŷo for *ìo* (*êo*), *byon* 15, 1.

In Unaccented Syllables:

an for *um*, *middan* 6, 4.
æ for *e*, *eallæs* 7, 1. Gen. sing.
e for *a*, *mæȝes* (nom. pl.) 21, 1; 23, *hereteame* 15, *healden* 1, *sweriȝen* 19.
a for *e*, *ȝefeohtan* 6, 4.
o for *a*, *ȝefullod* (E *ȝefulwad*) 2, *buton* 2; 3, 2; 20.
e, *biscope* 13.
um for *on*, *nyhtum* 8.
y for *e*, *ȝewitnysse* 3, 1; 7, 1 (cf. *ȝewitnesse* 13).

Also *wed* (*dd*) 8, *bebycȝe* (*ȝȝ*) 11, *manna* (*n*) 22, *ȝehealdenne* (*n*) 1, *wereȝilde* (*werȝ*) 15, *huslȝenȝa* (*ȝea*) 19, *berȝan* (*ȝean*) 22, *wisie* (*ȝe*) 5, *sweriȝen* (*ian*) 19 and *ȝeȝildanum* (*ȝeȝildan*) 16.

Ms. G shows a great mass of variations. The principal characteristic of the Ms. is the introduction of *y* for a great number of sounds of every sort of origin. This is in contrast to Bu. G is fairly consistent in its introduction of new forms and exhibits, we take it, the West-Saxon conditions or tendencies at its time. Examples follow [1]:

a for *æ*, *habbe* 11, 3; 12, 4; *habben* LXXXII, *habbon* 23.
æ (*a*), *stal* XC, *ofslaȝen* 21, 1; *ofslaȝenes* LXV, *ofslaȝenum* X.
ea (br. of *a*), *ȝaldorcræft* 30.
a, æ for *o* (before nasal), *man* (always), *land* (always), *handa, ȝefanȝenum* LVI, *ȝanȝe* CXIII, *ânfôn* 30, *anfenȝe* XII (cf. *onfenȝe* XVI), *andsæce* LXXXV, *naman* (always), *fram* (always), *ȝesamnodan* 49, 3; *ðan, mæniȝe* 49, 1; *þænne* LXXX; 28, 3; *ðæne* (eum) 45, (still *moniȝfealdum* 49, 3).
æ for *e* (*æ*), *ælðeodiȝ* always; for *a* (*æ*), *stæfe* 16.
e, ê for *æ, ê̂* *hwet* 24, 1, *seȝe* 8, *restedæȝ* 3, *befestað* XVIII, *stele* 28, *slepe* 29.
e for *y*, *brece* LXXXIX; *ê* for *ìe* (I uml. of *èo*), *flese* CXIII.
i for *io* (U uml. of *i*), *wituma* 12, 4; for *u*, *awiht* 26.
i, y for *y, e, i, ie* (after pal) *anȝilde(e)* C, *werȝild* CXVI, *deofolȝyld* 49, 5; *ȝylde, ȝyf, aȝyfe* 12, 3; *ȝyft* LXXV.
i for *y* (I uml. of *u*), *bicȝe* LXXV, *ȝebicȝe* 11, 1, *bebicȝað* LV, *ðurhðirliȝe* 11, 6; *drihten* 1.
y (*ie*, pal uml. of *eo, ea*), *riht* LXXXII, *rihtes* LII, LIII, *unrihte* 9, *rihte* 21, 1, *rihton* 49, 3; *slihte* XVII, XXIV.

---

[1] Arabic numerals refer to Introd. Examples without reference occur often. Forms in brackets occur in E or in W.-Sax. generally.

y for old *e*, Goth. *i*, *swyltan* 14, *lybbe* 17.

Teut. *i*, *byst*, *fryþe*, *fryðstowa* 13, 1, *ys*, *hys*, *hyt*, *hyne*, *hym*, *syððan*, *syndan*.

i (*y*) (borrowed words) *cyrice*, *eᶎypta* 1, 1.

eo, *io* (O uml. of *i*), *clypiᶎen* 48, *hyra* (cf. *hira*).

e, *brynᶎe* 11, 6; *ᶎecyrdon* 49, 1; *œwyrdlan*, *ᶎewyrde*.

eo, *e*, *i*, *wyrcum* XLVII, *swylce* (cf. *swilce* 11, 2), *ᶎehwylces* C, *ylcan*.

ie, (I uml. of *eo*), *hyre* 11, 4; 29.

e (I uml. of *a*), *sylle* 19, *ᶎesylle* 21, 3; *wyrᶎe* 15, 1.

ie (*i*, *y* I uml. of *ea*), *fyrd* XCV, *wylysces* LXXVI, *dyrnum* XCVI, *forhwyrfdon* (*e*) 49, 3.

ie, *i*, (*y* I uml. of *eo*), *cyrlisces*, *cyrliscre* XII; etc.

ŷ for *ê* (I uml. of *ô*), *ᶎehyne* 35.

îe (I uml. of *êa*), *cypmanna* LXIX, *cypmannum*, *nytena* XXII, *un-alyfedes* XCIII.

ê (I uml. of *êa*), *alyfe* 12, 3; *nydes* 13, 1; *ᶎymeleasnesse* XXXIII.

îe (I uml. of *êo*), *frynd* 28, *flyman* LXXIV, *ᶎehyre* 34, 1; *ᶎehyranne* 40, *ᶎetrywe* 28, 3; *ðyfðe* LXXXI.

îe for *ê*, *nietene* 31, *niedþearf* 49, 5; cf. above.

u for *y* (I uml. of *u*), *ᶎemune* 3.

y for *u* (uml. to *y*), *becyme* 42, *utancymenan* 47.

eo for *io* (*eo*), *seofoðan* 3, *seo*, *heo*, *feoh* 17, *freoh* 11, 1; *freonne* 15.

ye for *ie* (*e*), *nyehstan* 13, 2; *eo* for *ie* (I uml. of *eo*) *ᶎeornnesse* 13, 2.

In Unaccented Syllables:

a for *e*, *findan* 21, 1, *bebicᶎan* 23, *fryðstowa* 13, 1, *leasunᶎa* XXIX; etc.

o (*a*), *butan* (always), *ᶎemettan* LXIV, *sendan* 49, 3; *ᶎesamnodan* 49, 3; *syndan* 49, *ofworpad* 21, 3.

œ for *es* (*œ*), *nihtœ* CXVII; *y* for *i*, *wylysces* LXXVI, *scyldyᶎ* 17.

e for *a*, *orceapunᶎe* 11, 1; *utᶎanᶎen* 16, *healdenne* 49, 5; etc.

eo for *o*, *bisceopum* XV. Prob. *e* only indicates pronunc. '*sch*.'

o for *a*, *ᶎesamhiwon* LXXXII, for *e*, *habbon* 23.

u for *o*, *unbeweddude* 29, for *e*, *dearnunᶎa* LXXI, 6.

ea for *a*, *sunea* 12, 3; *ᶎewitnessea* 8; *a* for *ea*, *wyrcað* 3, 1; *bereccan* 15.

an for *um*, *minan* 13, 2.

e dropped, *wœpn* XVII, *dumbra* XIV, *niedhœmde* XXIII, XXVII.

Also *ᶎeahsodon* (*asc*) 49, 3, *spœce* (*sprœce*) 41, *œðenum* (*hœð*) 49, 2; *tihlan* (*htl*) CXV, *werfœhte* (*hðe*) XCVIII, *ceaste* (*cease*) 18, *wiste* (*ss*) 23, 1; *sceatum* (*tt*) XLVIII, *bicᶎe* (*ccᶎ*) LXXV, etc.

The text of Lamb. offers little of interest phonologically: *e* is frequently dropped from the end of a word, as in Ms. B, after *ᶎ*; in general however it shows nothing new as against the other Mss. Here again there are indications of a composite text. To a great extent the forms coincide with E, still there are many, especially in certain places, as IX seq., that greatly resemble B. In the part remaining of G variations from E are apt to coincide with G. Where Lamb resembles B, the variants from E are quite numerous, otherwise they are not great in number nor in importance. This being the case, none are adopted in the variant collections. Were their interest greater than it is, so old an edition would be but poor authority for phonological variants.

III. LITERARY OBSERVATIONS.

Chapter I.

THE COMPOSITION OF ÆLFRED'S CODE.

1. The purpose of this chapter is to examine Æ.'s code, to determine its sources, so far as possible in a purely literary consideration, and to explain its construction. We shall in so doing take occasion to compare translations and adaptations with their originals and to discuss any other literary questions of import. A word at the outset as to division of our monument. Former editions separate it into three parts: 1. Introduction [1]); 2. Laws of Ælfred; 3. Laws of Ine. The Mss. recognize none of these divisions. The best authority proceeds without paragraphing to the end of 48, makes a second paragraph of 49 to 49, 5, a third, which is numbered I, of 49, 6 to 49, 8, and a fourth, unnumbered, of 49, 9 and 10. This last is the Introduction Proper to the Laws in distinction from the Historical Introduction preceding it. With II begin the actual Laws and the division into numbered paragraphs, or chapters, continues without any further distinction to the end of the document. Our code has suffered in the past from a too zealous separation into parts, and we prefer as far as possible to regard it as a whole, though gathered from different sources. Yet, as for convenience of reference we retain the threefold division with its three sets of numbers, so merely for the purposes of our present consideration we may make the following division:

1. The Historical Introduction; To Introd. 49, 8.

---

[1]) Less aptly termed Ecclesiastical Laws and so referred to by Bosw.-Toller Dicty.

2. The Introduction Proper; 49, 9 and 10.
3. The Miscellaneous Laws; II(1)—XXXIX (43).
4. The Code concerning Bodily Injuries, XL(44)—XLIII (77).
5. The Laws called Ine's, XLIV (Ine Introd.) to End.[1])
The first part is partly translation — from the Mosaic Law and the Letter of the Apostles from Jerusalem — and partly original; it will require two sections for its consideration, the original parts being best considered first. Our remarks on 2. and 3. can be given in one section.

2. The Original Parts of the Historical Introduction: Its Construction; Comments.

Having completed his translation from the Mosaic Law, Æ. says (49): *Þis sindan ða domas þe se ælmihteʒa ʒod self sprecende wæs to moyse 7 him bebead to healdanne.* This is Æ.'s statement of his sufficient reason for putting these laws before his people, for, unlike all others, they were given by God himself and He ordered their fulfilment.[2]) Æ. proceeds, adapting incidentally Matt. V, 17,[3]) *7 siððan se âncenneda dryhtnes sunu ure ʒod þæt is hælend crist on middanʒeard cwom, he cwæð ðæt he ne come no ðas bebodu to brecanne ne to forbeodanne, ac mid eallum ʒodum to ecanne,* pointing out that these Mosaic Laws are not abrogated by Christ under the new dispensation, for He desired but to augment them with all good (laws).[4]) Then comes the second important point, *7 mildheortnesse 7 eaðmodnesse he lærde:* this prepares the way for the rendering of the Apostolic letter and indicates at the same time the reason for giving it, viz: that, having introduced the harsh injunctions of the Mosaic Law ('an eye for an eye, a tooth for a tooth'), Æ. avoids a too literal interpretation of them and modifies very greatly their effect by adding to represent the dispensation of Christ the peculiarly mild and encouraging precepts of the Apostolic

[1]) Strictly speaking 5. should be subdivided into (1) Ine's Introd. XLIV, and (2) Ine's Laws.
[2]) *Self* shows this to be Æ.'s intent.
[3]) Nolite putare quoniam veni solvere legem, aut prophetas: non veni solvere, sed adimplere. Vulg.
[4]) Better than Schmid, 'mit allem Guten zu vermehren'.

Letter. The two extracts together present a fairly complete view of Biblical teaching in these particulars.

Immediately upon the Letter follows the paragraph (49, 6—8) numbered I and designated in the chapter headings as '*Be ðon þæt mon ne scyle oþrum deman buton swa he wille þæt him mon deme*'. Only the first three sentences of this paragraph, however, are at all in the form of an injunction. This injunction, while recalling to mind Matt. VII, 1, 2,[1]) is closely connected with thé final clause of the Apostolic letter (7 *þæt ȝe willen þæt oðre men êow ne don, ne doð ȝe ðæt oþrum monnum*); it is in a manner deduced from it: *Ȝeðence he þæt he nanum men ne deme þæt he nolde ðæt he him demde, ȝif he ðone dôm ofer hine sohte*. It is as well the spirit of all law and justice, the underlying principle of all lawgiving: *Of ðissum anum dome mon mæȝ ȝeðencean*, says Ælfred, *þæt he æȝhwelcne on ryht ȝedemeð. Ne ðearf he nanra domboca oþerra.*

The author does not now pass, as he well might, at once to his own laws, or to the introduction to them; he wishes to construct, rather than imagine, the bridge that shall connect the Apostolic injunctions with his own ordinances, just as he had carefully joined the former to the Mosaic commandments. His next sentence joins on closely to the introductory sentences of the Letter. There we read: *ða æfter his ðrowunȝe ær þam þe his apostolas tofarene wæron ȝeond ealle eorðan to læranne, 7 þa ȝiet ða hie ætȝædere wæron, moneȝa hæðena ðeoda hie to ȝode ȝecerdon*. The part now reached begins: *Siððan ðæt þa ȝelamp þæt moneȝa ðeoda cristes ȝeleafan onfenȝon;* it continues: *þa wurdon moneȝa seonoðas ȝeond ealne middanȝeard ȝeȝaderode, 7 eac swa ȝeond anȝelcyn, siððan hie cristes ȝeleafan onfenȝon, haleȝra biscepa 7 êac oðerra ȝeðunȝenra witena.* Thus Æ. conducts the reader from the Apostles and their times to England and the middle ages. With a renewed reference to the compassion taught by Christ, he relates how these synods resolved that secular lords might accept a money fine for a first offense, except only in the case of betrayal of a lord[2]),

---

[1]) Nolite iudicare, ut non iudicemini. In quo enim iudicio iudicaveritis, indicabimini. Vulg.

[2]) We note here Æ.'s severity where the kingly power might be touched. Cf. Pauli (I, E) pp. 168 seqq.

against which he proceeds on scriptural grounds to deliver a severe denunciation, closing with an imitation, the sense being however quite new, of Matt. XXII, 37, 39.[1]) Relating then how fines for various offenses were fixed and recorded in the synod-books, he is ready to proceed to the Introduction Proper to his own Laws, which names these books as the first source of his compilation.

Good as are the grounds that Æ. alleges for introducing his Biblical extracts, and apt as the historical account is, that connects and follows them, an underlying reason is still, we think, left to be inferred. Only in the Preface to the Pastoral Care does Æ. express himself on this head. The same general purpose, however, undoubtedly inspires both undertakings. Æ. knew the ignorance of his advisers in the state to be more lamentable than that of his clergy. As he gave Gregory's great work to the latter for their instruction, so, on the occasion of formulating a code of laws, he opened to his statesmen and people in the tongue they could understand the ancient commandments of God through Moses and the recommendations of the Holy Apostles for the Christian conduct of life. We may note here at the outset that a very different idea of his Law-book occupied Æ.'s mind from that of a mere publication of a certain number of his ordinances for the use of his kingdom.

3. Comparison of Ælfred's Translations with the Vulgate: The Decalogue; The Rest of the Mosaic Law, with Lists of Omissions, Alterations, Augmentations; The Apostolic Letter; Summary.

There is, as might be expected, no original from which Æ.'s extracts from the Bible could have been taken as they stand. There are numerous changes and omissions due to Æ. himself. The Text of Exodus, however, that he altered for his purposes, was the Vulgate, not any Pre-Hieronymic text. This is shown not only by comparison with the existing Pre-Hieronymic fragments, but also by Ælfred's agreement with the Vulgate against the Septuagint (the original of all Pre-Hieronymic texts), wherever they interpret the Hebrew differently. The version of the

---

[1]) Diliges Dominum Deum tuum ex toto corde tuo .... Diliges proximum tuum, sicut teipsum. Vulg. Note that all the references point to studies in Matthew.

Turk, Ælfred the Great. 3

Epistle from Jerusalem is also undoubtedly taken from the Vulgate.[1]) That Æ. used a text altogether corresponding to the present Vulgate — the Clementine — is certainly not to be supposed, but his translation is far too free to allow of determining the peculiar readings of the Ms. before him, except in rare cases; we make our comparisons accordingly with the standard Vulgate text, which unquestionably answers well the purpose.

The Decalogue as given by Æ. must be omitted from any comparison of his adaptation with the original to determine its fidelity. In his chief deviation, viz: the omission of the entire Second and part of the Fourth and Tenth commandments, Æ. but conforms to the custom of the Church. Lambarde and other editors have pointed to the second Nicene council as the reason for the omission of the Second, though it is worth notice that Æ. adds as the tenth Chap. XX, v. 23, of similar purpose, but of much narrower scope.[2]) Just why he does this is hard to see. As to the commandments in the middle ages, we may quote from the Speaker's Commentary, ed. Cook, p. 337. "In those copies of the commandments which have been used in different branches of the church for the instruction of its members, the form has almost always been more or less abbreviated of a part or the whole of those which are most expanded in Exodus and Deuteronomy, namely the Second, Third, Fourth, Fifth, and Tenth." Just how much of Æ.'s paraphrase is original and how far he is following an older Latin paraphrase is an interesting question, but no evidence has been found upon it.[3]) In most cases Æ. merely omits parts, following otherwise the Vulgate text closely. He has, however, two renderings that are unknown to any Bible text:

(1) The change of *Dominus* (always transl. *Dryhten*) to *Crist* in "*Crist ȝeworhte heofonas* etc.", the proper translation being retained just below in 7 *forðon dryhten hine ȝehalȝode*. This can not, well authenticated as the reading is, be attributed to the mistake of a scribe. In all probability it is Æ.'s own

---

[1]) For the above information we are indebted to Dr. F. J. A. Hort.

[2]) That is, in Æ.'s view. To the Hebrew the two meant quite the same.

[3]) Dr. Hort kindly examined into this matter.

deliberate rendering. That such a rendering would be quite possible is shown, for example, by the A.-S. poem "Crist", where Christ, rising at the last day to deliver his judgment, describes how he created the world, going on later to relate his own birth and ministry upon earth.[1]) As the word *"Dominus"* is so often used in the New Testament for Christ, it is easy to see how confusion could creep in, and how in this case Æ. should translate the single word — there is no *"Deus"* with it here — by *Crist* instead of *Dryhten*.

(2) In the fifth commandment the last clause, *"quam Dominus Deus tuus dabit tibi"*, is put immediately after the first, changing the sense altogether, i. e. *Ara ðinum fæder 7 þinre medder, ða þe dryhten sealde.* This change is probably due to the ambiguity of *terra.* In Exodus it means "land" (limited portion of earth), but Æ. took it to mean the earth generally. This interpretation left no room for a reference of the following words to *"terram"* and so we may suppose that Æ. assumed them to refer to the first clause.[2]) The A.-S. relative would be the same, and the Latin relative, if not before him in some unrecognisable abbreviation, would not trouble Ælfred, especially as it agrees perfectly with the *"tuam"* at the end of the first clause. Æ. accordingly transposed the clauses to make the supposed reference clear.

The adaptation from the rest of the Mosaic Law may be subjected to a detailed examination to show Æ.'s relation to his original. It extends from Exodus XXI, v. 1 to XXIII, v. 13. The entire 36 verses of Chap. XXI are taken with deviations only in an occasional clause or expression. In XXII Æ. becomes more free, omitting part of 6 and of 7, changing 8, omitting 9, omitting part and changing the order of the clauses of 10 and 11, omitting 12—15, then altering a good deal in 16—29, omitting last part of 29 and all 30, but taking the last verse 31. In Chap. XXIII Æ. omits vv. 3 and 5, translating the rest to v. 9 very freely; omits then all to the last part of v. 13, with which he closes his adaptation from Exodus. From the subjoined lists of his deviations from his original, it

---

[1]) Cf. Grein, Bibl. d. Ags. Poesie, Vol. I (line 1380 seqq).
[2]) Dr. Hort offers this explanation.

will be seen that he handled his Biblical source with considerable
freedom, judiciously adapting rather than slavishly rendering
it. He seems almost invariably master of the sense and one
or two mistakes go rather to prove his independence. His work
throughout bears high testimony to his excellent judgment in
the use of his original. Following are the deviations:

Omissions: Clauses not necessary to the sense are often
omitted: XXI, 4, 6, 18—19 (with good discernment here, the
end of 19 being brought cleverly into more intelligible expression), 22, 30; XXII, 4, 5, 24. Other omissions affecting the sense
are to be noted: XXI, 9—10, *juxta morem filiarum faciet illi.*
Quod si alteram ei acceperit, 22 end, giving husband right
to fix penalty for injury to his wife; XXII, 8, Æ. carefully omits
applicabitur ad deos and also 9 where *deos* occurs again,
(cf. XXII, 20, *diis, to god geldum; diis, to ðinne dryhten.*) 12—15
entire, concerning goods committed to another's charge, 29—31
all omitted except first and last clauses. Such a commandment
as *primogenitum filiorum tuorum dabis mihi, viri sancti eritis mihi*
Æ. could hardly be expected to adopt. XXIII, 3, *Pauperis quoque non misereberis in iudicio* is rejected with evident reason.
Most interesting as showing at once Æ.'s practical purpose and
throwing light upon the spirit of his time is the omission of 5,
*Si videris asinum odientis te iacere sub onere, non pertransibis,
sed sublevabis cum eo.* We are reminded here of the difficulties
caused the Heliand poet not long before Æ.'s day by many
Christian conceptions and injunctions. At the end of 9 the
repeated reference to the bondage is omitted, also 10—12 conc.
tilling soil, keeping sabbath-day, etc. The choice of 13 to close
the extract is evidently for its repetition of the first commandment, with which Æ. opens.

Alterations: XXI, 2, *servum Hebraeum* to *cristenne þeow;*
8 is rearranged considerably, *populo autem alieno vendendi non
habebit potestatem* is transl. first, then that part of the verse
preceding it, *populo alieno* being a second time given; 20—21,
order of the given instances altered; 30, *quidquid fuerit postulatus* changed to *swa ðæt witan to ryhte finden;* XXII, 1, *quinque boves* to *twegen,* 3 end placed after v. 1 for the sake of
clearness, 7—8, for *furto ablata fuerint, si invenitur fur* Æ.
inserts *gif he hit self stæle,* for *si latet fur, gif he nyste hwa*

hit stæle. 10—11 is much altered: from *nullusque hoc viderit* is taken opposite sense, *ʒif he ʒewitnesse hæbbe*, and thereto is joined the end of 11 as *ne þearf he þæt ʒeldan;* then *nullusque hoc viderit* and the rest is given. 18, strange mistake of putting *quam virgines accipere consueverunt*, belonging to the preceding ordinance, but not translated with it, before *maleficos*, thus gaining the utterly different meaning of *þa fæmnan þe ʒewunia∂ onfôn ʒealdorcræftiʒan . . . ne læt þu ∂a libban*, a peculiar and very severe injunction. XXIII, 1, 2 is represented by a strong polemic against evil and seditious speech, that is hardly a translation, although it shows a clear idea of the meaning of the text; cf. Æ.'s Law XXIX (32). 4, in *si occurreris bovi inimici tui erranti, reduc ad eum, reduc* is changed to *ʒecy∂e*, an alteration of the same significance as the omission of v. 5 (which see). 6 is freely and strongly translated, 9 also is very free.

Augmentations: Mostly the addition, common in all Æ.'s transl., of synonyms and explanatory phrases: XXI, 10, *þæt is se weotuma aʒife he hire þone;* 13, *nedes ofsloʒe o∂∂e unwillum o∂∂e unʒewealdes.* Of more significance is *sie he feores wyr∂e 7 folc ryhtre bote, ʒif he fri∂stowe ʒesece*, a thoroughly A.-S. addition to the Latin *constituam tibi locum in quem fugere debeat.* 14, *per industriam, of ʒiernesse 7 ʒewealdes;* 16, *convictus noxae, 7 hit onbestæled sie þæt he hine bereccean ne mæʒe.* XXII, 3, *buton he nied dæda wære*, is Æ.'s own. 18, *maleficos, ʒealdorcræftiʒan 7 scinlæcan 7 wiccan;* 26—27, *si clamaverit, ʒif ∂u swa ne dest, þonne cleopa∂* etc.; 29, as if to compensate for the omission of *De bobus quoque* etc., *ʒonʒendes 7 weaxendes.* XXIII, 9, is much expanded.

The version of the Epistle from Jerusalem, taken from Acts XV, vv. 23—29, affords subject for a few comments. The only differences worth notice between Æ. and the Vulgate are that he omits the local address of the Epistle in v. 23, having just made use of it, that he alters *tradiderunt animas suas* into *wilnia∂ hiora sawla sellan* in v. 26, and that he adds a clause at the end. This final clause is very interesting. It does not come, as Thorpe and Schmid suppose, from Matt. VII, 12. It is a very ancient interpretation in the text of the Acts (vv. 20 and 29) found in Greek and several ancient versions, being as old as the second century. Here it is doubtless a bit of an old Latin text adhering to a Vulgate Ms. Such old Latin survivals in Vulgate Mss. are very common.[1])

Summary: We find that Æ. used for his historical introduction: Exodus XX, 1—3, 7—10 (beginning), 11—16, 17 (shortened), and 23; XXI entire; XXII, 1—5, 6—8 (in part), 10—11 (in part), 16—29, and 31. XXIII, 1, 2, 4, 6—9, and end of 13; — Acts XV, 23—29, including an ancient reading in 29 not belonging to the standard Vulgate text. The use, already noted[2]), of Matt. V, 17, VII, 1, 2 and XXII, 37, 39, in the original part of the Introduction may here be recalled to mind.

4. The Sources of the Laws as given in the Introduction Proper. Divisions of the Laws. II—XXXIX: The Miscellaneous Laws.

As Ine's Introduction told of those that had most assisted him in the preparation of his laws, so Æ. wishes to mention the sources from which his collection had been compiled. This he does, without any break, in close connection with his historical recital. This he had closed with the following words: *hie ða on monezum senoðum monezra menniscra misdæda bote zesetton 7 on moneza senoð bêc hie writan, hwær anne dom, hwær operne.* These clauses belong, we think, to the sense of the opening sentence of the part now under consideration, where Æ. proceeds: *Ic ða ælfred cyninz þâs togædere zezaderode 7 anritan het, moneze þara þe ure forezenzan heoldon ða ðe me licodon* (here is an anacoluthon which Ve. corrects with *reservavi*) *7 maneze þara þe me ne licodon ic ânwearp mid minra witena zeðeahte 7 on oðre wisan bebead to healdanne.* Æ. then goes on: *forðam ic ne dorste zeðristlæcan þara minra anuht fela on zewrit settan, forðam me wæs uncuð hwæt þæs ðam lician wolde ðe æfter ûs wæren,* and then finally, *ac ða ðe ic zemetle anðer oððe on ines dæze mines mæzes oððe on offan mercna cyninzes oððe on æþelbryhtes þe ærest fulluhte onfenz on anzelcynne, þa ðe me ryhtoste ðuhton ic þa heron zezaderode 7 þa oðre forlêt.* We have divided these sentences into three parts, to show how Æ. indicates three, or rather five, sources of his laws, yet the whole seems

---

[1]) For this interesting information we are also indebted to Dr. Hort.
[2] See pp. 31, 32, 33.

to belong together and its references are indefinite and interconnected one with another. While we take *þâs* to refer to ordinances recorded· in the *senoð-bêc,* yet the context indicates that in Æ.'s mind his laws as collected from them are foremost. The laws of synods were not altogether ecclesiastical and Æ.'s reference to the betrayal of a lord shows that he did not wish to be so understood. In fact Æ. seems to mean by them all the laws *þe ure forezenzan heoldon.* The laws of the three kings, though not the resolutions of ecclesiastical synods, were still both in their origin and content largely ecclesiastical and, in an indefinite way, Æ. includes them with the rest. All this must be borne in mind in noting, for convenience's sake, the following five sources: 1. Synodical Laws, 2. Æ.'s own Laws, 3. Laws of Ine, 4. Laws of Offa, 5. Laws of Æðelbirht. As to the use made of these sources, Æ.'s own statements lead us to expect that he adopted but few laws entirely his own [1]; most of his collection is therefore from the adoption or revision, as he indicates, of laws from the other sources. With a view to our future discussion of Ine's Laws, however, attention may here be drawn to the indefinite and inexact character of this whole paragraph, and the way in which the laws "of the days of Ine, Offa or Æðelbirht" are mentioned all together. As already shown, this mention of the laws of the three kings is to some extent a repetition of what is said at the beginning of the paragraph, a particularisation induced by and in contrast to the mention just made by Æ. of himself and his own laws. In like manner the clauses following this mention of the kings parallel those above after the first reference to the laws that Æ. had collected. No reference is made to a particular lawbook of any single king, and, evident as is their general intent, these concluding clauses, thus introduced, do not, we are convinced, furnish sufficient ground for the statement that Æ. must have revised or excerpted the code of each one of the kings and that the code of no one of the three could appear unrevised in Æ.'s compilation.

---

[1] It is quite likely that Æ. had in use some laws of his own before this code was compiled, whose earliest possible date is after many years of peace.

The division of the Laws has already been made at the outset in dividing the entire Code. It remains but to state its grounds. Ine's Laws are so called because Chap. XLIV, entitled *Be ines domum,* is evidently the formal introduction to the code of King Ine of Wessex. The placing of Æ.'s revision of Æðelbirht's code concerning bodily injuries, which XL—XLIII readily appears to be, in a separate section, is merely for purposes of treatment. Only in subject matter is it distinguished from the laws preceding it; formal distinction there is none. This leaves Chapters II (1)—XXXIX (43) to be considered together as "Miscellaneous Laws".

It is not our purpose in considering these laws to endeavour to search out a source for the single chapters. Such a treatment of them would be legal, rather than literary, in character. The object of our observations here can only be to verify by actual investigation the information as to the sources used already gathered from Æ.'s own words. A considerable use of Ine and Æb. is shown outside these miscellaneous laws. The examination of these yields rather indefinite results. The loss of Offa's code is of course serious hindrance. It is, however, pretty clear that Æ. could have adopted but few laws not suggested to him by an ecclesiastical or Biblical[1] source or by some law of the three kings; there are apparently not many entirely original laws of Æ. Yet in most of these the suggestion is all that is borrowed, the law is really Ælfred's and to him unquestionably is to be ascribed the whole character of this part of his code. How important a part in it Offa's Laws play, must probably remain an unanswered question. That a number of them were used by Æ. here, there can be no doubt, but probably they underwent, as others did, a thorough revision. The supposition of Palgrave[2] that Offa's Laws occupied in a second promulgation of Æ.'s code for Mercia the place in which Ine's Laws are found in what he calls "the statute for the West-Saxons", is to be positively rejected. There is no evidence of any sort for such an assumption, and the fact that

---

[1] Compare 9 with Intr. 18; 23—4 with Intr. 21; 32 with Intr. 8 and 40—41. Is 13 possibly suggested by Deut. XIX, 5, quoted by Gregory in Past. Care and found in Æ.'s transl., Chap. XXI?

[2] See I, E.

Ine's Laws occupy such a position as they do, affords, as will be shown[1]), no ground for alloting to Offa's Laws a like place in a supposititious publication of which neither in Ms., nor ancient translation, nor ancient tradition any trace whatever can be found.

5. XL—XLIII: Ælfred's Revision of Æðelbirht's Code concerning Bodily Injuries.

The second part of the laws is interesting by reason of the insight it gives into Æ.'s work as a reviser. Its source, or perhaps more accurately model — for the salient point, the penalty, is almost always altered by Æ. — is found in Chapters 32—72 of the Laws of Æðelbirht[2]) as preserved in the Textus Roffensis.[3]) Here we have a list of fines that follows in general the order of the parts of the body from head to foot. In some places, however, as 38, 56, 66, this order is broken; again provisions seem to be repeated, as 45, 49, while others that should occur are wanting. All these are meagre in expression, some doubtful in meaning. Æ.'s revision is in four chapters, but the fourth, under the convenient title, *Be monnes eaȝwunde 7 oðerra missenlicra lima*, includes a great number of provisions; the whole occupies 44—77 in the new numbering. 44—64 go in the most exact order from crown to toe. 44 adds to the penalties for an injury to the head in Æb. 36, 37; 45 is Æ.'s own, but cf. Æb. 33; 46 (ear) doubles fines of Æb. 40, 39; 47 (eye) revises Æb. 43, 44; 48 (nose) displaces Æb. 45, 48; 49 (tooth) revises Æb. 51; 50 (cheek) displaces Æb. 46, 47, 50. 51 (throat) is Æ.'s; so also 52 (tongue). 53 (shoulder) shows the same penalty as Æb. 38; for 54 and 55 (arm) cf. Æb. 53. In 56—60 Æ. fills out Æb. 54, 55 by alloting a provision to each finger and the nail thereof, a notable instance of his love of order. He now returns 61 to the trunk, cf. Æb. 61; then comes 62 (thigh) for Æb. 67, and 63 (shank) Æ.'s own provision; 64, cf. Æb. 70, 71, provides for each toe in exemplary detail. — This part is carried through with perfect regularity, as well as great

---

[1]) See below p. 46.
[2]) Publ. by Wilkins, p. 1, Thorpe, Vol. I, p. 1 and Schmid, p. 2.
[3]) See p. 14.

exactness and even fulness of expression, and constitutes, so far
as it goes, a perfect code by itself. To this Æ. adds a number
of miscellaneous regulations, most of which have no counter-
part in Æb. For 65 cf. Æb. 64, for 68 Æb. 38, for 71 Æb.
69. Many of these are of a complex character, referring to
different parts of the body at once, as 66, 1 and 71, some refer
to no part in particular, as 74.

This brief sketch of Æ.'s work here can hardly fail to
have brought to view its salient point, the strong sense of order
and clear conscious purpose that actuate it. The form of Æb.'s
provisions — a mere collection of curt notes — did not please
Ælfred, the order in which they were arranged was not satisfactory to him: he did not, therefore, content himself with
simply altering the size of the fines, but, in spite of the great
labour involved, constructed in place of the old code a new
one satisfactory to his sense of order and to his views of literary propriety.

6. XLIV—CXX: The Laws called Ine's: Their relation to the Code: Ms. Evidence; Views of Schmid; The Compendious Character of this Work; Right of Ine's Laws to be considered an Intrinsic Part of it; These Laws not revised by Ælfred, but interpolated by his Predecessors.

We have already in dividing the Laws drawn attention
to the fact that as Chapter XLIV appeared the introduction
to the Laws of Ine, and that the chapters following could accordingly be regarded as Ine's Laws. Not only has this natural
assumption in the past been freely made, but indeed all editors,
excepting Thorpe, have separated this part of the Code from
the rest, placing it then on chronological grounds before the
"Laws of Ælfred" as the "Laws of Ine". Authority for this
proceeding there is none. Six A.-S. Mss. and all the old Mss.
of the Ve.[1] agree in showing that Æ.'s code did not exist
without this part of it, and of Ine's Laws, independent of Æ.'s
code, there is no more trace than of Offa's. The evidence being
thus all on one side, no argument should be necessary, in spite
of the course taken by so many editors in contradiction to the

---

[1] Only Bromton and one or two other late adaptations of Ve. put
Ine's Laws first for the same reason as the edd.

Mss. Yet Schmid, the last editor of the Laws, not content with placing "Ine's Laws" before Ælfred's, goes so far as to refer[1]) to "die Vermuthung, dass Aelfred seine Gesetze für Westsachsen in Verbindung mit Ine's Gesetzen publiciren liess"! As Ine's Laws were otherwise unknown to us, this "supposition" may be stated to be correct!

Though for such a remark as this a refutation merely on Ms. grounds be sufficient, Sch.'s expressions in concluding his consideration of the question as to Æ.'s relation to the laws of the three kings, open a new field of controversy and demand that we show the position of these laws in the Mss. to be not unnatural, but altogether right, proper, and to be expected. Sch. says[2]): "Wir müssen uns bescheiden .... eine einigermassen sichere Antwort auf diese Frage geben zu können, nur müssen wir darauf aufmerksam machen, dass die Annahme am nächsten liegt, Aelfred habe gar keine Publication der beibehaltenen ältern Gesetze für nothwendig erachtet, sondern nur in sein Gesetz aufgenommen, was er ändern oder neu hinzufügen wollte. Es blieb Sache der Richter, das neue Gesetz mit den ältern geschriebenen und ungeschriebenen Rechtsnormen, wie sie in jedem Lande in Gebrauch waren, zu vereinigen". However well this statement might apply to other A.-S. kings, it involves in this case a real misconception of the nature and aims of the work. Æ.'s code was meant to be a legal compend. We gather indications and proofs of this from the most diverse sources. The spirit displayed by Æ. in his whole political and literary activity leads us to expect such a work from him, when once he takes the rôle of lawgiver. The purposes that caused him to strive so mightily to put all in the state on a firm and lasting basis, the aims shown in the translation of so many great works to raise the standard of learning among his people, lead us to expect of him now a different course from merely altering or adding a certain number of laws, leaving all the rest, along with the question of its retention or rejection, to his incompetent judges. More than this, Æ.'s own words in the Intr. are opposed to Schm.'s view.

---

[1]) See (I, E) p. XXXVII.
[2]) See (I, E) p. XL—XLI.

He says distinctly that he did take up into his code laws of his predecessors that he wished to retain; he expresses most clearly his preference for such laws before his own to make up this code. Strongest, however, is the evidence gathered from our consideration of the code itself. We see clearly from Æ.'s omissions and changes in his rendering of Biblical injunctions that, without putting them on a par with his own ordinances, he still intended them to be studied and observed by his people. This and his account of the work of the mediaeval synods, shows how in his eyes his compilation extended over the whole period from which any tradition of laws was preserved. And, as always, he gathered from the past to make good for the future, alive to the important question *hwæt þæs ðam lician wolde þe æfter ûs wæren.*

There is surely no possible ground for doubting the compendious character of this work, nor can there be any question as to the labour expended upon its compilation, evidenced by the revision just examined. That in such a work these laws, the standard law of the West-Saxon kingdom, should appear, seems on the face of it self evident. And the necessity of it becomes more clear from a comparison of them with the rest of the code. They are found to contain a large number of provisions, wanting otherwise in the code, yet absolutely necessary to it. In the first part we find ecclesiastical laws, laws concerning the rights of lordship, of inheritance; Æ. goes so far as to fix the responsibility for the misdeeds of a deaf mute; he mentions various special cases of assault, certain special cases of murder and two of theft[1]); but for the great mass of cases of theft, harbouring thieves, receiving stolen goods, etc., he has no provisions whatever. The omission of these in such a compend of law would be inexplicable. Their absence in this part of the collection is wholly justified, however, by their presence in great numbers among the laws that Æ. had reserved for the last place in his code. Æ.'s laws against stealing from a church are about the only possible additions to the remarkable collection already in his hands on that subject. Here thievery seems to be regarded from every imaginable

---

[1]) Viz: 6, 16, but 9, 2; 12; 22 bear more or less upon it.

point of view: robbery in general and forcible spoliation (10), a servant's theft (22), former theft of a new-made serf (48), theft with or without the wife's knowledge (7), theft of wood (44), of mast (49), of meat (17), of a man (53); then concerning a thief caught in the act (12), catching a thief (18, 37, 28), catching a thief and letting him go (36, 72, 73), harbouring a fugitive (30), concerning slaying a thief (16, 35), concerning stolen goods (47, 75, 35, 1, 46), not to mention a stranger taken for a thief (20) and the slaying of the same (21). To the subject of murder fewer chapters are devoted and Æ. accordingly introduces quite a number among the miscellaneous laws. There can be no question that Æ. collected his laws with regard to those already found in the code of Ine, to which he intended to give a place in his law-book. This is the reason that the newer part of his code rarely, if ever, comes in contact with this older part. Analogous is his course in omitting penalties for wounds from his miscellaneous laws, having resolved upon a revision of Æb.'s collection on that subject. As to the position given Ine's Laws, it may be that he regarded the rest of the laws as a compilation from sources older than Ine's time, or at least as old, whereas the code bearing Ine's name was the present standard law of the kingdom, and he therefore puts these after the Biblical extracts and lets Ine's Laws follow them. At all events, the position of the laws called Ine's as an intrinsic, inseparable, part of Ælfred's Code, attested to by all the Ms. tradition, is equally well established as consistent with the aims of the author and the character of his work.[1]

The relation of Æ. to this part of his code is, none the less, by no means so close as to the other parts of the compilation. There are substantial grounds for asserting that Æ. did not revise the laws of Ine. This is indicated by the retention of the original introduction, which points to the adoption of the code bodily; it is evidenced also by the retention in it of one or two provisions supplanted by similar ones in Æ.'s other laws (cf. Ine 45 with Æ. 40, and Ine 6, 2 with Æ. 15), it is put beyond peradventure by an examination of the entire code. We find in it not only utter disorder as to arrangement,

---

[1] Cf. Pauli (I, E) p. 165, near the foot, apparently unknown to Sch.

46

but the same subject treated from the same point of view in many places (cf. the list just given concerning theft), sometimes, as 18 and 37, 16 and 35, in particular, the same provision appears twice in nearly the same words. Compare the condition found here with the results of our examination of Æ.'s revision of Æb., and the impossibility of believing in any Ælfredian revision of Ine must appear. Only the chapter headings are Æ.'s work.[1]) We have already[2]) done what we could to reconcile Intr. 49, 9 with this fact; we will only add here that the absence in so inexact a statement of a special clause saying that this standard law of the kingdom had been taken up bodily into the code, is less to be wondered at if we consider that such a statement would be purely formal and have no practical value, in as much as this code was well known to West-Saxons and its retention complete was patent to all. Nor has, in fact, the idea of a revision found friends at any time. Schmid[3]) considers it, because of Æ.'s statement in 49, 9, to follow from Palgrave's statement that Ine's Laws are annexed to the statute of Alfred.[4]) Palgrave did not mean it so, however, for he says, "The laws of Offa have not been preserved in their original form, and we cannot distinguish them in the capitulary of the King of Wessex. But the Laws of Ina are annexed etc.", which shows that he believed Ine's Laws to be preserved here in their original form.

Though right as to an Ælf. revision, Pal. is wrong in considering, or permitting the inference, that these laws appear in their original form. They are preserved to us by Æ. in the form in which, as the current law of the kingdom, he found them in his day. But we doubt if one half the code really existed in Ine's time. Ine having been the first great West-Saxon law-giver, the code naturally retained his name, but through so long a period it received many accretions. The very condition that argues most strongly against an orderly Ælfredian revision is proof positive of a careless interpolation and augmentation by Æ.'s predecessors. Take away all long chapters and all chapters repeated from or suggested by preceding

---

[1]) Cf. below p. 47.   [2]) Cf. p. 39.
[3]) P. XL.   [4]) See I, E.

chapters, and perhaps something like the original code would be the result. It would, at all events, then gain a resemblance in form to the collection of legal notes known as Æðelbirht's Code, which undoubtedly bears the stamp of great antiquity.

7. Conclusion: Construction of the Code as a Whole; The Chapter Headings; Critical Comments.

The different parts of Æ.'s code that accdg. to our division we have now considered in order, had, if we consider the Introduction as one part, each its separate origin. The order of time in which the parts arose seems to be exactly the reverse of their order in the Code. Ine's Laws lay ready before Ælfred, the revision of Æðelbirht was resolved upon and probably made before the miscellaneous laws were collected, and, whether the translations in the Introd. were made before the completion of the code or not, they were destined unquestionably for it [1]), and the entire Introd., including the original parts, in all probability was not written until the rest of the work was done. Prefixed to the whole is the last of Æ.'s manifold labours in connection with this undertaking — the chapter headings. This set of headings is itself quite interesting. It belongs to the literary, rather than to the legal, character of Æ.'s work. Æ. found, we believe, no chapter headings in Ine. There are none to this day in the old Kentish laws. In the Pastoral Care and other Latin writings appear headings over the chapters indicating the contents of each. These are placed all before the text as a sort of synopsis or table of contents. Our headings are quite similar in form to those in P. C. and are possibly modelled directly after that translation. That they are not of legal origin seems to be shown also by the fact that they are not given to every law nor to laws alone. After the various parts of his code were in place and connected together Æ. wrote out this set of headings, covering loosely most of its contents. It begins not at the first law nor at the beginning of the code, but immediately after the translation; it includes Ine's introduction as a chapter and it leaves many a law to make one chapter with the law preceding it, without recognising

---

[1]) The Decalogue, as Wülker suggests, may well be an exception.

its subject in the heading. The set of titles thus made becomes here as in other works a sort of table of contents for the whole. According to it, not according to separate subjects or provisions, the division into chapters was then made.

The great value of this code for law and history has been sufficiently emphasized already by others and is not likely to be underestimated. From our own observations it is difficult to gather any homogeneous results, as each investigation lay in a different field. A word may be said however as to the literary significance of the work. One thousand years have elapsed since its composition; the ordinances of the Apostles were nearer to Æ. in time than are his laws to us. We must bear this in mind in forming an estimate of this undertaking. Let us think what it meant to form in that day such a conception of a code as his! The fidelity and prudence with which he carried out his plan are remarkable. In the selection and adaptation of extracts from the Bible, in the establishment of an historical connection between them and his laws, in the selection of the various laws to add to his conscientious revision of Ædelbirht and to the code already in his hands, Æ. displayed his for that time remarkable learning and his for all time admirable traits of mind, literary taste and judgment combined with political foresight. Yet to the largeness and worthiness of Æ.'s idea of a legal compend covering all human history the greatest recognition is due. The work itself is small, but it bears testimony to the greatness of its author.

Chapter II.
THE DATE OF THE CODE.

The question of the order in time of Ælfred's literary productions has had to be treated with practically no aid from direct testimony of any sort; to this fact, no doubt, is due the great difference of opinion on this point that has long subsisted. Pauli [1]) and Bosworth [1]) give the arrangement: Boethius, Beda,

---

[1]) See p. 8.

Orosius, Pastoral Care, referring to W^m of Malmesbury's [1]) remark
that the text of Boet. was glossed or explained for Æ. by Asser.
Ten Brink [2]), without mentioning his reasons, adopts the order:
Oros., Beda, Boet., P. C. A new light was thrown upon this
matter by the first detailed investigation of it, that of Wülker
in the Grundriss.[2]) Here the place of P. C. at the head of the
list is attested by expressions in Æ.'s preface, and that of Boet.
at the end by his additions to the text. Wülker further draws
attention to the varying relation of the rendering to the original,
and points out that a free treatment of the matter at hand
indicates increased literary experience. Thus Handbook, P. C.,
Beda and Oros. are put in the first period of peace, before 893,
while Boet., with the Soliloquies and 'De videndo Deo', is
assigned to the closing years of Æ.'s life, 897—901.

The arguments here offered and the conclusions reached
have justly commended themselves to those that have since had
occasion to deal with this question: Schilling [3]), Ebert, Körting,
Wichmann [4]) and Schmidt have in turn accepted them. Schilling
and Schmidt indeed have done more: their detailed examinations
of the relation between the A.-S. and Latin texts of Oros. and
Beda respectively have furnished strong confirmation of the
order given, which now seems as well established as such a
hypothesis can be. The character of each of the great translations is now definitely ascertained. In the P. C., which Æ.
in the preface declares to have been written by him as he
learned the meaning of the Latin from four clerical assistants,
words are treated quite freely, but each clause is translated
without any attempt at adaptation of the matter given. This
agrees well with Æ.'s statements. Not yet master of the Latin,
he could not give exact translations nor did he yet feel equal
to altering or handling freely the work before him. Although,
as Sweet [5]) says, P. C. is not a translation in our sense of the
term, neither is it an adaptation; it is a careful 'rendering·
of the sense of the Latin original. Beda, however, as Schmidt

---

[1]) See p. 8, Hardy, II, 122.   [2]) See p. 9.   [3]) For all these, see p. 9.
[4]) Wichmann adds to the list of Æ.'s works the doubtful 'Psalms',
which, on internal evidence as well as on W^m of Malmesbury's testimony,
he considers Æ.'s last production.
[5]) See p. 8.

shows [1]), is for the most part a remarkably literal translation. A large number of chapters, however, are omitted altogether, for which there is often some reason discernible [2]); there are also smaller omissions, alterations, condensations, but (a fact often remarked and lamented) only very slight attempts to add anything from the king's knowledge of the subject. The actual translation is generally far more literal than P. C. [3]), the work as a whole, however, is much more freely treated: apparently Æ. now understands, as he ought, the Latin much better, while his omissions make the first approach to the perfect freedom of adaptation which separates Oros., and still more Boet., from the other works.

In adopting the order given we have, unfortunately, but gained a basis for our consideration; the Laws have not been included in any actual investigations; in the 'Grundriss' alone are they given a definite place in a list of Æ.'s works. The reason is, of course, that this code has not, heretofore, been generally considered except in its place among A.-S. laws. In attempting a consideration of the question we must confess at the outset that its results, like the material at hand for it, are likely to be meagre and unsatisfactory. This work differs from those discussed in being for the most part original; it lacks too any allusions that might help to determine the date. We are confined, then, to general observations as to the subject of the work, to a search for possible allusions to it in other works, and to the comparison of its fragment of translation (in the Introduction) and its general literary tenour with the conditions noted in the other works.

No value can be attached to W[m.] of Malmesbury's statement that Æ. made laws amid the tumults of war.[4]) As Pauli and others have said, this code cannot have been made during actual war; it is a work of peace and its provisions are for a people at peace. Nor was this Code published immediately after peace was declared: whether or not Æ. gave some laws

---

[1]) Cf. p. 46 in Schmidt's work.
[2]) Cf. pp. 15—19 in Schmidt.
[3]) Cf. Schmidt, pp. 47—56.
[4]) Ille inter fremitus armorum et stridores lituorum leges tulit. See p. 8, Hardy (II, 122).

in the interim, this code cannot have been made before he
began his literary labours, of which the extracts from the Vulgate
were a fruit. The beginning of these labours is set- at Asser's
first visit in 887. To be sure, the Decalogue had probably
been rendered into A.-S. before Æ., but the rest was certainly
made by Æ. for these laws. This is shown [1]), for example, by
omissions in XXI, 22, XXIII, 3 and 5, by alterations in XXI, 2
and 30, XXII, 1, XXIII, 1, 2, etc.; indeed the whole character
of the translation attests this beyond peradventure. Such a
work of translation cannot have been undertaken by Æ. before
Asser's visit.

This conclusion brings us to the consideration of the by
no means insignificant argument from the subject of the work,
viz: that a code of laws ought properly to precede any other
of Æ.'s works, because of the much greater need of it, a need
that Æ., alive to less evident wants of his kingdom, should
have been the first to feel. This argument, in its bearing on
our code, is somewhat modified in effect by the fact just adduced that this work could not have been completed until some
years of peace had passed. If Æ. had waited so long, a year
more or less could hardly matter to him. Still when once Æ.
set himself to literarv tasks, a law-code should still have been
his first thought, and we may with propriety resolve to put
the code as near the beginning as other considerations permit.
On this ground, we take it, Wülker [2]) gives our code a place
between the Handbook and the P. C., thus making it the first
of Æ.'s extant works.

Our search for allusions to the Laws in Æ.'s other works
yields but little. In the oft-quoted Preface to P. C., Æ. dwells
at length upon the various translations of the Law (sio æ, the
Pentateuch): how it and the other books were translated from
Hebrew into Greek and Latin and how afterwards many other
Christian (i. e. Germanic) nations rendered them into their own
tongue. This seems to show that Æ.'s mind was then on such
work as he did for our Code, but it must he remembered that
the translations lately made in the Handbook may well have

[1]) Cf. pp. 36—37, and Text.
[2]) Grundriss, p. 398, foot-note.

4*

covered similar ground. Moreover, we can hardly say whether this would point to earlier or later work on the Laws, though we should incline to consider it indicative of the formation of the plan merely; were our Code with its Introduction already completed, it might well have received more definite notice in this place. Another possible allusion is brought forward by Schmidt's work. Having previously shown how Æ. was accustomed to alter statements introduced in the original by *usque hodie, hactenus,* and the like, to conform them to the facts as in his time, Sch. finds certain such passages literally translated.[1]) This he believes to have been done in many cases because the statement was still true in Æ.'s time: among these "Fälle, in welchen man mit ziemlicher Sicherheit behaupten kann, dass Æ. wörtlich übersetzte, weil er aus eigener Kenntnis oder durch Mitteilungen anderer wusste, dass die geschilderten Verhältnisse noch fortbestanden", appears the following: *Qui (Aedilberct) inter cetera bona, quae genti suae consulendo conferebat, etiam decreta illi iudiciorum, iuxta exempla Romanorum, cum consilio sapientium constituit; quae conscripta Anglorum sermone hactenus habentur et obseruantur ab ea.* II, 5. — *Se cyning (Æþelbyrht) betwih ða oþre ʒod ðe he his leodum ðurh ʒeþeaht ʒefremede, eac swylce he rihtra doma ʒesetnesse mid snotera ʒeþeahte ʒesette æfter Romana bysena ond ða het on enʒlisc awritan ða nu ʒena oþ ðis mid him hæfde ond ʒehealdene synd.* 506[25]. — If we concur, as there is every reason to do, in Schmidt's view that Æ. intentionally translated this as it stood, then it seems to indicate not only that Æ. was acquainted with Æb.'s laws, but that he knew them to be still in use, a fact well explained by the existence of our code, with its adaptation of a great part of them. This conjecture would, of course, put the Code before Beda.

Both these possible allusions would place the Laws near the beginning of Æ.'s literary labours, thus agreeing with the conclusion reached at the outset by a consideration of the subject and nature of the work. We must now endeavour to bring the matter, so far as possible, to a final determination by a consideration of the general literary character of the work,

---

[1]) Cf. Schmidt, p. 57.

and of the results of our comparison of the translated part with its original. At the close of the preceding chapter and at various points throughout it [1]), we have drawn attention to the skill with which Æ. handles the component parts of his code, shaping and adapting them to his purpose, and welding them together in a coherent whole. The work done here is far in advance of anything in other A.-S. codes. It leads us to look for a man of some literary experience, as well as natural talent. Extensive as it is, the P. C. exhibits little, if anything, of this sort. Though, of course, the author of P. C. might at that time have been in a position to do such work as this, still Æ. appears on the face of the matter to have been working then on a somewhat lower plane. Not until the Preface, written after the translation was completed, does he give proof of any literary skill, and here too there is nothing that can be said to excel the Introduction to the Laws, which might well have followed after a short time.

The condition of matters with regard to the translation is much the same. We find here a clear advance toward the Beda. There are discernible in our Introd. the two marks that distinguish that work from P. C., viz: general adherence to the words of the text, and occasional freedom in adapting the matter. As to the first point, the beginning of Chap. XXI and many other passages may be compared with Schmidt's instances from Beda [2]), which they at least approach. Here and in regard to the next point, we must not forget the great difference in size between the two translations. To show occasional adaptation, however, the changes [3]) in XXI, 2, 30, in XXII, 1, 7—8, and in XXIII, 4, and as well the omissions in XXI, 9—10, in XXII, 8, and in XXIII, 3, 5, may be put in evidence. They differ only in number and variety from those cited from the greater work [4]); the spirit is the same in both. In respect of augmentation, indeed, our work [5]) shows little

---

[1]) Cf. pp. 31, 32, 33, 36, 42.
[2]) Cf. Schmidt, pp. 50 seqq.
[3]) Cf. pp. 36—37 and Text.
[4]) Cf. Sch., pp. 19—24.
[5]) Cf. p. 37.

54

more than the same use of synomyms with P. C.[1]), exhibiting no
independent additions; Beda[2]), however, is little in advance
here. In other respects we have certainly been able to note
a difference between the Laws and P. C. Other causes than
increase in experience might explain such a change; in the
absence, however, of any other evident reason, we cannot but
ascribe it to some difference in time.

The conclusion from our literary examination is, then, that
the Laws come after P. C. In adopting this result, we follow
other indications at the expense of the argument that the Laws,
as the most necessary work, should naturally have come first.
But as we have already shown, the weight of this argument
is not great, when a small difference of time is in question.
Then too, Æ. had Ine's Laws and probably some of his own
already at hand. In the Introduction (49, 9 and 10) he tells·
us he prefers the old Laws, and shows that he regards his
own work as one of compilation and revision, saying nothing,
moreover, as Ine does, of the need for laws in his kingdom.
On the other hand, in P. C. he speaks most seriously of the
great demand for such a work to enlighten the shepherds of
his people. In view of all this, perhaps our Law-book seemed
at the time no more pressing a necessity than the other —
the code that was to help spiritual leaders in guiding men
aright.

We have no wish to put the Laws any later than this.
Not to mention the possible allusion to the Code in Beda, there
is no evidence which, in view of the consideration just discussed, should place it farther from the beginning of Æ.'s
labours, to the earlier stages of which it no doubt belongs.
Evidently Æ. had much of this work already at hand. The
plan of the Introd. he may have had in mind when he wrote
the Preface to P. C.; at all events, as already remarked[3]), it
is a result of the same educational purpose that animates the

---

1) Cf. Sweet (I, F), p. XLI.
2) Cf. Sch., pp. 30 seqq., also 37.
3) Cf. p. 33.

earlier work and is so earnestly expressed in the Preface. If we suppose the Introd. to have been prepared shortly after this, the publication of the completed Code may be set in the year 890. This seems a fair conclusion from the facts before us: it must, however, be remembered that the materials gathered for this work are inadequate to its final accomplishment, and that our conclusion is at best but a careful conjecture.

PART SECOND.

TEXT.

MANUSCRIPT E.

I. Be ðon þæt mon ne scyle oþrum deman buton swa he wille þæt him mon deme.

II. Be aþum 7 be weddum.

III. Be circena socnum.

IIII. Be borʒ bryce.

V. Be hlaford searwe.

VI. Be circena friðe.

VII. Be circan stale.

VIII. Be ðon þe mon on cynʒes healle feohte.

VIIII. Be nunnan hæmede.

X. Be bearn eacnum wife ofslæʒenum.

XI. Be twelfhyndes monnes wife forleʒenum.

XII. Be cirliscre fæmnan onfenʒe.

XIII. Be wudu bærnette.

XIIII. Be dumbera monna dǽdum.

XV. Be þam monnum þe beforan biscopum feohtað.

XVI. Be nunnena onfenʒe.

XVII. Be ðam monnum þe heora wæpen to monslyhte lænað.

XVIII. Be ðam þe munecum heora feoh buton leafe befæstað.

XVIIII. Be preosta ʒefeohte.

XX. Be eofetes andetlan.

XXI. Be hundes slite.

XXII. Be nietena misdædum.

XXIII. Be ceorles mennenes niedhæmede.

In red above: þis syndon þa domas ðe ælfred cyncʒ ʒeceas H |
I. ðam H | man GH | scule H | dêman H | butan GH | man him GH |
III. cyricena G | IV. borh Ot, burh GH | V. over searwe small but old
swice H | VI. cyricena G | fryþe G | VII. cyricena G, circean H | VIII. þon
þæt G, þam ðe H | man G | cyninʒes OtG, kyninʒes H | ʒefeohte, ʒe
above H | X. eac-num H | ofsleʒenum Ot, ofslaʒenum GH | XI.
.XII. hyndes G | mannes GH | XII. cirilscre Ot, cyrliscre G | an-

MANUSCRIPT B.

(These Headings are found on the margins of B,
which begins in the middle of IIII.)

Be cyninᵹes swicdome.
Be ciricene friðe.
Be ðam ðe steleð on ciric*ean.*
Be ðam þæt man feohteð on kyninᵹes healle.
Be ðam þe nunnan of mynstre utalædeð.
Be ðam ðæt man ofslea wif mid cilde.
Be hæmed ðinᵹu*m.*
Eft.
Be wude benete 7 Gif man afylled bið on ᵹemænu*m* weorce.
Be du*m*bra manna dædu*m.*
Be ðam þæt man toforan b*isceope* feohteð.
Be ðam ᵹif man of myran folan adrifþ oððe cu cealf.
Ðe oðru*m* his unmaᵹu ætfæsteð.
Be nunnena andfencᵹu*m.*
Be þam þe heore wepna lænað to manslihte.
Be þam þe munecan heore feoh befæstað.
Be preosta ᵹefeohte.
Be cyninᵹes ᵹerefan ðyfðe.
Be hundes slite.
Be nytena misdædu*m.*
Be ceorles me*n*nenes nydhemede.

---

fenᵹe G, onfænᵹe H | XIII. wuda H | XIV. du*m*bra OtGH, r above
H | manna GH | XV. ðan G | mannum GH | bisceopum OtG, biscope
H | XVI. anfenᵹum H | XVII. mannum GH | hiora, hi ab. Ot, hyra G |
wæpn G, wæpna H | monslihte G, manslyhte H | XVIII. þe man above
H | butan GH | befestað G | XX. ðeofes H | 7 detlan G, andettan H |
XXI. slyte Ot | XXII. nytena GH | XXIII, in H XXVI. ciorles H |
mennen H | niedhæmde G, nydhæmede H |

60

XXIIII. Be twyhyndum men æt hloþslyhte.
XXV. Be syx hyndum men.
XXVI. Be .XII. hyndum men.
XXVII. Be unȝewintredes wifmonnes ned hæmde.
XXVIII. Be swa ȝerades monnes sleȝe.
XXVIIII. Be folcleasunȝe ȝewyrhtum.
XXX. Be ȝod borȝum.
XXXI. Be ciepe monnum.
XXXII. Be cierlisces monnes byndellan.
XXXIII. Be speres ȝemeleasnesse.
XXXIIII. Be bold ȝetale.
XXXV. Be ðon ðe mon beforan ealdormen on ȝemote ȝe-
feohte.
XXXVI. Be cierlisces monnes flet ȝefeohte.

XXXVII. Be bôclondum.
XXXVIII. Be fæhðe.
XXXVIIII. Be mæsse daȝa freolse.
XL. Be heafod wunde.
XLI. Be feax wunde.
XLII. Be ear sleȝe.
XLIII. Be monnes eaȝwunde 7 oðerra missenlicra lima.
XLIIII. Be ines domum.
XLV. Be ȝodes ðeowa reȝole.
XLVI. Be cildum.
XLVII. Be sunnan dæȝes weorcum.
XLVIII. Be ciric sceattum.
XLVIIII. Be ciric sôcnum.
L. Be ȝefeohtum.
LI. Be stale.
LII. Be ryhtes bene.
LIII. Be ðam wrecendan ær he him ryhtes bidde.
LIIII. Be reaflace.

XXIV, in H XXIII. twyhindum Ot | slihte GH | — End of p. 65 in E |
XXV, in H XXIV | XXVI, in H XXV. twelf Ot | XXVII. tynȝewintredes
H | monnes wif Ot, wifmannes GH | niedhæmde G, nydhæmede H | XXVIII.
mannes GH | sleȝes G, slæȝe H | XXIX. leasunȝa G | XXXI. cypemannum
G, cyp-mannum H | XXXII. cyrlisces OtG | mannes GH | byndelan H |
XXXIII. ȝymeleasnesse GH | XXXV. þam GH | man GH | ealder H |
ȝemôte H | feohte H | XXXVI. cyrlisces G | mannes GH | flett H |

Be twyhyndu*m* men æt hloðslihte.
Be sixhyndu*m* m*en*.
Be twylfhendu*m* m*en*.
Be un*z*ewintrede wif mannes sla*z*e.

Be *z*odborh*z*um.
Be cypmannum.
Be ceorlisces mannes bindelan.
Be speres *z*ymeleaste.
Be bold *z*etale.
Be ða*m* ðe beforan aldorm*en* on *z*emote feohte.
Eft.
Be cyrlisces monnes flette *z*efeohte.
Be burhbryce.
Be boclande.

(Leaf wanting.)

Be heafodwunde 7 oðre liman. ” ”

Ines La*z*e.

Be ciric sceatte.
Be ciric socnu*m*.
Be *z*efeohtu*m*.
Be stale.
Be rihtes bene.
Be þa*m* wrecendan.
Be reaflace.

XXXVII. boclandum GH | XXXVIII. fæhðum G, fahþum H | XXXIX. freolsum H | XLII. earslæ*z*e H | XLIII. mannes GH | ea*z*ena wunde, ena above H | oððera Ot, oðra G, oðre H | mislicra G, mistlicra, t above H | XLIV. înes G | XLV. re*z*ule H | XLVII. wyrcum G | XLVIII. cyricsceatum G | XLIX. cyric G | — End of p. 66 in E — | LII. rihtes GH | LIII. he above line, appar. new E | man rihtes, vac. him G, hine man ryhtes H | — End of first fragment of Ot — |

LV. Be ðam monnum þe hiora ʒelondan bebycʒʒað.

LVI. Be ʒefonʒenum ðeofum.

LVII. Be ðam ðe hiora ʒewitnessa beforan biscope âleoʒað.

LVIII. Be hloðe.

LVIIII. Be heriʒe.

LX. Be þeofsleʒe.

LXI. Be forstolenum flæsce.

LXII. Be cirliscum ðeofe ʒefonʒenum.

LXIII. Be cyninʒes ʒeneate.

LXIIII. Be feorran cumenum men butan weʒe ʒemetton.

LXV. Be swa ofsleʒenes monnes were.

LXVI. Be ðon ðe monnes ʒeneat staliʒe.

LXVII. Be elðeodies monnes sleʒe.

LXVIII. Be wite ðeowes monnes sleʒe.

LXVIIII. Be ciepe monna fore uppe on londe.

LXX. Be fundenes cildes fostre.

LXXI. Be þon þe mon dearnenʒa bearn ʒestrienc.

LXXII. Be ðeofes onfenʒe æt ðiefðe.

LXXIII. Be ðon þe mon sweordes onlæne oðres ðeowe.

LXXIIII. Be ðon þe cierlisc mon flieman feormiʒe.

LXXV. Be ðon ðe mon wîf bycʒe 7 þonne sio ʒift tostande.

LXXVI. Be wilisces monnes lond hæfene.

LXXVII. Be cyninʒes horsweale.

LXXVIII. Be monslihte.

LXXVIIII. Be þeof slihte þæt he mote aðe ʒecyðan.

LXXX. Be ðeofes onfenʒe 7 hine ðonne forlæte.

LXXXI. Be cirlisces monnes ontyʒnesse æt ðiefðe.

LXXXII. Be þon ðe ryhtʒesamhiwan bearn hæbben 7 þonne se
wer ʒewite.

LV. þan G | mannum GH | hira G, heora, o above | ʒelandan GH, ʒe
above H | bebicʒað GH | LVI. ʒefanʒenum GH | þeofe G | LVII. þan
G | hyra G, heora, o above H | ʒewitnesse GH | bisceope G, biscope H.| LIX.
herʒe G, hereʒe, second e above H | LXII. cyrliscum G, cirliescum, e above H |
ʒefanʒenum GH | LXIII. kyninʒes H | LXIV. cumenan H | ʒemettan G, ʒemet-
tum, ʒe above H | LXV. ofslaʒenes GH, first e above H | mannes GH | LXVI.
þan G, þam H | mannes ʒestaliʒe, vac. neat G | LXVII. ælþeodiʒes GH,
æ over erasure H | mannes GH | LVIII. mannes GH | LXIX. cypmanna
G, cypemanna H | fôre G, fâre H | ûp G, upp H | land G, land stryne H |
LXXI. ðan G, þam H | man GH | dearnunʒa GH | ʒestriene, second e appar.
new G, ʒestri-ne H | LXXII. þeowes mannes, w over eras., mannes above

Be landbyᵹene.
Be ᵹefanᵹenum ðeofum.
Be þam þe heore ᵹewitnesse ᵹeleoᵹað.
hloðe.
Be herᵹe.
Be ðeofslæᵹe.
Be forstolenum flæsce.
Be ceorliscum ðeofum ᵹefanᵹenum.
Be cinᵹes ᵹeneate.
Be feorran cumenan men.
Be swa ofslaᵹenes mannes were.
Be ðam þe mannes ᵹeneat staliᵹe.
Be ælðeodiᵹes mannes slæᵹe.

Be cypmanna fare uppe land.
Be fundenes cildes fostre.
Be ðam þe dearnunᵹe bearn stryneð.
Be ðeowes mannes onfenᵹe æt ðyfðe.
Be ðam þe his sweord alæne oðres ðeowan.
Be þam þe cyrlisc man feormiᵹe flyman.
Be þam þe man wif bycᵹe 7 seo ᵹift wiðstande.
Be wylisces mannes londhæfene.
Be cininᵹes horswale.
Be manslihte.
Be ðeofslihte.
Be ðeofes andfenᵹe 7 hine swa forlæte.
Be ceorlisces monnes betoᵹenesse.
Be ðam ðe rihtᵹesamhiwan bearn habban.

H | ðyfðe GH | LXXIII. þan G, þam H | man GH | his above sweord H |
alæne H | ðeowan, n above H | LXXIV. þan G, þam H | cyrlisc G | man
GH | flyman GH | LXXV. þan G | þam above H | man GH | bicᵹe G,
bycᵹe H | seo GH | ᵹyft G | LXXVI. wylysces G | mannes GH, nes above
H | land GH | — End of p. 67 in E — | LXXVII. kyninᵹes H | LXXVIII.
man G, mann, last n above H | slyhte H | LXXIX. slyhte H | he þæt
môte aðe G, he mott þæt mid aðe, þæt above H | LXXX. þænne G, hine
man ðonne H | LXXXI. cyrlisces G, cierlisces H | mannes GH | ðyfðe G |
æt þyfðe betoᵹenisse H | LXXXII. ðan G, ðam H | riht GH | ᵹesamhiwon
G | habben G, habban H |

64

LXXXIII. Be unalefedum fære from his hlaforde.
LXXXIIII. Be ceorles weorðiʒe.
LXXXV. Be borʒes ondsæce.
LXXXVI. Be ceorles ʒærstune.
LXXXVII. Be wuda bærnette.
LXXXVIII. Be wuda onfenʒe butan leafe.
LXXXVIIII. Be burʒ bryce.
XC. Be stæl tyhtlan.
XCI. Be ðon þe mon forstolenne ceap befehð.
XCII. Be wite þeowum men.
XCIII. Be unaliefedes mæstennes onfenʒe.
XCIIII. Be ʒesiðcundes monnes ʒeþinʒe.
XCV. Be ðon ðe ʒesiðcund mon fierd forsitte.
XCVI. Be diernum ʒeðinʒe.
XCVII. Be forstolenes monnes forefonʒe.
XCVIII. Be werfæhðe tyhtlan.
XCVIIII. Be ewes weorðe.
C. Be ʒehwelces ceapes anʒelde.
CI. Be cierlisces monnes stale.
CII. Be oxan horne.
CIII. Be cuus horne.
CIIII. Be hŷr ʒeohte.
CV. Be ciric sceatte.
CVI. Be þon þe mon to ceape fordræfe.
CVII. Be ʒesiðcundes monnes fære.
CVIII. Be þon þe hæfð .XX. hida londes.
CVIIII. Be .X. hidum.
CX. Be .III. hidum.
CXI. Be ʒyrde londes.
CXII. Be ʒesiðcundes monnes dræfe ôf londe.
CXIII. Be sceapes ʒonʒe mid his fliese.

LXXXIII. ûnalyfedum G, unaʒelyfedum H | fram GH | LXXXIV. ciorles H | weorðiʒe, first e above H | LXXXV. andsæce GH | LXXXVI. ciorles H | LXXXVIII. wudu H | anfenʒe H | LXXXIX. burh GH | brece G | XC. stal GH | tihlan G | XCI. þam H | man GH | befehþ cêap H | XCII. mannum H | XCIII. unalyfedes GH | mæstenes GH | XCIV mannes GH | XCV. þan G, þam H | man GH | fyrd G, fyrde, e above H | XCVI. dyrnum GH | XCVII. mannes GH | forefenʒe G, forfenʒe H | XCVIII. werfæhte G | tihtlan GH | XCIX. eowes GH | C. ʒehwylces

Be unalyfedu*m* fare fra*m* his laforde.
Be ceorles worðiᵹe.
    (Included with above in B)
Be ða*m* þæt ceorlas habbað land ᵹemæne 7 ᵹærstunas.
Be wude bærnete.
Be wude andfenᵹe.
Be burhbryce.
Be staltiblan.

Be witeðeowu*m* mannu*m*.
Be unalefedu*m* mæstenu*m* andfencᵹe.
Be ᵹesiðcundes mannes ᵹeðinᵹe.
Be þa*m* þe ᵹesiðcund man fyrde forsitte.
Be dyrnun ᵹeþincðe.
Be forstolenes mannes forfenᵹe.
Be werfæhðe tyhlan.
Be eowe wyrðe.
Be ᵹehwylces ceapes wyrðe.
Be cyrlisces mannes stale.

Be hyr oxan.
Be ciricsceatte.
Be þa*m* þe man to ceace fordræfe.
Be ᵹesiðcundes mannes fare.
Be ða*m* þe hafð .XX. hida.
Be tyn hidu*m*.
Be ðreo*m* hi*dum*.
Be ᵹyrde.
Be ᵹesiðcundes.mannes drafe of lande.
Be sceapes ᵹanᵹe.

GH | anᵹilde GH | CI. cyrlisces G, cirlisces H | mannes tale G | mannes H | —
End of p. 68 of E — | CIII. cu G, cû- H | CIV. hyreᵹeohte H | CV. cyric
G, ciric H | sceatum G, sceattum H | CVI. ðan G, ðam H | man GH |
ceace GH | CVII. mannes GH | CVIII. ðan þe G, þam ðe H | landes
GH | CX. hidum, d like cl H | CXI. ᵹirde H | landes GH | CXII.
siðcundes G | mannes GH | lande G | CXIII. sceapos, a above H | ᵹanᵹe
GH, perh. orig. o H | flese G, flyse H |

CXIV. Be twyhyndum were.

CXV. Be wertyhtlan.

CXVI. Be werȝeld ðeofes forefonȝe.

CXVII. Be anre nihtes ðiefðe.

CXVIII. Be ðon ðe ðeowwealh frione mon ôfslea.

CXIX. Be forstolenes ceapes forefonȝe.

CXX. Be þon ȝif mon oðres ȝodsunu slea oððe his ȝodfæder.

CXV. tihlan G, tihtlan H | CXVI. werȝild GH | forefenȝe GH |
CXVII. anra G | nihtæ G | ðyfðe GH | CXVIII. þan G, ðam above H |
þeofwealh G | freonne m. G, friȝne man H | CXIX. forefenȝe G, forfenȝe
H | CXX. ðan G, þam H | man GH | ófslea H | Added in H: CXXI. Be
blaserum 7 be morðslihtum. | — Last 8 lines of p. 69 and all p. 70 blank
in E — |

Be twyhindum were.
Be wertyhlan.
Be werʒild ðeofes forefenʒe.
Be anre nihte ðyfte.
Be þam þe þeowwalh friʒne man ofslea.
Be forstolene ceape.
Be ʒodfæderes oððe ʒodsunes slæhte.

MANUSCRIPT E.

1.   Dryhten wæs sprecende ðas word to
1, 1. moyse 7 þus cwæð: Ic êom dryhten ðin god;
       Ic ðe utʒelædde of eʒipta londe 7 of hiora ðeow-
1, 2. dome.   Ne lufa ðu oþre fremde ʒodas ofer me.
2.   Ne minne noman ne ciʒ ðu on idelnesse, forðon þe
       ðu ne bist unscyldiʒ wið me, ʒif ðu on idelnesse ciʒst
3.   minne noman.   Ʒemyne þæt ðu ʒehalʒiʒe þone ræste-
3, 1. dæʒ;   wyrceað eow .vi. daʒas 7 on þam siofoðan
3, 2. restað eow: forðam on .vi. daʒum crist ʒeworhte
       heofonas 7 eorðan, sæs 7 ealle ʒesceafta þe on him
       sint, 7 hine ʒereste on þone siofoðan dæʒ, 7 forðon
4.   dryhten hine ʒehalʒode.   Ara ðinum fæder 7 þinre
       medder ða þe dryhten sealde þæt ðu sie þy lenʒ libbende
5. 6.   on eorþan.   Ne sleah ðu;   ne liʒe ðu dearnenʒa.
7. 8.   Ne stala ðu;   ne sæʒe ðu lease ʒewitnesse.
9.   Ne wilna ðu þines nehstan ierfes mid unryhte.
10. 11. Ne wyrc ðe ʒyldne ʒodas oððe sylfrene.   Ðis sint
11, 1. ða domas þe ðu him settan scealt: Ʒif hwa ʒe-
       bycʒʒe cristenne þeow, .vi. ʒear ðeowiʒe he, ðy siofo-
11, 2. ðan beo he frioh ôrceapunʒa;   mid swelce hræʒle

---

1. rihten, blank for D, G ‖ **1, 1.** eam H | drihten G ¦ îc G | utt ʒelæ
-de H | eʒypta GH | lande GH | hyra G, heora H ‖ **1, 2.** mê G ‖ **2.** naman
GH | ydelnesse H | forðam, vac þe H | byst GH | ʒecyʒst, ʒe above H |
naman GH ‖ **3.** ʒemune G, ʒemun H | ʒehalʒie GH | restedæʒ G, resten-
dæʒ H ‖ ˙ **3, 1.** wyrcað GH | syx H | ðone G | seofoðan GH | After eow
added ðu 7 ðin sunu 7 ðine dohter 7 ðin ðeowe 7 ðine wylne 7 ðin weorcnyten 7 se cuma þe bið binnan ðinan durum Lamb, tu, et filius tuus
et filia tua, servus tuus et ancilla tua, jumentum tuum et advena qui est
intra portas tuas Ve Vulg. ‖ **3, 2.** forðan G | syx H | heofenas H | sæ
G, 7 sæ H | hym G, heom H | sindon GH | seofoðan GH | forðan G, forðam
H | drihten G ‖ **4.** meder GH | drihten GH | sy H ¦ þe H ‖ **6.** dearnunʒa
G, deornunga H ‖ **8.** seʒe G | ʒewitnessea G | added wiþ ðinum nehstan

EXTRACTS FROM THE VULGATE AS USED BY ÆLFRED.

From the Book of Exodus.

XX, 1. 2. Locutus*que* est Dominus *cunctos* sermones hos: Ego
sum Dominus Deus tuus, qui eduxi te de terra Aegypti,
3. de *domo* servitutis. Non habebis deos alienos coram

(2) 7. me..... Non assumes nomen *Domini Dei tui* in
vanum;. nec enim habebit insontem *Dominus* eum,

(3) 8. qui assumpserit nomen *Domini Dei sui* frustra. Me-
9. mento ut diem sabbati' sanctifices. Sex diebus
10. operaberis et *facies omnia opera tua.* Septimo
autem die sabbatum Domini Dei tui est; non facies
11. omne opus *in eo* ..... Sex enim diebus fecit
Dominus coelum et terram *et* mare et omnia, quae
in eis sunt, et requievit in die septimo; idcirco *bene-
dixit* Dominus *diei sabbati et* sanctificavit eum.

(4) 12. Honora patrem tuum et matrem tuam, ut sis
longaevus super terram, quam Dominus *Deus tuus*
13. 14. 15. dabit tibi. Non occides. Non moechaberis. Non

(8) 16. furtum facies. Non loqueris *contra proximum tuum*

(9) 17. falsum testimonium. Non concupisces *domum* pro-

(10) 23. ximi tui, *etc.* . . Non facietis deos argenteos, nec *deos*

XXI, 1. aureos *facietis* vobis. Haec sunt iudicia quae pro-

(11) 2. pones eis: Si emeris servum *Hebraeum,* sex annis
3. serviet *tibi,* in septimo egredietur liber gratis. Cum

Lamb, contra proximum tuum Ve Vulg. ‖ 9. ȝewylna H | niehstan G,
nyhstan H | yrfes H ¦ unrihte G ‖ 10. wyce G | wyrc ðu þe H | ȝyldene
GH ‖ 11. sindon G, synt H | heom H ‖ 11, 1. ȝebicȝe G, ȝebycȝe H |
cristene H | syx H | þeowie H | ði G | seofoðan G | 7 on þam seofoðan
H | freoh G, freo H | ôrceapunȝe G, on ceapunȝe H ‖ 11, 2. swilce G,
7 mid swylce reafe H | inneode H | swilce G, swylce H | ȝa G | ût G,
utt H.

11, 3. he ineode, mid swelce ʒanʒe he ût.   Ʒif he wîf self
11, 4. hæbbe, ʒanʒe hio ut mid him; ʒif se hlaford him þonne
11, 5. wif sealde, sie hio 7 hire bearn þæs hlafordes; ʒif se
     peowa þonne cweðe: Nelle ic from minum hlaforde ne
     from minum wife ne from minum bearne, ne from minum
11, 6. ierfe; brenʒe hine þonne his hlaford to ðære dura þæs
     temples 7 þurhþyrliʒe his eare mid æle, to tâcne þæt
12.   he sie æfre siððan þeow.   Ðeah hwa ʒebycʒʒe his
     dohtor on þeowenne, ne sie hio ealles swa ðeowu swa
12, 1. oðru mennenu.   Nage he hie ût on elðeodiʒ folc to
12, 2. bebycʒʒanne.   Ac ʒif he hire ne recce, se ðe hie bohte,
12, 3. læte hie freo on elðeodiʒ folc.   Ʒif he ðonne alefe his
12, 4. suna mid to hæmanne, do hiere ʒyfta,   lociʒe þæt hio
     hæbbe hræʒl 7 þæt weorð sie hiere mæʒðhades, þæt
12, 5. is se weotuma aʒife he hire þone; ʒif he hire þara
13.   nan ne do, þonne sie hio frioh.   Se mon se ðe his
13, 1. ʒewealdes monnan ôfslea, swelte se deaðe.   Se ðe
     hine þonne nedes ôfsloʒe oððe unwillum oððe unʒewealdes
     swelce hine ʒod swa sende on his honda, 7 he hine ne
     ymbsyrede, sie he feores wyrðe 7 folcryhtre bote, ʒif
13, 2. he friðstowe ʒesece.   Ʒif hwa ðonne ôf ʒiernesse 7
     ʒewealdes ôfslea his þone nehstan þurh searwa, aluc ðu
     hine from minum weofode to þam þæt he deaðe swelte.
14.   Se ðe slea his fæder oððe his modor, se sceal deaðe
15.   sweltan.   Se ðe frione forstele 7 he hine bebycʒʒe 7
     hit onbestæled sie þæt he hine bereccean ne mæʒe,
15, 1. swelte se deaðe.   Se ðe werʒe his fæder oððe his
16.   modor, swelte se deaðe.   Ʒif hwa slea his ðone neh-

11, 3. habbe sylf G | silf H | heo GH | ût G ‖ **11, 4.** Gyf H | þonne
him H | si G, sy H | hêo G, heo H | hyre GH | ðas G ‖ **11, 5.** Gyf H |
— þonne End of p. 71 of E — cwæþe H | fram 4 times GH | yrfe GH ‖
11, 6. Brynʒe G, Brinʒe H | æt ðas temples dura G | ðurhðirliʒe G, þurh-
þyrlie H | âle G, ane æle H | sy H | syððan G ‖ **12.** ʒebicʒe GH | dohter
H | ôn ðeowenne G, to þeowte H | beo H | he G, heo H | alles H | þeow
H | oðre mennenu G, oðer þeow wifman H ‖ **12, 1.** hî G, hy H | utt H |
ælðeodiʒ GH | bebycʒanne G, syllanne H ‖ **12, 2.** hyre GH | hy H | hie
faran freo G Lamb, hy friʒe H | ælðeodig GH ‖ **12, 3.** alyfe GH | hys
H | sunea G, sune H | hæmenne H | dô G | hyre GH | ʒifta GH ‖ **12,4.** locie
G, 7 locie H | heo GH | habbe G | sy wurð H | hyre G, hire H | þæt his
H | sie wituma G, se wîtuma H | aʒyfe GH, vac. he H | hyre G, hire H |

quali veste intraverit, cum tali exeat; si hab ens
4. uxorem, *et uxor* egredietur simul. Sin autem dominus
dederit illi uxorem, *et perpererit filios et filias,* mulier
et liberi ejus erunt domini sui, *ipse vero exibit*
5. *cum vestitu suo.* Quod si dixerit servus: *Diligo*
dominum meum et uxores ac liberos, *non egre-*
6. *diar liber, offeret eum dominus diis, et* applicabitur ad ostium et postes, perforabitque aurem ejus
(12) 7. subula, et erit *ei* servus in saeculum. Si quis
vendiderit filiam suam in famulam, non *egredietur,*
8. sicut ancillae *exire consueverunt.* Si displicuerit
oculis *domini sui,* cui tradita fuerat, dimittet eam;
populo *autem* alieno vendendi non habebit potestatem,
9. *si spreverit eam.* Sin autem filio suo desponderit eam,
10. *iuxta morem filiarum faciet illi. Quod si alteram ei*
acceperit, providebit *puellae* nuptias, et vestimenta,
11. et pretium pudicitiae non negabit. Si *tria* ista non
(13) 12. fecerit, egredietur *gratis absque pecunia.* Qui percusserit hominem volens occidere, morte moriatur.
13. Qui autem non est insidiatus, sed Deus illum
tradidit in manus ejus, constituam tibi locum in quem
14. fugere debeat. Si quis per industriam occiderit
proximum suum et per insidias, ab altari meo evelles
(14) 15. eum, ut moriatur. Qui percusserit patrem suum
(15) 16. aut matrem, morte moriatur. Qui furatus fuerit
hominem et vendiderit eum, convictus noxae, morte
17. moriatur. Qui maledixerit patri suo vel matri,
(16) 18. morte moriatur. Si *rixati fuerint viri et* percusserit

---

þene H ‖ **12, 5.** hyre H | nanne ne dô H | sy H | heo GH | freoh GH ‖
13. man G | man þe, vac. se H | hys H | man GH ‖ **13,1.** hyne G | nydes G,
neades H | ofslea H | unʒewylles H | swylce GH | hyne H | sende swa H |
hys G | handa GH | hyne ymbe ne sierede GLamb, him ne syrwde ymbe,
ne above H | sy GH | rihtere H | fryðstowa G ‖ **13, 2.** Gyf GH | ʒeorn-
nesse GH | hys H | nyehstan G, nyhstan H | syrwunʒe H | alûc H | hyne
H | fram GH | minan G ‖ **14.** swyltan G | moder, swelte se deaþe
H ‖ **15.** freonne GH | forsteleþ H | 7 hine, vac. he GH | bebycʒe GH |
vac. 7 hit .... mæʒe Lamb | hit hym G | sy H | bereccan GH | mæʒ H ‖
15, 1. wyrʒe G, wyrie H | modor, vac. his G, moder H ‖ **16.** — slea End
of p. 72 of E — hys H | nyhstan H | ûtʒanʒen G, uttʒanʒan H | maʒe G |
be GH | stæfe GH | beʒyte GH | hwyle H | sylf GH.

stan mid stane oððe mid fyste 7 he þeah utʒonʒan
mæʒe bi stafe, beʒite him læce 7 wyrce his weorc ða

17. hwile þe he self ne mæʒe. Se ðe slea his aʒenne
þeowne esne oððe his mennen 7 he ne sie idæʒes dead,
ðeah he libbe twa niht oððe ðreo, ne bið he ealles

17, 1. swa scyldiʒ, forþon þe hit wæs his aʒen fioh. Ʒif
he ðonne sie idæʒes dead, ðonne sitte sio scyld on him.

18. Ʒif hwa on cease êacniende wif ʒewerde, bete þone

18, 1. æwerdlan swa him domeras ʒereccen. Ʒif hio dead

19. sie, selle sawle wið sawle. Ʒif hwa oðrum his eaʒe
oððo, selle his aʒen fore, toð fore têð, honda wið honda,
fet fore fet, bærninʒ for bærninʒe, wund wið wunde,

20. læl wið læle. Ʒif hwa âslea his ðeowe oððe his
ðeowenne þæt eaʒe ût 7 he þonne hie ʒedo âniʒʒe,

20, 1. ʒefreoʒe hie for þon. Ʒif he þonne ðone toð ôfaslea,

21. do þæt ilce. Ʒif oxa ofhnite wer oððe wîf þæt hie dead
sien, sie he mid stanum ofworpod 7 ne sie his flæsc eten;

21, 1. se hlaford bið unscyldiʒ. Ʒif se oxa hnitol wære
twam dagum ǽr oððe ðrim 7 se hlaford hit wisse
7 hine inne betynan nolde, 7 he ðonne wer oððe
wîf ofsloʒe, sie he mid stanum ofworpod, 7 sie se
hlaford ôfsleʒen oððe forʒolden, swa ðæt witan toryhte

21, 2. finden; sunu oððe dohtor ʒif he ofstinʒe, ðæs ilcan

21, 3. domes sie he wyrðe; ʒif he ðonne ðeow oððe ðeowmennen ôfstinʒe, ʒeselle þam hlaforde .xxx. scill.

22. seolfres, 7 se oxa *sie* mid stanum ofworpod. Ʒif hwa

---

17. his aʒenne slea þeowne esne oððe his wifman H | sy GH | lybbe G |
nyht H | byþ H | scyldyʒ G ; ðan G, ðam, vac. þe H | hys G | feoh G, þeow
H ‖ **17, 1.** ʒyf ðonne he idæʒes sie G, ʒif he þonne byþ H | seo GH ‖
18. Gyf G | ceaste GH | ʒewyrde G | ʒebete G | æwyrdlan G, æwyrdlan,
vac. þone H | hym G | demeras H | ʒetæcan GLamb, ʒereccan H ‖ **18, 1.** ʒyf
G | heo GH | sy GH | sylle GH ‖ **19.** ʒyf G | hwâ G | hys GH | oððô G,
ofdo H | sylle GH | for toð GH | handa twice GH | for st. wið G | fett
twice H | for GH | bærninʒe twice G, bærnunʒ, bærnunʒe H | læle G ‖ **20.**
ofslea H | þeowan H | þeowene H | ût G, utt H | hy H | ʒedô GH | âneaʒe G,
aneʒede H | freoʒe, ʒe above H | hî G, heo H | ðan G ‖ **20, 1.** ʒyf G |
toð, vac. ðone H | ofâslea G | dô GH | sylfe G ‖ **21.** Gyf G | hi G, hy
H | deade H | syn H | sy H | oftorfod H | sy H | êten G, ʒeeten H | byþ
H ‖ **21, 1.** oððe þrim ǽr G, ær oððe þrym H | sê G | nyste, ʒif he hit
ðonne wiste GLamb | wiste H | betynan, vac. inne G, innan H | sy GH |

alter proximum suum lapide vel pugno, et ille *mor-*
19. *tuus non fuerit, sed iacuerit in lectulo:* si sur-
rexerit et ambulaverit foris super baculum suum,
innocens erit, qui percusserit, ita tamen, ut operas
(17) 20. ejus et impensas in medicos restituat. Qui percusserit servum suum vel ancillam *virga,* et mortui fuerint
21. in manibus ejus, criminis reus erit; sin autem *uno*
die vel duobus supervixerit, non subiacebit poenae,
(18) 22. quia pecunia illius est. Si rixati *fuerint viri et*
percusserit quis mulierem praegnantem, *et abortivum*
quidem fecerit, sed ipsa vixerit: subiacebit damno,
quantum *maritus mulieris expetierit et* arbitri iudica-
23. verint. Sin *autem* mors ejus fuerit subsecuta, reddet
(19) 24. animam pro anima, oculum pro oculo, dentem pro
25. dente, manum pro manu, pedem pro pede, adusti-
onem pro adustione, vulnus pro vulnere, livorem pro
(20) 26. livore. Si percusserit quispiam oculum servi sui
aut ancillae et luscos eos fecerit, dimittet eos liberos
27. pro *oculo, quem eruit.* Dentem quoque si excusserit
servo vel ancillae suae, similiter *dimittet eos liberos.*
(21) 28. Si bos cornu percusserit virum aut mulierem, et
mortui fuerint, lapidibus obruetur et non comedentur
carnes ejus; dominus *quoque bovis* innocens erit.
29. *Quod* si bos cornupeta fuerit ab heri et nudiustertius, et contestati sunt dominum ejus, nec recluserit
eum, occideritque virum aut mulierem: *et* bos lapidibus
30. obruetur, et dominum ejus occident. *Quod si*
pretium fuerit ei impositum, dabit *pro anima sua*
31. quidquid fuerit postulatus. Filium *quoque* et filiam
si cornu percusserit, simili sententiae subiacebit.
32. Si servum ancillamque invaserit, triginta siclos
argenti domino dabit, bos vero lapidibus opprimetur.
(22) 33. Si quis aperuerit cisternam et foderit et non

---

ofworpen H, oftorfod Lamb | sy H | ofslaჳen G | se man forჳolden H |
wytan H | rihte GH | findan G, fyndaþ H || **21. 2.** dohter H | ჳyf G | stynჳe
H | sy he þæs ylcan domes G | sy H || **21, 3.** Gyf H | þeowan H | þeowne G,
þeowene H | ofstynჳe H | ჳesylle GH | þryttiჳ scll. H | — scill. End p. 73
in E — | sie from Ǥ, sy se oxa H | ofworpad G, ofworpen H, oftorfod
Lamb.

74

adelfe wæter pŷt oððe betynedne ontyne 7 hine eft ne
betyne, ȝelde swelc neat swelc ðæron befealle, 7 hæbbe
23.   him ðæt deade. Ȝif oxa oðres monnes oxan ȝewundiȝe 7 he ðonne dead sie, bebycȝȝen þone oxan 7 hæbben
him þæt weorð gemæne 7 êac ðæt flæsc swa ðæs deadan.
23, 1.   Ȝif se hlaford þonne wisse þæt se oxa hnitol wære
7 hine healdan nolde, selle him oðerne oxan fore 7
24.   hæbbe him eall ðæt flæsc. Ȝif hwa forstele oðres
oxan 7 hine ôfslea oððe bebycȝȝe, selle tweȝen wið 7
24, 1.   feower sceap wið anum; ȝif he næbbe hwæt he selle,
25.   sie he self beboht wið ðam fio. Ȝif ðeof brcce mannes
hûs nihtes 7 he weorðe þær ofsleȝen, ne sie he na
25, 1.   mansleȝes scyldiȝ. Ȝif he siððan æfter sunnan up-
ȝonȝe þis deð, he bið mansleȝes scyldiȝ 7 he ðonne
25, 2.   self swelte buton he nieddæda wære. Ȝif mid him
cwicum sie funden þæt he ær stæl, be twyfealdum
26.   forȝielde hit. Ȝif hwa ȝewerde oðres monnes winȝeard
oððe his æcras oððe his landes awuht, ȝebete swa
27.   hit mon ȝeeahtiȝe. Ȝif fyr sie ontended rŷt to
bærnanne, ȝebete þone æfwerdelsan se ðæt fŷr ontent.
28.   Ȝif hwa oðfæste his friend fioh: ȝif he hit self
28, 1.   stæle, forgylde be twyfealdum; ȝif he nyte hwa hit
stæle, ȝeladiȝe hine selfne þæt he ðær nân facn ne
28, 2.   ȝefremede. Ȝif hit ðonne cucu feoh wære 7 he secȝȝe
þæt hit here name oððe hit self âcwæle 7 ȝewitnesse
28, 3.   hæbbe, ne þearf he þæt ȝeldan; ȝif he ðonne ȝewitnesse næbbe 7 he him ne ȝetriewe, sweriȝe he þonne.

---

22. delfe G | pitt H | ontŷne G, untyne H Lamb | ȝylde GH | swylc
GH | swylc G, swa H | habbe H ‖ **23.** ôxa G | mannes GH | ȝewundie
H | sy GH | bebicȝan GH | ôxan G | habbon G, habben H | hîm G, heom
H ‖ **23, 1.** wiste GH | he hyne G | sylle GH | eal H ‖ **24.** bebycȝe G,
bebicȝe H | sylle GH | tweȝen, vac. wið G | IIII. G | wyþ H ‖ **24. 1.** ȝyf
G | nite H | hwet G | sylle GH | sy GH | sylf H | þan H | feo GH ‖ **25.**
wurðe H | ofslaȝen G | sy GH | he, vac. na G ‖ **25, 1.** ȝyf G | syððan
H | upȝanȝe G, uppȝanȝe H | sylf swelte G, þonne swylte, vac. self H |
butan GH | nyddæde H ‖ **25, 2.** ȝyf G | cwycum H | sy H | forȝylde he
G, forȝylde H ‖ **26.** hwâ G | ȝewyrde G, awyrde H | mannes GH | wynȝeard
H | hys G | æceras GH | awiht G, awyht H | man GH | ȝeæhtie H ‖ **27.** fir
H | sy H | rŷt G, ryht H, ryp Lamb | bærnenne H | æwyrdlan G, æwyrdlan
H | ontende G, ontendeþ, vac. fyr H ‖ **28.** hys G | frynd G, freond H |
feoh GH | ȝyf G | hyt G | sylf H | stele GH ‖ **28, 1.** ȝyf G | nite H | hyt

operuerit eam, cecideritque bos aut asinus in eam,
34.   reddet *dominus cisternae* pretium iumentorum;
(23) 35. quod autem mortuus est, ipsius erit.   Si bos *alienus*
bovem alterius vulneraverit et ille mortuus fuerit,
vendent bovem *vivum* et divident pretium, cadaver
36. autem mortui *inter se dispertient*.   Sin autem sciebat,
quod bos cornupeta esset *ab heri et nudiustertius*, et
non custodivit eum dominus suus, reddet bovem pro
XXII, 1. bove, et cadaver integrum accipiet.   Si quis furatus
(24)   fuerit bovem *aut ovem* et occiderit vel vendiderit,
quinque boves pro *uno bove* restituet et quatuor oves
(25) 2. pro una *ove*.   Si effringens fur domum *sive suffodiens
fuerit inventus*, et *accepto vulnere* mortuus fuerit,
3. *percussor* non erit reus sanguinis.   Quod si orto
sole hoc fecerit, homicidium perpetravit et ipse mo-
rietur.   Si non habuerit quod *pro furto* reddat, ipse
4. venundabitur.   Si inventum fuerit apud eum, quod
furatus est, vivens, *sive bos sive asinus sive ovis*, du-
(26) 5. plum restituet.   Si laeserit quispiam agrum vel vineam
*et dimiserit iumentum suum, ut depascatur aliena, quid-
quid optimum habuerit in agro suo vel in vinea* pro dam-
(27) 6. ni aestimatione restituet.   Si egressus ignis *invenerit
spinas et comprehenderit acervos frugum sive stantes se-
getes in agris*, reddet damnum qui ignem succenderit.
(28) 7.   Si quis commendaverit amico pecuniam *aut vas
in custodiam, et ab eo qui susceperat furto ablata*
8. *fuerint: si invenitur fur*, duplum reddet; *si latet fur,
dominus domus applicabitur ad deos, et* iurabit quod
9. non extenderit manum in rem proximi sui   ad per-
10. petrandam fraudem. . . . . . . *Si quis commendaverit
proximo suo asinum, bovem, ovem, et omne iumentum
ad custodiam*, et mortuum fuerit, aut debilitatum, vel
11. captum ab hostibus, nullusque hoc viderit: Iusiur-
andum erit *in medio, quod non extenderit manum ad*

G, hitt H | stele H | ȝâ ladiȝe G, ȝeladie H | sylfne H | facen G, fanc H |
ôn ne ȝefremede G, on ne fremede H ‖   **28, 2.** ȝif ðonne, vac. hit G |
— ðonne End of p. 74 in E. — | cwicu G | secȝe G, sæcȝe H | hyt G,
þæt hit H | sylf GH | he ȝewitnesse GH | ȝyldan GH ‖   **28, 8.** ȝyf G | ne
ȝetrywe G, ȝetreowe ne sy H | swerȝe G, swerie H | ðænne G ‖
6*

29. Ʒif hwa fæmnan beswice unbeweddode 7 hire mid-
slæpe, forʒielde hie 7 hæbbe hi siððan him to wife.

29, 1. Ʒif ðære fæmnan fæder hie ðonne sellan nelle, aʒife

30. he ðæt feoh æfter þam weotuman. Ða fæmnan þe
ʒewuniað onfôn ʒealdorcræftiʒan 7 scinlæcan 7 wiccan

31. ne læt þu ða libban; 7 se ðe hæme mid netene, swelte

32. he deaðe; 7 se ðe ʒodʒeldum ônsecʒe ofer ʒod anne,

33. swelte se deaðe. Utancumene 7 elðeodiʒe ne ʒeswenc
ðu no, forðon ðe ʒe wæron ʒiu elðeodiʒe on eʒipta londe.

34. Ða wuduwan 7 þa stiopcild ne sceððað ʒe, ne hie

34, 1. nawer deriað. Ʒif ʒe þonne elles doð, hie cleopiað
to me 7 ic ʒehiere hie, 7 ic eow þonne slea mid minum
sweorde, 7 ic ʒedô þæt eowru wîf beoð wydewan 7

35. eowru bearn beoð steopcild. Ʒif ðu fioh to borʒe selle
þinum ʒeferan þe mid þe eardian wille, ne niede ðu hine
swa swa niedlinʒ 7 ne ʒehene þu hine mid ðy eacan.

36. Ʒif mon næbbe buton anfeald hræʒl hine mid to wreonne
7 to werianne 7 he hit to wedde selle, ǽr sunnan setlʒonʒe

36, 1. sie hit aʒifen. Ʒif ðu swa ne dest, þonne cleopað he to
me 7 ic hine ʒehiere for ðon ðe ic eom swiðe mildheort.

37. Ne tæl ðu ðinne dryhten ne ðone hlaford þæs folces

38. ne werʒe þu. Ðine teoðan sceattas 7 þine frum ripan

39. ʒonʒendes 7 weaxendes aʒif þu ʒode. Eal ðæt flæsc
þæt wildeor læfen ne eten ʒe þæt ac sellað hit hundum.

40. Leases monnes word ne rec ðu no þæs to ʒehieranne,
ne his domas ne ʒeðafa ðu, ne nane ʒewitnesse æfter

41. him ne saʒa ðu. Ne wend ðu ðe no on þæs folces
unræd, 7 unryht ʒewill on hiora spræce 7 ʒeclysp ofer

---

29. beswyce GH | unbeweddude G | hyre G | slepe G | forʒylde GH |
heo H | habbe G | hî G, hy H | syððan H || **29, 1.** ʒyf G | hie, e above
G, heo H | syllan GH | ðæm witoman weotuman G || **30.** ʒewilniað H |
ânfôn G | ʒaldorcræft G Lamb, ʒaldercræftiʒan H | scinlacan H | þu hi libban
H || **31.** nietene G, nytene H | se GH || **32.** ʒyldum G, ʒyltum H | on-
sæcʒe H | of G | ænne H || **33.** Ûtan G | ǽlðeodiʒe G, ælþeodiʒe H | ʒe-
swænc H | þa st. nô G, ðone H | for þam H | îu G, vac. H Lamb | elðeo-
diʒe GH | ôn G | eʒypta GH | lande GH || **34.** wydwan G, wydewan H |
steopcild, vac. þa G, steopcyld H | sceaððan ʒe hie nahwer nê ne deriað
G, scyþþað 7 ne hy nawer deriað H || **34, 1.** hy H | clipiað H | ʒehyre
G, ʒehire H | hy H | ʒedô G | eow ʒedô H | eowre GH | wudewan H |
eowre GH | steopcyld, vac. beoð H || **35.** feoh GH | ʒesylle G Lamb, sylle
H | wylle H | nyd H | swa once GH Lamb | nydlinʒ H | ʒehyne G, ʒehyn

rem proximi sui: suscipietque dominus iuramentum, et
ille reddere non cogetur. . . . .
(29) 16. Si seduxerit quis virginem necdum desponsatam,
dormieritque cum ea: dotabit eam, et habebit eam
17. uxorem. Si pater virginis dare noluerit, reddet pe-
(30) cuniam iuxta modum dotis, *quam* virgines accipere
18. 19. consueverunt. Maleficos non patieris vivere. Qui
(32) 20. coierit cum iumento, morte moriatur. Qui immolat
(33) 21. diis, occidetur, praeterquam Domino soli. Advenam
non contristabis, neque affliges eum: advenae enim
(34) 22. et ipsi fuistis in terra Aegypti. Viduae et pupillo
23. non nocebitis. Si laeseritis eos, vociferabuntur ad
24. me, et ego audiam *clamorem* eorum: Et *indigna-*
bitur furor meus, percutiam*que* vos gladio, et *erunt*
(35) 25. uxores vestrae viduae, et filii vestri pupilli. Si pecuniam mutuam dederis *populo meo pauperi* qui
habitat tecum, non urgebis eum quasi exactor, nec
(36) 26. usuris opprimes. Si pignus a proximo tuo acceperis
27. vestimentum, ante solis occasum reddes ei. Ipsum
enim est solum, quo operitur *indumentum carnis*
eius, nec habet aliud in quo dormiat: si clamaverit
(37) 28. ad me, exaudiam eum, quia misericors sum. *Diis*
non detrahes, et principi populi tui non maledices.
(38) 29. Decimas tuas et primitias tuas non tardabis red-
30. dere: *primogenitum filiorum tuorum dabis mihi. De*
31. *bobus quoque, etc.* . . . . . . *Viri sancti eritis mihi*:
(39) carnem, quae a bestiis fuerit praegustata, non come-
XXIII, 1. ditis, sed proiicietis canibus. Non suscipies vocem
(40) mendacii: nec *iunges manum tuam ut* pro *impio*
(41) 2. dicas *falsum* testimonium. Non sequeris turbam

H | hyne G | eâcan G || **36.** man GH | butan GH | hræȝl, h above H |
oðða st. 7 GH | sylle GH | ȝanȝe GH | sy GH | hyt G | aȝyfen G || **36, 1.**
clypiað H | hyne G, hy H | ȝehyre H | ðam H | eam H | swyþe H || **37.**
— tæl ðu End of p. 75 of E — | drihten G | wyrȝ G, weriȝ H ||
38. sceattas, tas above H | þinne H | ȝanȝendes GH | aȝyf G || **39.** êal G, eall
·H | wylddeor H | læfan H | nê H | etan H | syllað GH || **40.** mannes GH |
rece G, recce H | na to ȝehyranne, vac. þæs G, þæs to ȝehiranne, vac. no
H | seȝe G || **41.** ȝewend, ȝe above H | nâ G, na H | folces, ol over
longer eras. H | ûnræd G | unriht G, on unriht H | hyra G, hiora, o above
H | spæce H | ȝeclæsp G, ȝeclebs H, ȝecleps Lamb | riht G | 7 on þæs G,

ðin ryht 7 ðæs unwisestan lare ne him ne ᵹeðafa.

42.   Ᵹif ðe becume oðres mannes ᵹiemelêas fioh on hond,

43.   þeah hit sie ðin feond ᵹecyðe hit him. Dem ðu swiðe emne. Ne dem ðu oðerne dôm þam weleᵹan, oðerne ðam earman; ne oðerne þam liofran 7 oðerne þam

44. 45. laðran ne dem ðu. Ônscuna ðu â leasunᵹa. Soð fæstne man 7 unscyldiᵹne ne âcwele ðu þone næfre.

46.   Ne onfoh ðu næfre mêdsceattum, for ðon hie ablendað ful ôft wisra monna ᵹeðoht 7 hiora word onwendað.

47.   Þam elðeodeᵹan 7 utancumenan ne læt ðu no uncuðlice wið hine ne mid nanum unryhtum þu hine ne

48.   drece. Ne swerᵹen ᵹe næfre under hæðne ᵹodas ne on nanum ðinᵹum ne cleopien ᵹe to him.

49.   Þis sindan ða domas þe se ælmihteᵹa ᵹod self sprécende wæs to moyse 7 him bebead to healdanne 7 siððan se âncenneda dryhtnes sunu ure ᵹod þæt is bælend crist on middanᵹeard cwom, he cwæð ðæt he ne come no ðas bebodu to brecanne ne to forbeodanne, ac mid eallum godum to ecanne, 7 mildheortnesse 7 eaðmod-

49, 1. nesse he lærde. Ða æfter his ðrowunᵹe ær þam þe his apostolas tofarene wæron ᵹeond ealle eorðan to læranne, 7 þa ᵹiet ða hie ætᵹædere wæron, moneᵹa hæðena ðeoda hie to ᵹode ᵹecerdon; þa hie ealle ætsomne wæron, hie sendan ærendwrecan to antiohhia

49, 2. 7 to syrie cristes æ to læranne; þa hie ða onᵹeaton þæt him ne speow, ða sendon hie ærendᵹewrit to him. Þis is ðonne þæt ærendᵹewrit þe ða apostolas sendon ealle to antiohhia 7 to syria 7 to cilicia, ða sint nu

---

and þæs unwisestan lare þu ne ᵹeþafa, un above, dot and long eras. after lare H || **42.** becyme G | ᵹymeleas GH | feoh G | handa, a crossed G, hand H | hyt G | sy H | fiond H | ᵹecyþ H | hym G || **43.** ðû G | swiðe rihte 7 swiðe emne G Lamb, swiþe ryhtne dom H | 7 above ne H | dôm G | ðæm G | earm-an H | leofran G, leofon over eras. H | laðan H | dæm H | ðû G || **44.** þu âleasunᵹa G, also E, ða leasunᵹa H || **45.** mann G | âcwelle G, acwel- H | ðæne, o above æ G || **46.** þu above H | metsceattum H | ðon þe H | hî G, hy H | âblendað G | manna GH | hyra G, heora H | awendaþ H || **47.** ælþeodeᵹan G, ælþeodiᵹan H | utancymenan G | ðû G | nâ GH | ûncuðlice G | wiþ ðone G | nânum G | ûnrihtum G | drecce G || **48.** sweren ᵹê G, swerizen ᵹe, i ab. H | hæðene GH, first e ab. H | ôn G | næneᵹum G | clypiᵹen G, clipien H | ᵹê H | hym G, heom H || **49.** syndan G, sindon H | ælmihtiᵹa GH | sylf GH | heald-

ad faciendum malum: nec in iudicio plurimorum
3. acquiesces sententiae, ut a vero devies. *Pauperis*
(42) 4. *quoque non misereberis in iudicio.* Si occurreris bovi
5. inimici tui *aut asino* erranti, *reduc ad eum. Si*
videris asinum odientis te iacere sub onere, non per-
(43) 6. *transibis, sed sublevabis cum eo.* Non declinabis in
(44) 7. iudicium pauperis. Mendacium fugies. Insontem et
(46) 8. iustum non occides, *quia aversor impium.* Nec ac-
cipies munera, quae etiam excaecant prudentes, et
(47) 9. subvertunt verba *iustorum.* Peregrino molestus non
eris, *scitis enim advenarum animas: quia et ipsi pere-*
10. *grini fuistis in terra Aegypti. Sex annis seminabis*
12. 13. *etc. . , . . Sex diebus operaberis etc. . . . . Omnia*
(48) *quae dixi vobis, custodite. Et* per *nomen* externorum
deorum non iurabitis, neque audietur ex ore vestro.

---

ende G, healdenne H | syððan G | acenneda GH | drihtnes G, ʒodes H |
ûre G | vac. ure ʒod H | ys G | hælende GH | côm G, on woruld becom H | —
cwæð End of p. 76 in E — | nâ G, na H | word, bebodu new above H |
icanne G, ʒeecenne H | and, d ab. H ‖ **49,1.** ðâ G | tô G | lærranne G | ʒyt
GH | hy H | ætʒædere, first e ab. H | mæniʒe G, maneʒa H | hæðena, e ab. H |
hy H | ʒecyrdon G, ʒecirdon to ʒode H | ðâ G | hî G, hy H | Hy H | sendon
GH | ærendracan H | tô G | antiochia GH | tô G | siria G, syria H | æ̂
GH ‖ **49, 2.** hî G, hy onʒeaton, a ab., vac. ða H | þæt him belampe Lamb,
quid inter eos ageretur Ve | hî G, hy over eras. H | ærendʒewrit . . . þæt
on margin H | tô G | hîm G | Paragraph G | ys þæt vac. þonne G | færend-
ʒewritt, f crossed, last t from e, H | sendan H | tô G | antiochia GH | 7 siria,
vac. to G | cilitia H | sind GH | nû G | æðenum G, hæðenum, e ab. H | tô
G | cryste H | ʒecyrred G, ʒecyrrede H.

49, 3. of hæðenum ðeodum to criste ʒecirde: ða apostolas
7 þa eldran broðor hælo eow wyscað, 7 we êow cyðað
þæt we ʒeascodon þæt ure ʒeferan sume mid urum
wordum to eow comon 7 eow hefiʒran *wisan budan* to
healdanne þonne we him budon 7 eow to swiðe ʒe-
dwealdon mid ðam manniʒfealdum ʒebodum, 7 cowra
sawla ma forhwerfdon, þonne hie ʒeryhton. Ða ʒe-
somnodon we us ymb ðæt 7 ûs eallum ʒelicode ða,
þæt we sendon paulus 7 barnaban, ða men wilniað

49, 4. hiora sawla sellan for dryhtnes naman; mid him
we sendon iudam 7 silam þæt eow þæt ilce secʒʒen:

49, 5. þæm halʒan ʒaste wæs ʒeðuht 7 ûs þæt we nane
byrðenne on eow settan noldon ofer þæt ðe eow ned-
ðearf wæs to healdanne, þæt *is* ðonne þæt ʒe forberen
þæt ʒe deofolʒeld ne weorðien, ne blod ne ðicʒʒen ne
asmorod, 7 from diernum ʒeliʒerum, 7 þæt ʒe willen
þæt oðre men êow ne don, ne doð ʒe ðæt oþrum
monnum.

.I.

49, 6. Of ðissum anum dome mon mæʒ ʒeðencean þæt
he æʒhwelcne onryht ʒedemeð. Ne ðearf he nanra
domboca oþerra. Ʒeðence he þæt he nanum men ne
deme þæt he nolde ðæt he him demde, ʒif he ðone

49, 7. dôm ofer hine sohte. Siððan ðæt þa ʒelamp þæt moneʒa ðeoda cristes ʒeleafan onfenʒon, þa wurdon moneʒa
seonoðas ʒeond ealne middanʒeard ʒeʒaderode, 7 eac
swa ʒeond anʒelcyn, siððan hie cristes ʒeleafan onfenʒon, haleʒra biscepa 7 eac oðerra ʒeðunʒenra witena;
hie ða ʒesetton for ðære mildheortnesse þe crist lærde
æt mæstra hwelcre misdæde þætte ða weoruld hlafordas
moston mid hiora leafan buton synne æt þam forman

49, 3. and, d ab. H | ieldran G, yldran H | broþra H | wyrcað G |
ʒeahsodon G, ʒeaxodon H | ûre G | tô G | coman H | hefiʒran wisan budan
GH Lamb, Vulg. text in Ve (mistake in E here) | healdonne H | hym G |
tô G, vac. H | swyðe H | ʒedwe-ldon H | moniʒfealdum G | mâ H | forh-
wyrfdon GH, h ab. H | heo H | rihton G, ʒerihton H | Parag. G | ʒesamnodan
G, ʒesamnoden H | wê G | ûs G | ûs ða eallum ʒelicode G, us eallum ða
ʒelicode þa, þa ab. H | sendan G | willað G, ða ʒewilniað, vac. men H |
hyra G, hira H | saula G | to above syllanne H | drihtnes G ‖ **49, 4.** hym
G | sendað G, sendon, on ab. H | hy above eow H | secʒað G, secʒan
H ‖ **49, 5.** þam GH | byrþene GH | ðeow niedþearf is G, nydðearf H |

From the Acts of the Apostles.

XV, 23. Apostoli et seniores fratres *his qui sunt Antiochiae et Syriae et Ciliciae fratribus ex gentibus* salutem.

24. Quoniam audivimus quia quidam ex nobis exeuntes, turbaverunt vos verbis, evertentes animas vestras,

25. quibus non mandavimus: placuit nobis collectis in unum, *eligere viros, et* mittere *ad vos cum claris-*

26. *simis nostris* Barnaba et Paulo, hominibus, qui *tradiderunt* animas suas pro nomine Domini *nostri*

27. *Jesu Christi.* Misimus *ergo* Judam et Silam, qui

28. et ipsi vobis verbis referent eadem. Visum est *enim* Spiritui sancto et nobis nihil ultra imponere

29. vobis oneris quam haec necessaria: ut abstineatis vos ab immolatis simulacrorum, et sanguine, et suffocato, et fornicatione, [et quod vobis non vultis fieri, non faciatis aliis,] *a quibus custodientes vos, bene agetis. Valete.*

MS. H.   .I.

49, 6. On ðyssum anum dome man mæჳ ჳeþencan ðæt he æჳhwylcne dom on ryht ჳedeme. Ne þearf he nanre domboca oþera cêpan. ჳeðænce he ðæt he nanum men ne deme þæt he nolde ðæt man him

49, 7. demde, ჳif he þone dom ofer hine ahte. Syþþan ðæt þa ჳelamp ðæt maneჳa ðeoda cristes ჳeleafan underfenჳon, Ða wurdon maniჳe synoðas ჳeond ealne middaneard ჳeჳaderode, and eac swylce on anჳelcynne syððan hy cristes ჳeleafan onfenჳon, haliჳra biscopa and eac oðerra ჳeðunჳenra witena. Hy þa ჳesetton for ðære mildheort*nesse* ðe crist lærde æt mæstra ჳehwylcere misdæde ðæt ða woruld hlafordas moston mid heora leafan butan synne æt þam forman ჳylte ðæra fiohbota onfon butan æt hlaford

---

49, 6. ðyssum, first s above | dom above | ჳedeme, ჳe above | cêpan above ‖ **49, 7.** cynnesyððan Ms. | ჳeleafan, ჳe ab. | eras. before haliჳra | -heornesse Ms. | ჳehwylcere, second e ab. | eras. after ðæt | heora, o ab. | leafan, n ab. | æt hlaford ab. | mildheortnesse above ne ჳedemde.

---

healdenne G, healde-ne H | is from GH | forberan GH | deofolჳyld G, diofolჳyld H | weorðian G, wurðian H | ðicჳan GH | fram GH | — from End p. 77 of E — | dyrnum GH | willan H | do H | — ðæt End of Ms. G — | mannum H ‖ **49, 6.** sohte, soh new over flaw E ‖

ʒylte þære fiohbote ônfon þe hie ða ʒesettan, buton æt
hlaford searwe hie nane mildheortnesse ne dorston ʒecweðan, forþam ðe ʒod ælmihtiʒ þam nane ne ʒedemde
þe hine oferhoʒdon, ne crist ʒodes sunu þam nane ne ʒedemde þe hine to deaðe sealde, 7 he bebead þone hlaford

49, 8. lufian swa hine; hie ða on moneʒum senoðum mo-
neʒra menniscra misdæda bote ʒesetton, 7 on moneʒa
senoð bêc hie writan hwær anne dom hwær oþerne.

49, 9. Ic ða ælfred cyninʒ þâs toʒædere ʒeʒaderode 7
awritan het, moneʒe þara þe ure foreʒenʒan heoldon
ða ðe me licodon 7 maneʒe þara þe me ne licodon ic
âwearp mid minra witena ʒeðeahte 7 on oðre wisan
bebead to healdanne, forðam ic ne dorste ʒeðristlæcan
þara minra awuht fela on ʒewrit settan, forðam me
wæs uncuð hwæt þæs ðam lician wolde ðe æfter ûs
wæren, ac ða ðe ic ʒemette awðer oððe on ines dæʒe
mines mæʒes oððe on offan mercna cyninʒes, oððe on
æþelbryhtes þe ærest fullubte onfenʒ on anʒelcynne þa
ðe me ryhtoste ðuhton ic þa heron ʒeʒaderode 7 þa

49, 10. oðre forlêt. Ic ða ælfred westseaxna cyning eallum
minum witum þas ʒeeowde, 7 hie ða cwædon þæt him
þæt licode eallum to healdanne.

.II.

1. Æt ærestan we læráð þæt mæst ðearf îs þæt æʒhwelc

1, 1. mon his að 7 his wed wærlice healde. Ʒif hwa to hwæðrum
þissa ʒenied sie onwoh oððe to hlaford searwe oððe to
ænʒum unryhtum fultume, þæt is þonne ryhtre to âleo-

1, 2. ʒanne þonne to ʒelæstanne. ʒif he þonne ðæs weddie
þe him ryht sie to ʒelæstanne 7 þæt aleoʒe, selle mid
eaðmedum his wæpn 7 his æhta his freondum to ʒe-
healdanne 7 beo feowertiʒ nihta on carcerne on cyninʒes
tune, ðrowiʒe ðær swa biscep him scrife 7 his mæʒas

1, 3. hine feden ʒif he self mete næbbe. Ʒif he mæʒas
næbbe oððe þone mete næbbe, fede cyninʒes ʒerefa

1, 4. hine. Ʒif hine mon to ʒenedan scyle 7 he elles nylle,

49, 9. âwearp End of p. 78 in E | mercna, erc new over flaw ‖ **1, 2.**
Ʒif . . . ʒelæstanne, line skipped by E; revised from H.

searwe ðe hy ða ʒesetton, ðam hy nane mildheortnesse ne dorston ʒecweðan, for ðam ðe ʒod ælmihtiʒ
ðam nane mildheortnesse ne ʒedemde ðe hine oferhoʒodon, Ne crist ʒodes sunu ðam nane ne ʒedemde
ðe hyne to deaðe ʒesealde, and he bebead þone
49, 8. hlaford lufian swa hine selfne. Hy ða on maniʒum
synoþum maneʒa menniscra misdæda bote ʒesettan, and
on maneʒra synoþbec hy writon hwær ænne dôm, hwær
49, 9. oþerne. Ic ða ælfred cyninʒ ðas toʒædere ʒeʒaderode, and awriten het maniʒe ðara þe ure foreʒenʒan
heoldon þara ðe me lycedan, and moniʒe ðara ðe
me ne lycedon ic awearp mid minre witena ʒeðeahte,
and on oðre wisan bebead to healdenne. Forðam
ic ne dorste ʒeðristlæcan ðara minra awuht feola
on ʒewrit settan. Forðon me wæs uncuþ hwæt ðæs
þæm lician wolde þe æfter us wæron. Ac þa ða
ic ʒemette aþær oððe on Ines dæʒe mines mæʒes,
oððe on offan myrcena cyninʒes, oþþe on æþelberhtes
þe æres fulluht onfenʒ on anʒelcynne, ða ðe me ryhtest
þuhton, ic ða heron ʒeʒaderode, and ða oþre forlett.
49, 10. Ic þa ælfred westseaxena cynʒ eallum minum
witum þas ʒeowde, 7 hy þa cwædon, þæt heom
þæt licode eallum wel to healdene.
.II.
1. Æt ærestan we lærað ðæt mæst þearf is, þæt
1, 1. æʒhwilc man his að 7 his wedd wærlice healde. Ʒif
hwa to hwæðerum þisra ʒenyd sy onwoh, oþþe to
hlaford searwe, oððe to æniʒum unrihtum fultume,
þæt þonne rihtre is to aleogenne þonne to ʒelæstanne.
1, 2. Ʒif he þonne ðæs weddie þe hym riht sy to ʒelæstanne 7 þæt aleoʒe, sylle mid eadmedum hys wæpn
7 his æhta his freondum to ʒehealdenne 7 beo .XL.
nihta on carcerne æt cyninʒes tune, þrowie ðær swa
biscop him scrife, 7 his maʒas hine fedan, ʒif he
1, 3. sylf mete næbbe. Ʒif he maʒas næbbe oððe þone
1, 4. mete, fede cyninʒes ʒerefa hine. Ʒif hine man to

49, 8. synoþum ab. ‖ **49, 9.** ðælfred Ms. | þara ab. ðe | lycedon, y
new | awearp, a ab. | on ab. oðre | feola, o ab. | Ines, I over i | myrcena, e
ab. | ryhtest, est over eras. | forlett, ett over eras.

ʒif hine mon ʒebinde, þoliʒe his wæpna 7 his ierfes;

1, 5. 6. ʒif hine mon ôfslea, licʒʒe he orʒilde. Ʒif he ût
·oðfleo ær þam fierste 7 hine mon ʒefô, sie he feowertiʒ

1, 7. nihta on carcerne swa he ǽr sceolde. Ʒif he losiʒe,
sie he âfliemed 7 sie âmænsumod ôf eallum cristes

1, 8. ciricum. Ʒif þær ðonne oþer mennisc borʒ sie, bete
þone borʒ bryce swa him ryht wisie 7 ðone wed bryce
swa him his scrift scrife.

.III.

2. Gif hwa þara mynster hama hwelcne for hwelcere
scylde ʒesece þe cyninʒes feorm to belimpe oððe oðerne
frione hiered þe ârwyrðe sie, aʒe he þreora nihta fierst

2, 1. him to ʒebeorʒanne, buton he ðinʒian wille. Ʒif
hine mon on ðam fierste ʒeyfliʒe mid sleʒe oððe
mid bende oððe þurhwunde, bete þara æʒhwelc mid
ryhte ðeodscipe, ʒe mid were ʒe mid wite, 7 þam hiwum
hundtwelftiʒ scill. ciric friðes to bote 7 næbbe his aʒne
forfonʒen.

.IIII.

3. Gif hwa cyninʒes borʒ abrece, ʒebete þone tyht
swa him ryht wisie 7 þæs borʒes bryce mid .V. pundum
mærra pæninʒa; ærcebiscepes borʒes bryce oððe his
mund byrd ʒebete mid ðrim pundum; oðres biscepes
oððe ealdormonnes borʒes bryce oððe mund byrd
ʒebete mid twam pundum.

.V.

4. Gif hwa ymb cyninʒes feorh sierwe ðurh hine oððe
ðurh wreccena feormunʒe oððe his manna, sie he his

4, 1. feores scyldiʒ 7 ealles þæs ðe he aʒe; ʒif he hine
selfne triowan wille, do þæt be cyninʒes werʒelde:

4, 2. swa we êac settað be eallum hadum, ʒe ceorle ʒe eorle,
se ðe ymb his hlafordes fiorh sierwe, sie he wið ðone
his feores scyldiʒ 7 ealles ðæs ðe he aʒe oððe be his
hlafordes were hine ʒetriowe.

1, 6. nihta End of p. 79 in E ‖ **4, 1.** werʒelde End of p. 80 in E.

Continuation of Variants from p. 85.

4, 2. settað, vac be | ymbe, e above | hys | syrwie, i ab | ʒetreowie, new s
betw. w and i B, ʒetrewsie H.

ʒenydan scyle 7 he elles nylle, ʒif hine man ʒebinde,
1, 5. þolie his wæpna and his yrfes; ʒif hine man ofslea,
1, 6. lecʒe orʒylde. Ʒif he ut oðfleo ær þan fyrste 7 hine
man ʒefô, sy he .XL. nihta on carcerne, swa he ær
1, 7. sceolde. Ʒif he þonne losie, sy he aflymed, 7 sy he
1, 8. amansemod, of eallum cristes cyricum. Ʒif ðær ðonne
oþer mennisc borh sy, bete þone borh brice swa him
riht wisie, 7 þone wed brice .swa him his scrift scrife.
.III.

2. Ʒif hwa þæra mynster hama hwylcne ʒesece for
hwylcere scylde þe cyninʒes feorm to belimpe, oþþe
oðerne freonne hyred þe arwyrðe sy, aʒe he ðreora
nihta fyrst him to ʒebeorʒanne, butan he þinʒian wille.
2, 1. Ʒif hine man on þam fyrste ʒeyflie mid slæʒe, oððe
mid bende, oððe þurh wunde, bete ðæra æʒhwylc mid
rihte þeowscipe, ʒe mid were ʒe mid wite, 7 þam hiwum
.CXX. scll. cyric friðes bote, 7 hæbbe his aʒen for-
fanʒen.

.IIII.

3. Ʒif hwa cyninʒes borh abrece, ʒebete þone tihtlan
swa him riht wisie, 7 þæs borʒes bryce mid .V. pundum
mærra peninʒa. Ercebiscopes borʒes bryce oððe his
*MS. B. mund byrd ʒebete mid .III. pundum. *Oþres bisceopes
oððe ealdormannes borʒes bryce oððe mundbyrd, ʒebete
mid .II. pundum.

4. Gyf hwâ ymb cyninʒes feorh syrwie, ðurh hine
oððe wrecena feormunʒe, oððe his manna, sy he his
4, 1. feores scyldiʒ, 7 ealles ðæs þe he aʒe; ʒyf he hine
sylfne treowsian wylle, do þæt be cyninʒes werʒylde.
4, 2. Swa we eac settað be eallum hadum, ʒe ceorle ʒe
eorle: Se ðe ymbe his hlafordes feorh syrwie, sy he
wiþ ðone his feores scyldiʒ, 7 ealles þæs þe he aʒe,
oððe be his hlafordes were hine ʒetreowie.

1, 5. sceolde, first e above ‖ Oþres begins B; now given in full,
with notes on B and Variants from H. H has generally ʒif, scll., always
the chapter number. — ‖ 3. biscopes | ealder- | brice | his mundbyrd |
Eras. bef. II in B, twam H ‖ 4. All or most of first line of chapters caps
in B | eard new ab. wrecena B, þurh wrecena H ‖ 4, 1. treowan | dô ‖

.VI.

5.   Eâc we settað æʒhwelcere cirican ðe biscep ʒehalʒode ðis frið, ʒif hie fâh mon ʒeierne oððe ʒeærne þæt
hine seofan nihtum nan mon ût ne teo; ʒif hit þonne
hwa dô, ðonne sie he scyldiʒ cyninʒes mundbyrde 7
þære cirican friðes, mare ʒif he ðær mare ôfʒefo,
ʒif he for hunʒre libban mæʒe, buton he self ûtfeohte.

5, 1.   Ʒif hiwan heora cirican maran þearfe hæbben, healde
hine mon on oðrum ærne 7 ðæt næbbe ðon ma dura

5, 2.   þonne sio cirice; ʒewite ðære cirican ealdor þæt

5, 3.   him mon on þam fierste mete ne selle.   Ʒif he self
his wæpno his ʒefan utræcan wille, ʒehealden hi hine

5, 4.   .XXX. nihta 7 hie hine his mæʒum ʒebodien.   Eac
cirican frið, ʒif hwelc mon cirican ʒesece for ðara ʒylta
hwylcum þara ðe ær ʒeypped nære 7 hine ðær on

5. 5.   ʒodes naman ʒeandette, sie hit healf forʒifen.   Se ðe
stalað on sunnan niht oððe on ʒehhol oððe on eastron
oððe on ðone halʒan þunres dæʒ on ʒanʒdaʒas, ðara
ʒehwelc we willað sie twy bote swa on lencten fæsten.

.VII.

6.   Gif hwa on cirican hwæt ʒeðeofige, forʒylde þæt
anʒylde 7 ðæt wite swa to ðam anʒylde belimpan wille

6, 1.   7 slea mon þa hond ôf ðe he hit mid ʒedyde;   ʒif
he ða hand lesan wille 7 him mon ðæt ʒeðafian wille,
ʒelde swa to his were belimpe.

.VIII.

7.   Gif hwa in cyninʒes healle ʒefeohte oððe his wæpn
ʒebrede 7 hine mon ʒefô, sie ðæt on cyninʒes dome,

7, 1.   swa deað swa lif swa he him forʒifan wille;   ʒif he
losiʒe 7 hine mon eft ʒefô, forʒielde he hine self â
be his wereʒilde 7 ðone ʒylt ʒebete swa wer swa wite
swa he ʒewyrht aʒe.

5, 5. twy bote, wy new over rubbed place ‖   **6, 1.** ʒif he End of
p. 81 in E.

Continuation of Variants from p. 87.

ciric-an | wîte | belimpan | wille | 7, poss. s. crossed and erased B | man | on
marg. æt oþrum cerre, new B | mid dyde, stæl above ‖ **6, 1.** alysan, first
a ab. | wille | ʒeðafyan | wille ‖ **7.** healle | ʒefeohte, ʒe ab. | wæpen, vac
his | ʒebrêde perhaps B | ʒefô, ʒe ab. | dôme | wille ‖ **7, 1.** man eft ʒefô,
eft ab. | sylfne, ne ab. | werʒilde.

5. Eac we settaðᵈ æʒhwylcere cyricean ðe bisceop ʒehalʒode ðis friðᵈ. Gif ʒefahmon ciricean ʒeyrne, oðᵈe ʒeærne, þæt hine seofon nihtum nan man ut ne têo; ʒyf hit ðonon hwa do, ðonne sy he scyldiʒ cyninʒes mundbyrde, 7 ðære cyricean friðes, mare ʒyf he ðær mare ofʒefô, ʒyf he for hunʒre libban mǽʒ, buton he

5, 1. sylf ut feohte. Gyf hiwan hêora ciricean mare ðearfe hæbben, healde hine mon on oðrum huse 7 þæt næbbe

5, 2. ðon ma dura ðonne seo cyrice; ʒewite ðær cyricean

5, 3. ealdor, þæt him mon on fyrste mete ne sylle. Gyf he sylf his wæpno his ʒefân utrǽcan, ʒehealdan hi hine ðrittiʒ nihta, 7 hi hine his maʒum ʒebeoden.

5, 4. Eac cyricean friðᵈ ʒyf hwylc man cyricean ʒesêce, for ðara ʒylta hwylcum þæra ðe ær ʒeypped nære, 7 hine ðær on ʒodes naman ʒeandette, sy hît healf for-

5, 5. ʒyfen. Se ðe stalaðᵈ ôn sunnan niht, oðᵈ on ʒeol, oðᵈe on eastron, oðᵈe on ðone halʒan þunres dǽʒ, 7 on ʒanʒ daʒas, ðara ʒehwylc we willaðᵈ, sy twy bote, swa on lencten fæsten.

6. Gyf hwâ on cyricean hwæt ʒeþeofiʒe, forʒylde þæt anʒylde, 7 þæt wite swa to ðam anʒylde ʒelimpan wylle, 7 slea mon ða hand ôf, ðe he hit mid ʒedyde.

6, 1. Gyf he ða hand lysan wylle, 7 him mon þæt ʒeþafian wylle, ʒylde swa to his were belimpe.

7. Gyf hwa on kyninʒes halle ʒefeohte, oðᵈe his wæpne ʒebrede 7 hine mon ʒefo, sy þæt on cyninʒes dome,

7, 1. swa deaðᵈ, swa lif, swa he him forʒyfan wylle; ʒyf he losiʒe 7 hine mon eft ʒefô, forʒylde he hine sylfne be his werʒylde, 7 þone ʒylt ʒebête, swa wer swa wite, swâ he ʒewyrht aʒe.

---

5. æʒhwylcere, first e ab. | cirican | biscop | faʒman | ciricean above, but old B, hy H | utt, last t above | ðonon, ne ab. on B, ðonne H | dô | vac ðonne bef. sy | cirican | ofʒefô | mǽʒ, e above new B, mæʒe H | butan | utt, t ab. ‖ 5, 1. heora, o ab. | cirican | ærne for huse | ðonne, ne ab. | seo above circe ‖ 5, 2. þære | cirican | on þam fyrste mete, mete above ‖ 5, 3. — sylf, end of p. 13 in B — wæpna | ʒefân | wylle above lighter B, wille H | .XXX. | ʒebodie ‖ 5, 4. cyric-an | is new ab. B | ciric-an | þæra | þæra ab. ðe | forʒifen ‖ 5, 5. oþþe | ʒeol in text, al. ʒeohhol on margin | hal-ʒan | 7 new BH | æʒhwylc | swa, al above new B | swa lencten, eras. betw. words H ‖ 6.

.VIIII.

8. Gif hwa nunnan of mynstere utâlede buton kyninȝes lefnesse oððe bisc*epes* ȝeselle hundtwelftiȝ. scill. healf cyninȝe, healf biscepe 7 þære cirican hlaforde ðe

8, 1. ðone munuc aȝe;   ȝif hio lenȝ libbe ðonne se ðe hie

8, 2. utlædde, naȝe hio his ierfes owiht;   ȝif hio bearn ȝestriene, næbbe ðæt ðæs ierfes ðon mare ðe seo

8, 3. modor;   ȝif hire bearn mon ofslea, ȝieldc cyninȝe þara medren mæȝa dæl, fædren mæȝum hiora dæl mon ȝife.

.X.

9. Gif mon wîf mid bearne ôfslea þon*ne* þæt bearn in hire sie, forȝielde ðone wifman fullan ȝielde 7 þæt

9, 1. bearn be ðæs fædren cnosles were healfan ȝelde;   â sie þæt wite .LX. scill. oð ðæt anȝylde ârise to .XXX. scill., s) siððan hit to ðam ârise þæt anȝylde, siððan sie

9, 2. þæt wite .CXX. scill.;   ȝeo wæs ȝoldðeofe 7 stodðeofe 7 beoðeofe 7 maniȝ witu maran ðon*ne* oþru, nu sint ealȝelic buton manðeofe .CXX. scill.

.XI.

10. Gif mon hæme mid twelfhyndes monnes wife, hundtwelftiȝ. scill. ȝebete ðam were, syxhyndum men hundteontiȝ. scill. ȝebete, cierliscum men feowertiȝ. scill. ȝebete.

.XII.

11. Gif mon on cirliscre fæmnan breost ȝefô, mid .V.

11, 1. scill. hire ȝebete;   ȝif he hie oferweorpe 7 mid ne

11, 2. ȝehæme, mid .X. scill. ȝebete;   ȝif he mid ȝehæme,

11, 3. mid .LX. scill. ȝebete;   ȝif oðer mon mid hire læȝe

11, 4. ær, sie be healfum ðæm þon*ne* sio bot;   ȝif hie mon teo, ȝeladieȝe hie be sixteȝum hida oððe ðoliȝe be

---

8, 8. ȝielde, e over i ‖ 10. wife hund End of p. 82 in E ‖
11, 4. ȝeladieȝe (ȝe apart in Ms.), confusion of -die and -diȝe.

Continuation of Variants from p. 89.

but 7 þæt sy ... sylle 18, 1. added Lamb ‖ 11. cyrliscre | fæmnan above |
ȝefô | .V. | hire ab. ȝebete B | Before 11, 1 appears: ȝyf he mid ȝehæmede,
tyn scill. ȝebete in B, underlined and partially erased ‖ 11, 1. — Gyf End
of p. 15 in B — oferweorpe hy, hy ab. | mid .X. ‖ 11, 2. mid .LX. | hit
ȝebete ‖ 11, 8. ȝe on margin before læȝe | ær | healfum ðæm ðonne seo
bóte, ðonue ab. ‖ 11, 4. hy ȝeladiȝe hy | .LX. | hida | healfre ðære bote.

· 8. Gyf hwa nunnan of mynstre utalǽde butan cyninʒes leafe oððe bisceopes, ʒesylle hundtwentiʒ scill., healf cyninʒe, healf bisceope, ðære cyrice hlaforde, þe þa

8, 1. nunnan aʒe. Gyf heo lenʒ libbe þonne se ðe hêo

8, 2. utlæde, naʒe heo yrfer nawiht. Gyf hêo bearn ʒestryne, næbbe þæt þæs yrfes na mare þonne seo moder.

8, 3. Gyf man hire bearn ofslêa, ʒylde cyninʒe þæra medra maʒa dæl; fædren maʒum hêora dæl man aʒyfe.

9. Gyf man wif mid bearne ofslea, ðonne þæt bearn in hire sy, forʒylde ðone wifman fullan ʒylde, 7 þæt

9, 1. bearn be ðæs fædren cnosles were halfan ʒylde; a sy þæt wite syxti scill. oþ þæt anʒylde arise to ðrittiʒ scill.; syððan hit to ðæm arîse þæt anʒylde, syþþan

9, 2. sy þæt wite hundtwelftiʒ; hwilon wæs ʒoldþeofe 7 stodðeofe 7 *beoþeofe*, 7 maniʒ witu maran þonne oðru; nu synd ealle ʒelice, butan manþeofe hundtwelftiʒ scill.

10. Gif mon hæme mid twelfhyndes mannes wîfe, hundtwelftiʒ scill. ʒebete man were. Syxhyndum *men* hundteontiʒon scill. ʒebete. Ceorliscum *men* feowertiʒum scill. ʒeb*ete*.

11. Gyf man on ceorliscne fænan breost ʒefo, mid fîf

11, 1. scill. ʒebete..... Gyf he hiʒ oferweorpe 7 mid ne

11, 2. ʒehæme, tyn scill. ʒebete; ʒyf he mid ʒehæme, syxti

11, 3. scill. ʒebete. Gif oðer man mid hire lǽʒe ǽr, sy be

11, 4. healf*um* seo bot; ʒyf hi man teo, ʒehladiʒe hî be

11, 5. sixtiʒ*um* hidu*m*, oððe þolie be healfere bote; ʒyf

8. ûtalæde | biscopes | .CXX. | —cyninʒe healf End of p. 14 in B — biscope 7 ciric-an, vac. ðære || 8, 1. se þe, þe ab. | ûtlædde | his yrfes awuht || 8, 2. ʒestri-ne | naʒe | þes | irfes | ðe for na | ðe modor || 8, 3. hire bearn man | þam cyninʒe, þam ab. | ðara | meddren, last d ab. | mæʒa | mæʒum | hiora, o ab. | aʒife || 9. hwa wif ofslea mid bearne | hyre sy, sy ab. | forʒilde | ðone, e over eras. B | heo for ðone wifman | healfan || 9,1. .LX. | .XXX. | siððan | .CXX. scill. || 9, 2. ʒeo | 7 beo þeofe, vac. B, from marg. and H | maneʒu | sint | ealle ʒelice, 2nd and 4th e above | man, a second n above B | .CXX. || 10. man | .XII. | hyndes, y out of u B | .CXX. | ʒebete man þam were, man ab. | Syx hyndum, both y's out of u B | .C. | scill, i made into y B | Cyrliscum | .XL. | ʒebete above | vac. ʒebete,

11, 5. healfre þære bote; ʒif borenran wifmen ðis ʒelimpe, weaxe sio bôt be ðam were.

.XIII.

12.   Gif mon oðres wudu bærneð oððe heaweð unaliefedne, forʒielde ælc ʒreat treow mid .V. scill. 7 siððan æʒhwylc sie, swa fela swa hiora sie, mid .V. pæninʒum,

13.   7 .XXX. scill. to wite; ʒif mon oðerne æt ʒemænan weorce ôffelle unʒewealdes, aʒife mon þam mæʒum þæt treow, 7 hi hit hæbben ær .XXX. nihta of þam lande oððe him fô se to se ðe ðone wudu aʒe.

.XIIII.

14.   Ʒif mon sie dumb oððe dêaf ʒeboren þæt he ne mæʒe synna onsecʒʒan ne ʒeandettan, bete se fæder his misdæda.

.XV.

15.   Gif mon beforan ærcebiscepe ʒefeohte oððe wæpne

15, 1. ʒebreʒde, mid .L. scill. 7 hundteonteʒum ʒebete; ʒif beforan oðrum biscepe oððe ealdormen ðis ʒelimpe,

16.   mid hundteonteʒum .scill. ʒebete. Ʒif mon cu oððe stodmyran forstele 7 folan oððe cealf ôfadrife, forʒelde mid

17.   .scill. 7 þa moder be hiora weorðe; ʒif hwa oðrum his unmaʒan oðfæste 7 he hine on ðære fæstinʒe forferie, ʒetriowe hine facnesse ðe hine fede, ʒif hine hwa hwelces teo.

.XVI.

18.   Gif hwa nunnan mid hæmeð þinʒe oððe on hire hræʒl oððe on hire breost butan hire leafe ʒefô, sie

18, 1. hit twybete swa we ær be læwdum men fundon; ʒif beweddodu fæmne hie forlicʒʒe, ʒif hio sie cirlisc, mid .LX. scill. ʒebete þam byrʒean 7 þæt sie on cwic æhtum feoʒodum 7 mon næniʒne mon on ðæt ne selle.

18, 2. Ʒif hio sie syxhyndu, hundteontiʒ .scill. ʒeselle

---

14. he, e old over i ‖ 16. cu oððe End of p. 83 in E.

underlined and feowertiʒum written above prob. new B, mid scyllinge H | moder | weorðe ‖ 17. 7 he hine, he ab. | ʒetreowiʒe, new s before iʒe B, ʒetreowsie, sie ab. H | facnes | ðe, se before it new B, se ðe H | ʒif hine hwa ‖ 18. on before hire hræʒl | butan | ʒefô | twybote | mannum ‖ 18, 1. beweddo, eras. at end B, beweddod H | hy | cierlisc | mid .LX. | ðam þe ʒebyrie, vac. hit | næniʒne ‖ 18, 2. syx | .C. | ʒesylle ðam ðe, ðe above, also hit lighter B, ʒebete ðam þe hit ʒebyrie H.

borenran wifmen þis ʒelimpe, wexe seo bôt be ðam
were.

12.　Gyf man oðres wudu bærneð oððe heaweþ unalyf-
edne, forʒylde ælc ʒreat treow mid fif scill. 7 syþþan
æʒhwylc sy, swa feola swa heora sy, mid fif peneʒum
13.　7 þrittiʒ scill. to wite.　Gyf man oðerne æt ʒemænan
weorce offealle unʒewealdes, aʒyfe man þam maʒon
þæt treow, 7 lî hit hæbben ær þrittiʒ nihta of ðæm
lande, oððe him fo to se ðe ðone wudu aʒe.

14.　Gyf mon sy dumb oððe deaf ʒeboren þæt he ne
mæʒe his synna ʒeandettan ne ætsacan, bete se fæder
his misdæda.

15.　Gyf man beforan ercebisceope ʒefeohte, oððe wæpne
15, 1.　ʒebrede, mid fiftiʒum scill. 7 hundteontiʒum ʒebete.　Gyf
beforan oðrum bisceope oððe ealdormen ðis ʒelimpe,
16.　mid hundteontigum scill. ʒebete.　Gyf man cu oððe
stodmære forstele 7 folan oððe cealf ofadrife, forʒylde
17.　mid sixtiʒ scill. 7 þa modor be heora wyrðe.　Gyf
hwâ oðrum his unmaʒan oðfæste, 7 he hine on ðære
fæstinʒe forferie, ʒetreowiʒe hine facnesse ðe hine fede,
ʒyf hwâ hine hwylces têo.

18.　Gyf hwa nunnan mid hæmed ðinʒe, oððe hire
hræʒl, oððe on hire breost, buton hire leafe ʒefô, sy
18, 1.　hit twibote, swa we ær be læwedum men fundon.　Gyf
beweddo fæmne hêo forlicʒe, ʒyf hêo sy ceorlisc, syxtiʒ
scill. ʒebete ðam þe hit ʒebyriʒe 7 þæt sy on cwycæhtum
feoʒodum 7 man næninʒne man on þæt ne sylle.
18, 2.　Gyf hêo sy sixhynde, hundteontiʒ scill. ʒesylle

11, 5. borenran, æðel ab. B | 3if þis bett bor. wifmen ʒelimpe, bett ab. |
weaxe ‖　12. .V. | siþþan | ælc swa, vac. sy | moniʒ for feola | þær for
heora | .V. | peninʒum | .XXX. ‖　13. weorce ab. | aʒife | maʒum | hy |
.XXX. | fô | se þe, þe ab. ‖　14. man | vac. his bef. synne | onsæcʒan
ne ʒeandettan H, ʒeondettan ne onsecʒan Lamb. ‖　15. ærcebisceope |
.L. scll. ʒebete 7 .C. ‖　15, 1. biscope | ealdormenn | .C. ‖　16. cû | —
cu oððe End of p. 16 in B — | stodmyran | ofadrifeð | forʒilde | sixtiʒ

18, 3. þam byrʒean;   ʒif hio sie twelfhyndu, .CXX. scill.
ʒebete þam byrʒean.

.XVII.

19.   Gif hwa his wæpnes oðrum onlæne þæt he mon
mid ôfslea, hie moton hie ʒesomnian, ʒif hie willað, to
19, 1. þam were;   ʒif hi hie ne ʒesamnien, ʒielde se ðæs
wæpnes onlah þæs weres ðriddan dæl 7 þæs wites
19, 2. ðriddan dæl;   ʒif he hine triewan wille þæt he to
19, 3. ðære læne facn ne wiste, þæt he mot;   ʒif sweord
hwita oðres monnes wæpn to feormunʒe onfô oððe
smið monnes andweorc, hie hit ʒesund beʒen aʒifan,
swa hit hwæðer hiora ær onfenʒe, buton hiora hwæðer
ær þinʒode þæt he hit anʒylde healdan ne ðorfte.

.XVIII.

20.   Gif mon oðres monnes munuce feoh oðfæste butan
ðæs munuces hlafordes lefnesse 7 hit him losiʒe, þoliʒe
his se ðe hit ær ahte.

.XVIIII.

21.   Ʒif preost oðerne mon ôfslea, weorpe mon to handa
7 eall ðæt he him hames bohte 7 hine biscep onhadiʒe
þonne hine mon of ðam mynstre aʒife, buton se hlaford
þone wer forðinʒian wille.

.XX.

22.   Gif mon on folces ʒemote cyninʒes ʒerefan ʒeyppe
eofot 7 his eft ʒeswican wille, ʒestæle on ryhtran hand
ʒif he mæʒe; ʒif he ne mæʒe, ðolie his anʒyldes.

.XXI.

23.   Gif hund mon toslite oððe abite, æt forman misdæde ʒeselle .VI. scill., ʒif he him mete selle, æt æfteran
23, 1. cerre .XII. scill., æt ðriddan .XXX. scill.   Ʒif æt ðissa
misdæda hwelcere se hund losiʒe, ʒa ðeos bôt hwæðre

---

20. Ends with p. 84 in E.

Continuation of Variants from p. 93.

hande underlined and him over it B, handa H | 7 part. erased B | eal, 2 nd
new 1 B | mid him | onhadiʒe | mon | þæm | aʒife | forðinʒian | wille || **22.**
man | folces, es ab. | ʒe eofot yppe, cf. E | ryhtran | maʒe | maʒe | anʒildes |
and tô to ðam wite added || **23.** abîte | mysdæde | æt æfterran ci-rre | þriddan
ci-rre || **23, 1.** ʒyf, here prob. he erased B | ðissa | hweþere, 2 nd e ab.

18, 3. ðam ðe to ӡebyrian.   Gyf heo sy twelfhynde, hund-
twelftiӡ scill. ӡebete ðam ðe to ӡebyriӡe.

19.   Gyf hwa his wæpne oðrum læne þæt he mid man
ofslea, hi moton hi ӡesanian, ӡyf hî wyllað, to ðæm
19, 1. were;   ӡyf heo hi ne ӡesamnian, ӡylde se ðæs wæpnes
onlænde þæs weres ðridda dæll, 7 *þæs wites ðriddan*
19, 2. *dæl*;   ӡyf he hine triwian wylle þæt he to ðære læne
19, 3. facne nyste, þæt he mot.   Gyf sweord hwîta oðres
mannes wepen to feormunӡe underfô, oððe smið mannes
andweorc, hi hit ӡesund beӡen aӡyfen, swa hit hwæðer
heora ær underfenӡe, buton heora hweðer ǽr ðinӡode
þæt he hit anӡylde healdan ne þorfte.

20.   Gyf mon oðres monnes muneke feoh befæste, buton
þæs munekes hlafordes hleafe, 7 hit him losiӡe, þolie
his se ðe ær ahte.

21.   Gyf preost oðerne man ofslêa, weorpe man to
hande 7 eal þæt he him mid hâmes brohte, 7 hine
biscop unhadie ðonne hine man of ðem mynstre aӡyfe,
buton se hlaford ðone wer foreðinӡian wylle.

22.   Gyf mon on folces ӡemote cyninӡes ӡerefan ӡeyppe
þeofðe, 7 his eft ӡeswican wille, ӡestǽle on rihtran
hand, ӡyf he mæӡe; ӡyf he ne mæӡe, þoliӡe his anӡyldes.

23.   Gyf hund man toslite oððe abite, æt forman mis-
dǽde ӡesylle .VI. scill., ӡyf he him mete sylle, æt ðam
23, 1. oðran cyrre .XII. scill., æt ðridda*n* .XXX. scill.;   ӡyf
æt ðisra misdæda hwylcere se hund losiӡe, ӡa ðeos

18, 3. hio | .XII. | .CXX. | hit lighter above ӡebyriӡe B, hit ӡebyrie
H ‖   **19.** wæpn | man mid | hy | hy | ӡesam-nian | willað ‖   **19, 1.** hy heo
ӡesamni-an nellen | ӡilde | onlan | ðriddan | dæl | 7 þæs wites ðriddan dæl
vac. B Lamb., from H ‖   **19, 2.** triwian, new s betw. wi B, trywan H |
wille | to ðære fore 7 to ðære læne | facn ‖   **19, 3.** wæpn | onfô H, underfô
Lamb. | hy | — beӡen End of p. 17 in B — | aӡifen | heora hwæðer,
o ab. | onfenӡe H, underfenӡe Lamb. | heora, o ab ‖   **20.** hlafordes under-
lined and aldres over it B | Ӡif man oþres mannes munuce butan his hla-
fordes leafe feoh befæste, mannes and his above | losie | ðolie ‖   **21.** to

23, 2. forð. Ȝif se hund ma misdæda ȝewyrce 7 he hine
hæbbe, bete be fullan were swa dolȝbote swa he wyrce.
.XXII.

24. Gif neat mon ȝewundiȝe, weorpe ðæt neat to
honda oððe foreðinȝie.
.XXIII.

25. Gif mon ceorles mennen to ned hæmde ȝeðreatað,
mid .V. scill. ȝebete þam ceorle 7 .LX. scill. to wite;

25, 1. ȝif ðeow mon þeowne to ned hæmde ȝenede, bete
mid his eowende.
.XXIIII.

26*. Gif mon twyhyndne mon unsynniȝne mid hloðe
ofslea, ȝielde se ðæs sleȝes andetta sie wer 7 wite 7 æȝ-
hwelc mon ðe on siðe wære ȝeselle.XXX. scill. to hloð bote.
.XXV.

27. Gif hit sie syxhynde mon, ælc mon to hloð bote
.LX. scill. 7 se slaȝa wer 7 fulwite.
.XXVI.

28. Gif he sie twelfhynde, ælc hiora hundtwelftiȝ

28, 1. scill., se slaȝa wer 7 wite; ȝif hloð ðis ȝedô 7 eft
oðswerian wille, tio hie ealle 7 þonne ealle forȝielden
þone wer ȝemænum hondum 7 ealle ânwite swa to
ðam were belimpe.
.XXVII.

29. Gif mon unȝewintrædne wifmon to niedhæmde
ȝeðreatiȝe, sie ðæt swa ðæs ȝewintredan monnes bot.

30. Ȝif fædren mæȝa mæȝleas mon ȝefeohte 7 mon ôfslea 7 þonne, ȝif medren mæȝas hæbbe, ȝielden ða
þæs weres ðriddan dæl, *ðriddan dæl ða ȝeȝildan 7 for*

30, 1. *ðriddan dæl* he fleo; ȝif he medren mæȝas naȝe,
ȝielden þa ȝeȝildan healfne, for healfne he fleo.

---

26. ofslea, eras. of er? betw. of & slea. || 28. scill. End of p. 85 in
E. ||· 30. words skipped in E supplied from H, where and in Lamb.
full sense is to be got. *Thorpe-Schmid put 29, 30, 31 before 26.

Continuation of Variants from p. 95.
28, 1. ȝedô | oþswerian | wille | teo man hy, man ab. | forȝilden | wær |
ȝemænum | ân wîte | bef. belimbe new to B | belimpe || 29. ȝewintredan ||
30. fæddren, second d ab. | maȝa, æ new ab. B, mæȝa H | mæȝleas | 7
man | he new ab. meddren B | meddren, first d ab. | mæȝas | ȝilden | —
ȝeȝilden End of p. 19 in B — | words supplied from H || 30, 1. after
ȝyf new he B | maȝes, es over eras. | naȝe | ȝilden | healfne and for.

23, 2. bôt ðeah hwæðere forð. Gyf se hund ma misdæda ʒewyrce 7 he hine hæbbe, bete be fullan were swa dolhbote swa he ʒewyrce.

24. Gyf neat man ʒewundiʒe, weorpe þæt neat to handa oððe foreðinʒie.

25. Gyf man ceorles mennen to nyd hæmede ʒeðreataþ, mid fif scill. ʒebete ðam ceorle 7 syhtiʒ scill. to wite.

25, 1. Gyf ðeow man ðeowne to nyd hæmede ʒenyde, bete mid his eowende.

26. Gyf man twyhynde man unsynniʒne mid hloþe ofslêa, ʒylde se ðæs slæʒes andetta sy wer 7 wite 7 ælc mon ðe on syþe wære ʒesylle ðrittiʒ scill. to loð bote.

27. Gif hyt sy syxhynde man, ælc to hloð bote feowertiʒ 7 se slaʒa were 7 fulwite.

28. Gyf he sy twelfhynde, ælc heora hundtwelftiʒ
28, 1. scill., se slaʒa wer 7 wite; ʒyf hloð ðis ʒedô, 7 eft ætswerian wylle, teo hî ealle 7 ðonne ealle forʒylden ðone wer ʒemæne handum 7 ealle anwite swa to ðam were belimbe.

29. Gyf man unʒêwintredne wifman to nyd hæmede ʒeþreatiʒe, sy þæt swa ðæs ʒewintredes mannes bot;

30. ʒyf fædren maʒa mæiʒleas mon ʒefeohte 7 mon ofslêa 7 ðonne, ʒyf meddren maʒas hæbbe, ʒylden þa ðæs weres ðriddan dǽl, ðriddan dǽl ða ʒeʒyldan 7 for

30, 1. ðriddan dæl he flêo; ʒyf medren maʒas næbbe, ʒylden ða ʒeʒylden heafne, for healfne he fleo.

23, 2. dolhbote, on marg. oððe new B, after swa, hwætt new above B, both in Lamb. || 24. mannes neat | — þæt neat End of p. 18 in B — | fore ʒeþinʒie, ʒe ab. || 25. as .XXVI. put after 26, 27, 28 in H, 29 follows it in Ve. Lamb. | ciorles | .V. | ciorle | .LX. || 25, 1. ʒenide | hyde for eowende || 26. ofslea mid hloþe | ʒilde | se ðe þæs sleʒes, ðe ab. | wer, secoñd new r | æʒhwylc for ælc † ðara for mon | on ðæm syþe | ʒeselle | .XXX. | hloþbote || 27. ælc man | feowertiʒ, scill. ab. new B, .LX. scll. H | wer | full, last l ab. || 28. .XII. | .CXX. | 7 new bef. se B, and H ||

.XXVIII.

31. Gif mon swa ʒeradne mon ofslea, ʒif he mæʒas
næʒe, ʒielde mon healfne cyninʒe healfne þam ʒeʒildan.

.XXVIIII.

32. Gif mon folc leasunʒe ʒewyrce 7 hio on hine ʒeresp
weorðe, mid nanum leohtran ðinʒe ʒebete þonne him
mon aceorfe þa tunʒon ôf, þæt hie mon na undeorran weorðe moste lesan ðonne hie mon be þam were ʒeeahtiʒe.

.XXX.

33. Gif hwa oðerne ʒodborʒes oncunne 7 tion wille
þæt he hwelcne ne ʒelæste ðara ðe he him ʒesealde,
aʒife þone foreað on feower ciricum, 7 se oðer, ʒif he
hine treowan wille, in .XII. ciricum do he ðæt.

.XXXI.

34. Eâc is ciepe monnum ʒereht, ða men ðe hie up
mid him læden ʒebrenʒen beforan kyninʒes ʒerefan on
folc ʒemote 7 ʒerecce hu maniʒe þara sien, 7 hie
nimen þa men mid him þe hie mæʒen eft to folc ʒe-

34, 1. mote to ryhte brenʒan, 7 þonne him ðearf sie ma
manna ûp mid him to habbanne on hiora fore, ʒecyðe
symle swa ôft swa him ðearf sie in ʒemotes ʒewitnesse
cyninʒes ʒerefan.

.XXXII.

35. Ʒif mon cierliscne mon ʒebinde unsynniʒne, ʒebete
35, 1. mid .X. scill.; ʒif hine mon beswinʒe, mid .XX. scill.
35, 2. ʒebete; ʒif he hine on henʒenne alecʒʒe, mid .XXX.
35, 3. scill. ʒebete; ʒif he hine on bismor to homolan be-
35, 4. scire, mid .X. scill. ʒebete; ʒif he hine to preoste
35, 5. bescire unbundenne, mid .XXX. scill. ʒebete; ʒif he
35, 6. ðone beard ôfascire, mid .XX. scill. ʒebete; ʒif he
hine ʒebinde 7 þonne to preoste bescire, mid .LX. scill.
ʒebete.

34, 1. swa him ðearf sie End of p. 86 in E.

Continuation of Variants from p. 97.
simle | him bef. ðearf | on for in | ʒewitnesse || **35.** man ab. cierliscne |
man | — ʒebinde End p. 20 in B — | unsynniʒne | .X. || **35, 1.** :XX. ||
35, 2. henʒenne | .XXX. scillinʒa || **35, 3.** on bysmer above | bescire ||
35, 5. new on marg. of B | ofascyre || **35, 6.** to above new B, to preoste
H | syxtig, new feowertiʒ above B, .LX. H.

31.   Gyf mon swa ʒeradne man ofslêa, ʒyf he maʒas naʒe, ʒylde man healfe kyninʒe, healfne þam ʒeʒyldan.

32.   Gyf mon folc leasunʒe ʒewyrce, 7 heo on hine ʒeræf weorðe, mid nanum leohtran ðinʒe ʒebete þonne him mon aceorfe ða tunʒan ôf, þæt heo mon na undeorran wurde moste lesan þonne hêo mon be ðæm were ʒeehtiʒe.

33.   Gyf hwâ oþerne ʒodborʒes oncunne 7 teon wylle þæt he hwylcne ne ʒelæste ðara ðe he him ʒesealde, aʒŷfe ðone foreað on feower cyricum, 7 se oþer ʒyf he hine treowian wylle, innan twelf cyricum do he þæt.

34.   Eac is cypemonnum ʒereht ða men þe hi up mid heom lædað ʒebrinʒan beforan cyninʒes ʒerefan on folc ʒemote 7 ʒerecca hu monie ðæra syn, 7 hi nimen þa men mid heom ðe hiʒ maʒon eft to folc ʒe-

34, 1. mote *to ryhte* brinʒan, 7 þonon heom þearf sy *ma manna* up mid heom to habbanne on heora fôre, ʒecyðe symble swa oft swa ðearf sy in ʒemotes ʒewitnysse cyninʒes ʒerefan.

35.   Gyf mon ceorliscne mon ʒebinde unscyldiʒne, ʒe-
35, 1. bete mid tyn scill.; ʒyf hine man beswinʒe, mid twentiʒ
35, 2. scill. ʒebete; ʒyf he hine on henʒene ʒebrinʒe, mid
35, 3. ðrittiʒ scill. ʒebete. Gyf he hine on bismor to homelan
35, 4. bescyre, mid .X. scill. ʒebete. Gyf he hine to preoste
35, 5. bescyre unbundenne, mid .XXX. scill. ʒebete. *Gif he*
35, 6. *þone beard ofascere, mid .XX. scill. ʒebete.* Gyf he hine ʒebinde, 7 þonne preoste bescyre, mid syxtiʒ scill. ʒebete.

---

31. ʒilde | healfne were þam cyninʒe, wære þam ab. | ʒeʒildan ‖ **32.** wêorðe ʒerǽf H, ʒeræ fLamb. | bef. ʒebete new ne B | man | hy | môn nâ | wurde, ð uncrossed B, weorðe H | alysan | vac. hêo | man | þǽm, m ab. | ʒeeahtiʒe ‖ **33.** wille | aʒife | for-âþ | ciricum, 2d i above | treowan | wille | on .XII. | ciricum | do þæt on margin ‖ **34.** mannum | bef. ða men new þæt inserted B | hy | lædan | ʒebrinʒe | ʒerecce | moniʒe | hy | up mid him | hy | to ryhte vac. B, from H, where ʒemote to above | brenʒan ‖ **34, 1.** þonne | him | ma manna from H | him | to for on | heora, o ab. |

.XXXIII.

36.   Eac is funden, ᵹif mon hafað spere ofer eaxle 7
hine mon on asnaseð, ᵹielde þone wer, butan wite;

36, 1. . ᵹif beforan eaᵹum asnase, ᵹielde þone wer; ᵹif hine
mon tio ᵹewealdes on ðære dæde, ᵹetriowe hine be
þam wite 7 mid ðy þæt wite afelle, ᵹif se ord sie

36, 2. ufor þonne hindeweard sceaft; ᵹif hie sien bu ᵹelic,
ord 7 hindeweard sceaft, þæt sie butan pleo.

.XXXIIII.

37.   Gif mon wille of boldᵹetale in oðer boldᵹetæl
hlaford secan, do ðæt mid ðæs ealdormonnes ᵹewitnesse

37, 1. þe he ær in his scire folᵹode; ᵹif he hit butan his
ᵹewitnesse do, ᵹeselle se þe hine to men feormie .CXX.
scill. to wite: dæle he hwæðre ðæt, healf cyninᵹe in
ða scire ðe he ær folᵹode, healf in þa ðe he oncymð;

37, 2. ᵹif he hwæt yfla ᵹedon hæbbe ðær he ær wæs,
bete ðæt se ðe hine ðonne to men onfo 7 cyninᵹe .CXX.
scill. to wite.

.XXXV.

38.   Gif mon beforan cyninᵹes ealdormen on ᵹemote
ᵹefeohte, bete wer 7 wite swa hit ryht sie 7 beforan

38, 1. þam .CXX. scill. ðam ealdormen to wite; ᵹif he folcᵹemot
mid wæpnes bryde ârære, ðam ealdormen hund twelftiᵹ

38, 2. scill. to wite; ᵹif ðises hwæt beforan cyninᵹes ealdormonnes ᵹinᵹran ᵹelimpe oððe cyninᵹes preoste, .XXX.
scill. to wite.

.XXXVI.

39.   Gif hwa on cierlisces monnes flette ᵹefeohte, mid

39, 1. syx scill. ᵹebete ðam ceorle; ᵹif he wæpne ᵹebrede

---

37. in above his scire, but old ǁ **37, 2.** Ends with p. 87 in E; page
rough, causing large spaces betw. syllables.

Continuation of Variants from p. 99.

to men under on fô, þonne on marg., under above | .CXX. ǁ **38.** man |
ealder | feohtaþ, aþ out of æh B, ᵹefeohte H | wer, second r added new
B | ryht | .CXX. | ealdermen | to wite etc. from H ǁ **38, 1.** before hundt-
welftiᵹ new 7 B | .CXX. ǁ **38, 2.** First difference in chapters betw. B and
EH | ðyses | ealder | ᵹi-nᵹran | .XXX. | scillinᵹas ǁ **39.** ciorlisces | ᵹebete
mid .VI. scll. ðam ciorle ǁ **39, 1.** ᵹebre-de.

36.   Eac is funden, ʒyf mon hæfð spere ofer eaxle 7
36, 1. hine man onsnǣseþ, ʒylde þone wer buton wite. *Gif*
beforan eaʒum, ʒylde þone wer. Gyf hine man teo
ʒewealdes on þære dæde, ʒetreowie hine be ðam wite
7 mid ðam þæt wite afylle, ʒyf se ord ufor ðonne
36, 2. hindeweard sceaft; ʒyf hî syn buta ʒelice, ord 7
hindeweard sceaft, þæt sy butan pleo.

37.   Gyf mon wylle of bold ʒetæle in oðer bold ʒetæl
hlaford secan, do þæt mid ealdormannes ʒewitnysse
37, 1. þe he ær in his scire folʒode.   Gyf he hit buton his
ʒewitnysse dô, ʒesylle *se ðe* hine to men feormie, hundtwelftiʒ scill. to wite; dæle he hwæðere þæt, healf cyninʒe in þam scire þe he ær folʒode, healf in þa þe
37, 2. he cymð.   Gyf he hwæt to yfele ʒedon hæfð ðær
he ær wæs, bete þæt se ðe hine ðonnon to men underfo,
7 cyninʒe hundtwelftiʒ scill. to wite.

38.   Gyf mon beforan cyninʒes ealdormen on ʒemote
feohtaþ, bete wer 7 wite, swa hit riht sy, 7 beforan
38, 1. ðam hundtwelftiʒ scill. ðam ealdormen *to wite; ʒif*
he folces ʒemot mid wæpnes bryde arære, þam ealdermen
hundtwelftiʒ scill. to wite.

38, 2.   Gyf ðisses hwæt beforan cyninʒes ealdormannes
ʒinʒran ʒelimpe, oððe cyninʒes preoste, ðrittiʒ scill. to
wîte.

39.   Gyf hwa on ceorlisces mannes flette ʒefeohte, mid
39, 1. .VI. scill. ʒebete ðam ceorle; ʒyf he wæpne ʒebrede

---

36. ʒefunden, ʒe ab. | man | hafað | eaxlen, n ab. | on asnæseð, on
above | ʒilde | butan ‖   **36, 1.** words new on margin B | eaʒum asnæse |
ʒilde | ʒetreowie, betw. wi new s B, ʒetrywe H | ðæm | þy for ðam | 7
þis beo new ab. ʒyf B | after ord new si B, sy H | þreo fingre ufor ‖
36, 2. ac new ab. ʒyf B | hy | bû | ʒelic ‖   **37.** man of bold ʒetæle wille, wille
first l above | dô | ðæs ealdermannes | ʒewitnysse, ysse over eras. but old
B, ʒewitnesse H | ǣr | on for in ‖   **37, 1.** butan | ʒewitnesse | dô | ʒesylle,
ylle over eras. but olʒ B | se ðe new ab. hine B, se þe H | hyne' | feormiʒe |
.CXX. | þæt hweðere, 2nd e above | þam bef. cyninʒe new B, þam above
H | on for in | ða | folʒade | new 7 above | on for in | þonne oncymð, þonne
ab. H, on new B ‖   **37, 2.** — hæfð End of p. 21 in B — | bete ðætþonne se ðe hine

39, 2. ꝺ no feohte, sie be healfum ðam;   ȝif syxhyndum
þissa hwæðer ȝelimpe, ðriefealdlice *arise be ðære cier-*
liscan bote, twelfhyndum men twyfealdlice be þæs syx-

40.   hyndan bote;   cyninȝes burȝ bryce bið .CXX. scill.,
ærcebiscepes hundniȝontiȝ scill., oðres biscepes ꝺ ealdormonnes .LX. scill., twelfhyndes monnes .XXX. scill.,
syxhyndes monnes .XV. scill., ceorles edorbryce .V.

40, 1. scill.;   ȝif ðisses hwæt ȝelimpe ðenden fyrd ute sie

40, 2. oððe in lencten fæsten, hit sie twybote;   ȝif mon in
lenctenne haliȝ ryht in folce butan leafe alecȝȝe, ȝebete mid .CXX. scill.

.XXXVII.

41.   Se mon se ðe bocland hæbbe ꝺ him his mæȝas
læfden, þonne setton we þæt he hit ne moste sellan of
his mæȝburȝe, ȝif þær bið ȝewrit oððe ȝewitnes ðæt
hit ðara manna forbod wære þe hit on fruman ȝe-
strindon ꝺ þara þe hit him sealdon þæt he swa ne
mote ꝺ þæt þonne on cyninȝes ꝺ on biscopes ȝewitnesse ȝerecce beforan his mæȝum.

.XXXVIII.

42.   Eac we beodað se mon se ðe his ȝefan hamsittendne
wite þæt he ne feohte ær ðam he him ryhtes bidde;

42, 1.   ȝif he mæȝnes hæbbe þæt he his ȝefân beride ꝺ
inne besitte, ȝehealde hine .VII. niht inne ꝺ hine ôn
ne feohte, ȝif he inne ȝeðolian wille ꝺ þonne ymb .VII.
niht, ȝif he wille on hand ȝan ꝺ wæpenu sellan, ȝehealde hine .XXX. nihta ȝesundne ꝺ hine his mæȝum

42, 2. ȝebodie ꝺ his friondum;   ȝif he ðonne cirican ȝeierne,
sie ðonne be ðære cirican are, swa we ær bufan cwædon;

39, 2. Line skipped; revised from B ‖   **40.** hundniȝontiȝ begins 2nd
Ot. fragm. (cf. Ap. A) from which foll. variants: hundniȝontiȝ, d above
old | bisceopes | vac. monnes after syxhyndes? | lenctenne haliȝ, ne ha
over eras. but old E ‖   **41.** ȝestryndon | bisceopes ‖   **42.** sittende | —
wite þæt End of p. 88 in E — ‖   **42, 1.** ȝyf | maȝum ‖   **42, 2.** cirican ðonne?
cf. cyricean ðonne Lamb | sie, i above.

39, 2. 7 ne feohte, sy be healfu*m* ðam. Gyf .VI. hyndu*m* ðissa hweðer ʒelimpe, ðryfealdlice arise bæ ðære cyrliscan bote, twelfhyndu*m* men twifealdlice be ðæs syx-

40. hyndu*m* bote. Cyninʒes burh bryce bið hundtwelftiʒ scill. Erceb*isceopes* hundniʒonti scill. Oþres bisceopes 7 éaldormannes syxtiʒ scill. Twelfhyndes mannes ðrittiʒ scill. Syxhyndes mannes fiftene scyll. *Ceorles*

40, 1. *eoderbryce fif scill.* Gyf ðisses hwæt ʒelimpe ðonne

40, 2. fyrd ute sy oððe in lenctene, *si hit twibote. Gif mànn on lenctene* haliʒ riht in folce buton leafe alecʒe, ʒebete mid̦ hundtwelftiʒum scillinʒum.

MS. H. .XXXVII.

41. Se man se þe bocland hæbbe 7 him þonne his yldran læfdan, þonne setton we ðæt he hit ne mot syllan of his mæʒburʒe, ʒif ðær bið ʒewritt oððe ʒewitnesse ðæt hit ðara manna fodbod wære ðe hit on fruman ʒestrindon 7 ðara ðe hit him sealdon ðæt he swa ne mote 7 þæt þonne on cyninʒes ʒe on biscopes ʒewitnesse ʒerecce beforan his maʒum.

.XXXVIII.

42. Eac we bedað, se man se ðe his ʒefân hamsittende wite, ðæt he ne feohte, ær ðam ðe he him ryhtes

42, 1. bidde. Ʒif he mæʒnes hæbbe, ðæt he his ʒefân berîde and hine inne besitte, ʒehealde hine seofan niht inne 7 him on ne feohte, ʒif he inne ʒeðolian wille, 7 þonne ymbe seofan niht, ʒif he wille ond hand ʒan and his wæpnu syllan, ʒehealde hine .XXX. nihta ʒesundne 7

42, 2. hine his freondum 7 his maʒum bebeode. Ʒif he þonne ciricean ʒyrne, sy ðonne be þære ciricean âre, swa we

---

39, 2. before .VI. new on B | syx | hynd, y out of u B | ðissa above hwæðer | ðri-fealdlice, first e ab. | cierliscan | .XII. | twy- | syxhyndan ‖ **40.** Cyninʒes, a bigger red C put before old C B | brice | .CXX. | Ercebiscopes | .XC. | biscopes | ealder | .LX. | .XII. hyndes | .XXX. | .XV. | ceorles etc. from margin of B, new | edorbrice | V. ‖ **40, 1.** þysses | lenʒten fæsten | si hit etc. from margin B, new | hit sy twybote ‖ **40, 2.** man | lenʒten | ryht H, haliʒrift Lamb | on for in | butan | leafe above | alecʒe, c above | — scillinʒum End of p. 22 in B, next leaf lost — ‖ **41.** þonne above | ʒewitnesse, se above | ʒestri-ndon ‖ **42, 1.** inne above besitte | feohte, o above | ʒeðoli-an | ymbe, e ab. | his above wæpnu | 7 his maʒum above ‖ **42, 2.** ciricean, 2nd i ab. | ciricean, 2nd i ab.

42, 3.   ʒif he ðonne þæs mæʒenes ne hæbbe þæt he hine inne besitte, ride to þam ealdormen, bidde hine fultumes; ʒif he him fultuman ne wille, ride to cyninʒe ær he

42, 4. feohte. Eac swelce ʒif mon becume on his ʒefân 7 he hine ǽr hamfæstne ne wite, ʒif he wille his wæpen sellan, hine mon ʒehealde .XXX. nihta 7 ·hine his freondum ʒecyðe; ʒif he ne wille his wæpenu sellan, þonne mot he feohtan on hine; ʒif he wille on hond ʒan 7 his wæpenu sellan 7 hwa ofer ðæt on him feohte, ʒielde swa wer swa wunde swa he ʒewyrce 7 wite 7

42, 5. hæbbe his mæʒ forworht.   Eac we cweðað þæt mon mote mid his hlaforde feohtan orwiʒe, ʒif mon on ðone hlaford fiohte, swa môt se hlaford mid þy men feohtan;

42, 6.   æfter þære ilcan wisan mon mot feohtan mid his ʒeborene mæʒe, ʒif hine mon on woh onfeohteð, buton

42, 7. wið his hlaforde, þæt we ne liefað,   7 mon mot feohtan ôrwiʒe, ʒif he ʒemeteð oþerne æt his æwum wife betynedum durum oððe under anre rêon, oððe æt his dehter æwumborenre, oððe æt his swister borenre oððe æt his medder ðe wære to æwum wife forʒifen his fæder.

.XXXVIlII.

43.   Eallum frioum monnum ðas daʒas sien forʒifene butan þeowum monnum 7 esne wyrhtan: .XII. daʒas on ʒehhol 7 ðone dæʒ þe crist ðone deofol oferswiðde 7 scs. ʒreʒorius ʒemynd dæʒ 7 .VII. daʒas to eastron 7 VII ofer, 7 an dæʒ æt sce. petres tide 7 sce. paules 7 on hærfeste ða fullan wican ǽr sca. marian mæssan 7 æt eallra haliʒra weorðunʒe anne dæʒ, 7 .IIII. wodnesdaʒas on .IIII. ymbren wicum ðeowum monnum eallum sien forʒifen þam þe him leofost sie to sellanne æʒhwæt ðæs ðe him æniʒ mon for ʒodes noman ʒeselle oððe hie on æneʒum hiora hwilsticcum ʒeearnian mæʒen.

42, 3. ʒyf ‖   **42, 4.** after ʒecyþe, ʒyf ‖   **42, 5.** cwæðað ‖   **42, 6.** lyfað ‖   **42, 7.** oððe æt his swister borenre, written above in E, yet prob. same hand | sweoster borenre | forʒyfen | XXXVIIII, last I invisible E | — 42, 7 ends with p. 89 in E — ‖   **43.** forʒyfene | oferswiþde, d above | weorþun, End of second Ot. fragment, cf. Ap. A.

Continuation of Variants from p. 103.
marian | ænne | .IIII. | .IIII. | forʒifen | leofast | æniʒ man | heora, o above | ʒeearni-an | maʒen.

42, 3. ær bufan cwædon. ꝣif he ðonne ðæs mæꝥnes næbbe
ðæt he hine inne besitte mæꝛe, ride to ðam ealdormen
7 bidde hine fultumes; ꝛif he him fultomian nelle, ride
42, 4. to cyninꝛe ær he feohte. Eac swylce ꝛif man becyme on his ꝛefân 7 he hine ær þam fæstne ne wite,
ꝛif he wille his wæpen syllan, hine man ꝛehealde
.XXX. nihta 7 hine his freondum ꝛecyðe 7 ꝛif he nelle
his wæpen sellan, ðonne mot he feohtan on hine. ꝣif
he wille on hand ꝛân 7 his wæpen sellan 7 ꝛif hwa
ofer ðæt on hine feohte, ꝛylde swa wer swa wite, swa
ðær he ꝛewyrce 7 wite ðæt he hæbbe his mæꝛ for-
42, 5. worht. Eac we cweðaþ *þæt* man mote mid his hlaforde feohtan on wiꝛe. ꝣif mon on þone hlaford feohte,
42, 6. swa mot se hlaford mid þam men feohtan. Æfter
ðære ilcan wisan man mot feohtan mid his ꝛeborenum
mæꝛe, ꝛif him man on wôh onfeohteð, butan wið his
42, 7. hlaforde, ðæt we ne lyfað,   7 man mot feohtan or-
wiꝛe ꝛif he oðerne ꝛemeteð mid his æwum wife be-
tynede durum oððe under anre reon, oþþe mid his
dehter æwum borenre, oððe mid his swister æwumborenre, oððe mid his meder þe wære to æwum wife
forꝛifen his fæder.
                        .XXXVIIII.
43.   Eallum freo mannum ðas daꝛas syn forꝛifenne
butan ðeowum mannum 7 esne wyrhtum: .XII. daꝛas
on ꝛehhol 7 ðone dæꝛ ðe crist oferswiðde ðone deofol
MS.B. 7 scs. ꝛreꝛorius ꝛemynd dæꝛ 7 seofon *daꝛas to eastron
7 seofen ofer 7 an dæꝛ æt sce. petres tide 7 sce.
paules 7 on herfeste ða fullan wucan ær sca. maria
mæssan. And æt ealra haliꝛra weorðunꝛe an dæꝛ 7
feower wodnesdaꝛas on feower ymbren wucum ðeowum
mannum eallum synd forꝛyfen ðam ðe him leofest sy
to syllanne æꝛhwæt ðæs ðe him man for ꝛodes naman
ꝛesylle oððe heo on æniꝛum heora hwilstyccum ꝛear-
nian maꝛan.

42, 3. 7 above bidde | fultomian, i ab. || 42, 4. 7 he hine, he above |
after ꝛecyðe, 7 above || 42, 7. betynede- | anre, n ab. | oððe mid his
swister æwumborenre on margin — cf. note on E. Lamb. has æwum ||
43. freo- | above ꝛehhol, ꝛeol | seofon ends extract from H, now given
variant from B | eastrum | .VII. | to for æt | tide after paules | hærfest |

.XL.

44.   Heafod wunde to bote, ʒif ða ban beoð butu ðyrel,
44, 1. .XXX. scill. ʒeselle him mon;   ʒif ðæt uterre ban bið
þyrel, ʒeselle .XV. scill. to bote.

.XLI.

45.   Gif in feaxe bið wund inces lanʒ, ʒeselle anne
45, 1. scill. to bote;   ʒif beforan feaxe bið wund inces lanʒ,
tweʒen scill. to bote.

.XLII.

46.   Gif him mon âslea oþer eare of, ʒeselle .XXX.
46, 1. scill. to bote;   ʒif se hlyst oðstande þæt he ne mæʒe
ʒehieran, ʒeselle .LX. scill. to bote.

.XLIII.

47.   Gif mon men eaʒe ofâslea, ʒeselle him mon .LX.
scill. 7 VI. scill. 7 VI. pæninʒas 7 ðriddan dǽl pæninʒes to
47, 1. bote;   ʒif hit in ðam heafde sie 7 he noht ʒeseon ne
48. mæʒe mid, stande ðriddan dæl þære bote inne;   ʒif
mon oðrum þæt neb ôfaslea, ʒebete him mid .LX. scill.;
49. ʒif mon oðrum ðone toð on foran heafde ôfaslea, ʒebete
49, 1. þæt mid .VIII. scill.;   ʒif hit sie se wonʒtoð, ʒeselle
49, 2. .IIII. scill. to bote;   monnes tux bið .XV. scill. weorð;
50.   ʒif monnes ceacan mon forslihð, þæt hie beoð fo-
50, 1. rode, ʒebete mid .XV. scill.   Monnes cinban, ʒif hit
51. bið toclofen, ʒeselle mon .XII. scill. to bote.   Ʒif
52. monnes ðrotbolla bið þyrel, ʒebete mid .XII. scill.   Ʒif
monnes tunʒe bið of heafde oþres monnes dædum dôn,
53. þæt biþ ʒelic 7 eaʒan bot;   ʒif mon bið on eaxle
wund þæt þæt lið seaw ûtflowe, ʒebete mid .XXX.
54. scill.   Ʒif se earm bið forad bufan elmboʒan, þær
55. sculon .XV. scill. to bote.   Ʒif ða earm scancan beoð
56. beʒen forade, sio bot bið .XXX. scill.;   ʒif se ðuma

---

47. after .LX. scill. at end of line appar. ʒes erased E ‖   **49, 2.** tux
bið End of p. 90 in E ‖   **50.** ceacan, first c above.

Continuation of Variants from p. 105.

.XV. scll. ‖   **50, 1.** Mannes | cinn, last n ab. | .XII. ‖   **51.** byð | þyrel |
ʒebete ðæt | .XII. ‖   **52.** mannes | dedum | ʒedôn, ʒe ab. | Here 1½ in.
erased in B; prob. þæt bið ʒelic was written twice | eaʒan ‖   **53.** man bið
on ða eaxle | ʒewunded, ʒe, ed above | .XXX. ‖   **54.** forod | þæm above
el-boʒan | .XV. ‖   **55.** .XXX. ‖   **56.** se þuma | aslæʒen | sceal, a above |
.XXX.

44.   Heafod wunde to bote, ȝyf ða ban beoð butu þyrle,
44, 1. .XXX. scill. ȝesylle him mon; ȝyf þæt uttre ban biþ
ðyrl, ȝesylle fihtyne scill. to bote.

45.   Gyf in feaxe bið wund ynces lanȝ, ȝesylle anne
45, 1. scill. to bote; ȝyf he beforan feaxe bið wund, ynces
lanȝ, tweȝen scillinȝas to bote.

46.   Gyf him man ofaslea þæt oðer eare of, ȝesylle
46, 1. him ðrittiȝ scill. to bote; ȝyf se lyst ætstande, ðæt
he ne mæȝ ȝehyran, ȝesylle syxti scill. him to bote.

47.   Gyf mon men eaȝe ofaslea, ȝesylle him mon syxti
scill. 7 syx scill. 7 syx peneȝas 7 ðriddam dæl peniȝes
47, 1. to bote; ȝyf hit in ðan heafde sy 7 he noht ȝeseon
ne mæȝe mîd, stande driddan dæl ðære bote inne.
48.   Gif mann oðrum þæt nebb ofaslea, ȝebete hit mid
49.   feowertiȝ scill. Gyf man oðrum ðone toð on foren
49, 1. heafde ofslea, ȝebetað þæt mid eahta scill. Gyf hit sy
49, 2. ðe wonȝtoð, ȝesylle feower scill. to bote; monnes tux
50.   biþ syxtyne scill. weorð. Gyf man mannes ceacan
50, 1. forslea, þæt heo beon forede, fiftyne scill. ȝebete.
51.   Monnes cinban ȝyf hit bið toclofen, ȝesylle mon
52.   twelf scill. to bote. Gyf mannes ðrotbolla bið ðyrl,
53.   ȝebete mid twelf scill. Gyf mannes tunȝe bið of
54.   heafde oðres monnes dædum ȝedon, þæt bið ȝelic 7
55.   eaȝon bot. Gyf mon on eaxle bið ȝewunded, þæt
56.   þæt liðseaw utflowe, ȝebete mid ðrittiȝ scill. Gyf
se earm bið forad bufan ðam elboȝan, ðær sculon
fiftyne scill. to bote. Gyf ða earmscancan beoð
beȝen forade, seo bot bið ðrittiȝ scill. Gyf ðe ðuma

---

44. butu beoð | butu þyrle X written over eras. in same hand B |
ðyrle, e ab. | ȝesylle .XXX. scll. him mon || 44, 1. utre | byð | .XV. ||
45. wund bið ynces | 45, 1. vac. he | .II. || 46. asclea | þæt above oðer |
of well erased B, vac. of H | .XXX. || 46, 1. hlyst | opstande | mæȝe |
ȝehiran | .LX. scll. him to bote ȝesylle || 47. his eaȝe | .LX. | .VI. | .VI.
peninȝas || 47, 1. on ðam | mæȝe End of p. 23 in B | se þriddan || 48.
from margin of B, new | man | ôfaslea him for hit | .LX. || 49. oþrum of-
aslea on foran heafde ðone toð | ȝebete | .VIII. || 49, 1. wanȝ toþ ȝebete
mid .IIII. scll. || 49, 2. mannes | .XV. || 50. mannes ceacan mau | for-
slea, erasure at end B, forslyhð H | hy | forede, last e above | ȝebete mid

56, 1. biⸯ ôfaslæʒen, þam sceal .XXX. scill. to bote. Ʒif se

57. næʒl biⸯ ôfasleʒen, ⸯam sculon .V. scill. to bote. Ʒif
se scytefinʒer biⸯ ôfasleʒen, sio bôt biⸯ .XV. scill.,

58. his næʒles biⸯ .III. scill; ʒif se midlesta finʒer sie
ôfasleʒen, sio bot biⸯ .XII. scill. 7 his næʒles bot biⸯ

59. .II. scill. Ʒif se ʒoldfinʒer sie ôfasleʒen, to þam sculon
.XVII. scill. to bote, 7 his næʒles .IIII. scill. to bote.

60. Ʒif se lytla finʒer biⸯ ôfasleʒen, ⸯam sceal to bote
.VIII. scill. 7 an scill. his næʒles, ʒif se sie ôfasleʒen.

61. Ʒif mon biⸯ on hrif wund, ʒeselle him mon .XXX.

61, 1. scill. to bote. Ʒif he ⸯurhwund biⸯ, æt ʒehweⸯerum

62. muⸯe .XX. scill. Ʒif monnes ⸯeoh biⸯ þyrel, ʒeselle

62, 1. him mon .XXX. scill. to bote; ʒif hit forad sie, sio

63. bot eac biⸯ .XXX. scill.; ʒif se sconca biⸯ þyrel be-

63, 1. neoⸯan cneowe, ⸯær sculon .XII. scill. to bote. Ʒif he
forad sie beneoⸯan cneowe, ʒeselle him .XXX. scill.

64. to bote; ʒif sio micle ta biⸯ ôfasleʒen, ʒeselle him

64, 1. .XX. scill. to bote; ʒif hit sie sio æfterre ta, .XV.

64, 2. scill. to bote ʒeselle him mon; ʒif seo midleste ta

64, 3. sie ôfasleʒen, þær sculon .VIIII. scill. to bote; ʒif hit

64, 4. biⸯ sio feorþe ta, ⸯær sculon .VI. scill. to bote. Ʒif

65. sio lytle ta sie ôfasleʒen, ʒeselle him .V. scill. Ʒif
mon sie on þa herⸯan to ⸯam swiⸯe wund þæt he ne
mæʒe bearn *ʒestrienan,* ʒebete him ⸯæt mid .LXXX. scill.

66. Ʒif men sie se earm mid honda mid ealle ofâcorfen

66, 1. beforan elmboʒan, ʒebete ⸯæt mid .LXXX. scill.; æʒhwelcere wunde beforan feaxe 7 beforan sliefan 7 bene-

67. oⸯan cneowe, sio bot biⸯ twy sceatte mare. Ʒif sio
lendenbræde biⸯ forsleʒen, þær sceal .LX. scill. to bote;

67, 1. ʒif hio biⸯ onbestunʒen, ʒeselle .XV. scill. to bote;

67, 2. ʒif hio biⸯ ⸯurhⸯyrel, ⸯonne sceal ⸯær .XXX. scill.

64, 2. midleste ta End of p. 91 in E — || **65.** *ʒestrienan* from H ||

Continuation of Variants from p. 107.

.XXX. || **64.** miccle, first c above | tâ | ofaslaʒen | man | .XX. || **64, 1.** Ʒif
seo æftere tâ sy ofaslæʒen, ʒesylle him man .XV. || **64, 2.** tâ | ofaslæʒen |
sculon | .IX. || **64, 3.** tâ | ⸯær | .VI. || **64, 4.** tâ biⸯ | ofaslæʒen | him.V.,
vac. mon || **65.** man | herⸯan | ʒewunded, ʒe, ed above | ʒestrienan for
beʒytan | .LXXX. scillinʒum || **66.** after earm, mid handa mid ealle | ofacorfen |
el-boʒan | .LXXX. || **66, 1.** æʒhwylcre | slyfan | biⸯ | twy sceatte mare || **67.**
bræde | .LX. || **67, 1.** — onbestunʒen End of p. 25 in B — | .XV. scll. to bote ||

56, 1. biÐ ofaslaȝen, Ðæm sceall Ðrittiȝ scill. to bote. Gyf
57. se næȝel biÐ ofaslaȝen, seo bot biÐ fif scill. Gyf se
scytefinȝer biÐ ofaslaȝen, seo bot biÐ fiftyne scill. 7
58. his næȝles beoÐ .IIII. scill. Gyf se midleste finȝer
sy ofaslaȝen, seo bot biÐ .XII. scill. 7 his næȝles .II.
59. scill. Gyf se ȝoldfinȝer sy ofaslæȝen, to Ðæm sculon
60. seofentyne scill. to bote 7 his næȝles .IIII. scill. Gyf
se lytle finȝer sy ofaslaȝen, Ðam sceal to bote niȝon
61. scill., 7 an scill. his næȝles, ȝyf he sy ofaslaȝen. Gyf
61, 1. mon rif wund biÐ, ȝesylle him mon Ðrittiȝ scill. Gyf
62. he Ðurhwund biÐ, æt æȝÐran muÐe twentiȝ scill. Gyf
monnes Ðeoh biÐ Ðurl, ȝesylle him man Ðrittiȝ scill. to
62, 1. bote; ȝyf hit forad sy, seo bot biÐ .XXX. scill.
63. Gyf se scanca biÐ Ðurl beneoÐan cweowe, Ðær
63, 1. sculon twelf scill.; ȝyf he forad sy beneoÐan cnêowe,
64. ȝesylle him Ðritti scill. to bote. Gyf mycle ta biÐ
64, 1. ofaslaȝen, ȝesylle him mon twentiȝ scill. to bote. Gyf
64, 2. hit sêo æftere tâ sy, fiftene scill. to bote. Gyf seo
midlæste tâ sy ofaslaȝen, Ðær scylan niȝon scill. to
64, 3. bote. Gyf hit biÐ seo feorÐe tâ, Ðar sculon syx scill.
64, 4. to bote. Gyf seo lytle tâ sy ofaslaȝen, ȝesylle him
65. mon fif scill. to bote. Gyf mon sy on Ða hærÐan to
Ðan swiþe ȝewundod þæt he ne mæȝe bearn beȝytan,
66. ȝebete him þæt mid hundeahtatiȝ scill. Gyf men
sy se earm ofacoruen beforan elmboȝan, ȝebete þæt
66, 1. mid hundeahtatiȝ scill.; æȝhwylcere wunde beforan
feaxe 7 beforan slefan 7 beneoÐan cneowe, seo bot
67. byÐ twyȝȝylde mare; ȝyf seo lendenbreda biÐ for-
67, 1. slæȝen, þær sceal syxtiȝ scill. to bote. Gyf heo biÐ
onbestunȝen, fihtene scill.;

---

56. 1, næȝl | ofaslæȝen, Ðan sculon. V. scll. to bote | eras. after fif B ||
57. ofaslæȝen | .XV. | biÐ. V. || 58. midlæsta | biÐ | ofaslæȝen | næȝles
bot biÐ .II. || 59. biÐ for sy | .XVII. | his næȝles III in same hand over
eras. B | .IIII. End of p. 24 in B | scll. to bote || 60. litla | biÐ for
sy | ofaslæȝen | Ðæm above | sceal, a above | .IX. scll. | he, prob. orig.
hit, B, se H | biÐ for sy | ofaslæȝen, .I. scll. | 61. mon on rife ȝe-
wunded, on, e, ȝe, ed new above B, man biÐ on hrife wund H | man |
.XXX. | scll. to bote || 61, 1. æȝÐrum | .XX. || 62. mannes | Ðurl, y
stroke new B, þyrel H | .XXX. || 62, 1. biÐ eac || 63. Ðurl, y stroke
new B, þyrel H | cneowe | .XII. | scll. to bote || 63, 1. biÐ for sy | man

68.   to bote. Ʒif mon biðֿ in eaxle wund, ʒebete mid .LXXX.

69.   scill., ʒif se mon cwic sie;   ʒif mon oðrum ða hond utan forslea, ʒeselle him .XX. scill. to bote, ʒif hine

69, 1.   mon ʒelacnian mæʒe;   ʒif hio healf on weʒ fleoʒe,

70.   þon*ne* sceal .XL. scill. to bote; ʒif mon oþrum rib forslea binnan ʒehaldre hyde, ʒeselle .X. scill. to bote.

70, 1.   Ʒif sio hyd sie tobrocen 7 mon ban ôfâdo, ʒeselle

71.   .XV. scill to botc.   Ʒif monnes eaʒe him mon ôfaslea, oðֿðe his hand oððe his fot, ðær ʒæð ʒelic bot to eallum, .VI. pæninʒas 7 .VI. scill. 7 .LX. scill. 7

72.   ðriddan dæl pæninʒes.   Ʒif monnes sconca bið ôfasleʒen wið ðæt cneou, ðær sceal .LXXX. scill to bote.

73.   Ʒif mon oðrum ða sculdru forslea, ʒeselle him mon

74.   .XX. scill. to bote.   Ʒif hie mon inbeslea 7 mon ban

75.   ôfado, ʒeselle mon ðæs to bote .XV. scill.   Ʒif mon ða ʒreatan sinwe forslea, ʒif hie mon ʒelacnian mæʒe

75, 1.   þæt hio hal sie, ʒeselle .XII. scill. to bote;   ʒif se mon healt sie for þære sinwe wunde 7 hine mon ʒe-

76.   lacnian ne mæʒe, ʒeselle .XXX. scill. to bote;   ʒif ða smalan sinwe mon forslea, ʒeselle him mon .VI. scill.

77.   to bote;   ʒif mon oðrum ða ʒeweald forslea uppe on þam sweoran 7 forwundie to þam swiðe þæt he naʒe þære ʒeweald 7 hwæðre lifie swa ʒescended, ʒeselle him mon .C. scill. to bote, buton him witan ryhtre 7 mare ʒereccan.

.XLIIII.

Ic ine mid ʒodes ʒife wesseaxna kyninʒ mid ʒeðeahte 7 mid lare cenredes mines fæder 7 heddes mines biscepes 7 eorcenwoldes mines biscepes mid eallum minum ealdormonnu*m* 7 þæm ieldstan witum minre ðeode 7 êac micelre ʒesomnunʒe ʒodes ðeowa wæs smeaʒende be ðære hælo urra sawla 7 be ðam

---

76. — ʒif ða End of p. 92 in E — |

Continuation of Variants from p. 109.

p. 26 in B — | sweoran | forwundiʒe | ðæra | vac. ðeah | hwæðere, first e above | libbe | ʒescynded | him .C. scll., vac. mon | butan | mare ʒereccan 7 ryhtre || **Introd.** Here Ines cyninʒes asetnysse in H | ine appar. over eras, but old B, yne H | westseaxena, second e above | cænredes | biscopes | eorcenwaldes | biscopes | ealder | witum | micelre | ʒesamnunʒe |

67, 2. ʒyf heo biÐ ÐurhÐurl, Ðonne sceal Ðrittiʒ scill. to bote.

68.   Gyf mon biÐ on eaxle ʒewundad, ʒebete mid

69.   hundeahta*ti* scill., ʒyf se mon cwic sy. Gyf man on oÐru*m*
Ða hand uton forslea, ʒesylle him .XX. scill. to bote. Gyf

69, 1. hine man ʒelacnian mæʒe. Gyf he healf on weʒ fleoʒe,

70.   Ðonne sceal syxtiʒ scill. to bote. Gyf man oÐru*m* ribb
forslêa binnan ʒehalre hyde, ʒesylle tyn scill. to bote.

70, 1.   Gyf seo hyd sy tobrocen 7 man ban ofadô, ʒesylle

71.   fiftyne scill.   Gyf mon him *eaʒe* ofslêa oþþe his hand
oÐÐe his fott, Ðær ʒæÐ ʒelic bot tô eallu*m*, syx peneʒas

72.   7 syx scill. 7 syxtiʒ scill. 7 driddan dæl peniʒes.   Gyf
mannes sceanca biÐ ofaslaʒen wiÐ þ*æt* cneow, Ðær sceall

73.   hundeahtati scill. to bote.   Gyf man oÐru*m* Ða sculdru

74.   forslea, ʒesylle him mon .XX. scill. to bote.   Gyf hine
mon inbeslêa 7 man ban ofadô, ʒesylle mon Ðæs to bote

75.   fiftyne scill.;   ʒyf mon Ða ʒreatan synewe forslêa, ʒyf
hine man ʒelacnian mæʒe þ*æt* he hal sy, ʒesylle twelf

75, 1. scill. to bote.   Gyf se mon healt sy for Ðære synewe
wunde 7 hine mon ʒelacnian ne mæʒe, ʒesylle .XX.

76.   scill. to bote;   ʒyf Ða *smalan* synewan man forslêa,

77.   ʒesylle hi*m* man syx scill. to bote.   Gyf man oÐrum Ða
ʒewald forslêa uppe on Ðam sweore 7 forwundie to Ðam
swiÐe þ*æt* he naʒe þær ʒeweald 7 Ðeah hwæÐere lifiʒe
swa ʒescend, ʒesylle him mon hund scill. to bote,
buton him witan rihtre 7 mare ʒereccan.

     Ic ine mid ʒodes ʒyfe wessexena cyninʒ mid ʒe-
Ðeahte 7 mid lare cenredes mines fæder 7 heddes
mines bisceopes 7 erconwoldes mines bisceopes 7 mid
eallu*m* minu*m* ealdormannu*m* 7 Ðam yldestan witan
minre Ðeode 7 eac mycelre somnunʒe ʒodes þeowena

67, 2. Ðurl, y stroke new B, þyrel H | sceal, a ab. | þær above .XXX. ‖
68. man | ʒewundod, ʒe, od above ǀ hundeahta, ti added new above B,
.LXXX. H | man ‖   69. utan ‖   69, 1. heo for he | syxtiʒ, on marg. new
feowertiʒ B, .XL. H ‖   70. ribb, last b above | .X. ‖   70, 1. bân | ofadô |
.XV. scll. to bote ‖   71. eaʒe supplied in an eras. in B, mannes eaʒe him
man ofaslea H | fôt | ʒeÐ | .VI. | .VI. | .LX. | peni-ʒes ‖   72. scanca |
ofaslæʒen | sceal, a above | .LXXX. ‖   74. hine, n above | man | bân | ofadô |
.XV. ‖   75. man | sinwe | ʒelacni-an | he- B, heo H | .XII. ‖   75, 1. se
above man | sinwe | .XX., on marg. new .XXX. B, .XXX. H ‖   76. smalan,
s appar. new and 1 over eras. B | sinwe | .VI. ‖   77. — oÐrum End of

staþole ures rices þætte ryht æw 7 ryhte cynedomas
ðurh ure folc ʒefæstnode 7 ʒetrymede wæron þætte
næniʒ ealdormonna ne us underʒeðeodedra æfter þam
wære awendende ðas ure dômas.

.XLV.

1.   Ærest we bebeodað þætte ʒodes ðeowas hiora
ryhtreʒol on ryht healdan; æfter þam we bebeodað
þætte ealles folces æw 7 domas ðus sien ʒehealdene.

.XLVI.

2.   Cild binnan ðriteʒum nihta sie ʒefulwad; ʒif hit
swa ne sie, .XXX. scill. ʒebete; ʒif hit ðonne sie dead
butan fulwihte, ʒebete he hit mid eallum ðam ðe he aʒe.

.XLVII.

3.   Ʒif ðeowmon wyrce on sunnandæʒ be his hlafordes hæse, sie he frioh 7 se hlaford ʒeselle .XXX.
3, 1. scill. to wite.   Ʒif þonne se ðeowa butan his ʒe-
3, 2. witnesse wyrce, þolie his hyde; ʒif ðonne se friʒea
ðy dæʒe wyrce butan his hlafordes hæse, ðolie his
freotes.

.XLVIII.

4.   Ciricsceattas sîn aʒifene be sce. martines mæssan;
ʒif hwa ðæt ne ʒelæste, sie he scyldiʒ. LX. scill. 7
be .XII.fealdum aʒife þone ciric sceat.

.XLVIIII.

5.   Gyf hwa sie deaðes scyldiʒ 7 he cirican ʒeierne,
5, 1. hæbbe his feorh 7 bete swa him ryht wisiʒe; ʒif hwa
his hyde forwyrce 7 cirican ʒeierne, sie him sio swin-
ʒelle forʒifen.

.L.

6.   Gif hwa ʒefeohte on cyninʒes huse, sie he scyldiʒ
ealles his ierfes 7 sie on cyninʒes dome, hwæðer he
6, 1. lîf aʒe þe naʒe.   Ʒif hwa on mynster ʒefeohte, .CXX.

Introd. æfter þam wære begins Bu. fragm. (cf. App. B), now given
variant from E | **1.** healden | þæm | ʒehealdenne || **2.** .XXX. | nyhtum |
ʒefullod | buton | þæm || **3.** werce | freoh || **3, 1.** ʒewitnysse || **3, 2.** bu-
ton | vac. his before hlafordes | — 3, 2 ends with p. 93 in E — || **4.** sien |
scildiʒ || **5.** vac. he before cirican | ʒeænne | habbe | wisie || **5, 1.** for-
werce | ʒeirne || **6.** kininʒes | habbe for aʒe ||

Continuation of Variants from p. 111.

preost eras. and new si B || **4.** aʒifene | martines | .LX. | .XII. | aʒife |
ciric | sceatt || **5.** 7 cirican, vac. he. || **5, 1.** ciricean, second i ab. | ʒeirne |
forʒifen || **6.** on cyninʒes huse ʒefeohte | hweþer || **6, 1.** .CXX. ||

wæs smeaʒende be ðære hæle ure sawla ꝥ be ðam
staðole ures rices þæt riht æwe ꝥ rihte cynedomas
þurh ure folc ʒefæstnode ꝥ ʒetrymede wæron þæt
næniʒ ealdormanna ne us underʒeðeodendra æfter ðem
wære awendende ðas ure domas.

1. Ærest we bebeodað þæt ʒodas þeowas heora riht
reʒol ʒyman ꝥ on riht healdon; æfter ðam we beodað
þæt ealles folces æw ꝥ domas ðus syn ʒehealdene.

2. Cild binnan .XXX. nihta sy ʒefullad; ʒyf hit swa
ne sy, .XXX. scill. ʒebete; ʒyf hit ðonne sy dead
butan fulluhte, ʒebete he hit mid eallum ðam ðe he aʒe.

3. Gyf ðeowmon wyrce on sunnandæʒ be his hlafordes
hæse, sy he freo ꝥ se hlaford ʒesylle .XXX. scill. to
3, 1. wite;   ʒyf þonne se ðeowa butan his ʒewitnysse
3, 2. wyrce, þolie his hyde, oððe hydʒyldes;   ʒyf ðonne se
friʒea ðy dæʒe wyrce buton his hlafordes hæse, ðolie
his freotes, oððe sixtiʒ scill. ꝥ preost twyscyldi.

4. Cyricsceattas syn aʒeuene be sce. martynes mæssan;
ʒyf hwa þæt ne ʒelæste, sy he scyldiʒ feortiʒ scill. ꝥ
be twelffealdum aʒyfe ðone cyricsceat.

5. Gyf hwâ sy deaðes scyldiʒ ꝥ he cyricean ʒeyrne,
5, 1. hæbbe his feorh ꝥ bete swa him riht wisie;   ʒyf hwâ
his hyde forwyrce ꝥ cyricean ʒeyrne. Sy him seo
swinʒle forʒyfen.

6. Gyf hwa ʒefeohte on cyninʒes huse, sy he scyldiʒ
ealles his yrfes ꝥ sy on cyninʒes dome hwæðer he lif
6, 1. aʒe ðe naʒe. Gyf hwa on mynstre ʒefeohte, hund-

þeowa | þæt, te added above B, ðætte, te above H | ryht | ryhte | ʒetrymede,
new m after y at end of line B | þætte, te ab., for þæt (næniʒ) | ealder |
þam for ðem ‖ 1. heora, o ab. | ryht reʒol on riht healden, vac. ʒyman
ꝥ H, found in Lamb. | þætte, te ab., for þæt | æw, w erased B, æw H ‖
2. Cyld | nihtum | ʒefullod | ʒebete hit, vac. he | âʒe ‖ 3. man | — dæʒ
be End of p. 27 in B — | freoh ‖ 3, 1. ʒewitnesse | on margin oððe
hyd ʒyld H, found in Lamb ‖ 3, 2. friʒea, ʒe above | butan | ðoliʒe |
oððe .LX. scll. ꝥ preost twyscildiʒ on margin H, found in Lamb | after

6, 2. scill. ӡebete;   ӡif hwa on ealdormonnes huse ӡefeohte
oððe on oðres ӡeðunӡenes witan, .LX. scill. ӡebete he
6, 3. 7 oþer .LX. ӡeselle to wite.   Ӡif ðonne on ӡafol-
ӡeldan huse oððe on ӡebures ӡefeohte, .CXX. scill. to
6, 4. wite ӡeselle 7 þam ӡebure .VI. scill.   7 þeah hit sie
on middum felda ӡefohten, .CXX. scill. to wite sie
6, 5. aӡifen. Ӡif ðonne on ӡebeorscipe hie ӡeciden 7 oðer
hiora mid ӡeðylde hit forbere, ӡeselle se oðer .XXX.
scill. to wite.

.LI.

7.   Gif hwa stalie swa his wîf nyte 7 his bearn, ӡe-
7, 1. selle .LX. scill. to wite;   ӡif he ðonne stalie on ӡewitnesse ealles his hiredes, ӡonӡen hie ealle on ðeowot;
7, 2.   .X. wintre cniht mæӡ bion ðiefðe ӡewita.

.LII.

8.   Gif hwa him ryhtes bidde beforan hwelcum scîr-
men oððe oþrum deman 7 âbiddan ne mæӡe 7 him
wedd sellan nelle, ӡebete .XXX. scill. 7 binnan .VII.
nihton ӡedô hine ryhtes wierðne.

.LIII.

9.   Gif hwa wrace dô ær ðon he him ryhtes bidde,
þæt he him onnime aӡife 7 forӡielde 7 ӡebete mid
.XXX. scill.

.LIIII.

10.   Ӡif hwa binnan þam ӡemærum ures rices reaflâc
7 niednæme dô, aӡife he ðone reaflac 7 ӡeselle .LX.
scill. to wite.

.LV.

11.   Gif hwa his aӡenne ӡeleod bebycӡӡe ðeowne oððe
friӡne, ðeah he scyldiӡ sie, ofer sæ, forӡielde hine
his were.

.LVI.

12.   Gif ðeof sie ӡefonӡen, swelte he deaðe oððe his
lif be his were man aliese.

6, 2. scll. | vac. he after ӡebete ‖ **6, 3.** mon for ðonne | ӡafolӡildan | bure for ӡebure ‖ **6, 4.** middan | ӡefeohtan ‖ **6, 5.** bið on ӡebeorscipe ‖ **7, 1.** ӡewitnysse | eallæs ‖ **7, 2.** beon | þeofðe | ӡewitæ or ӡewitte? ‖ **8.** hine | wed | mid .XXX. | nyhtum | weorðe ‖ **9.** wræce | him on End of p. 94 in E | forӡylde ‖ **11.** bebycӡe | scildiӡ ‖ **12.** monna liese or læse ‖

6, 2. twelftiȝ scill. ȝebete. Gyf hwâ in ealdormannes huse feohte, oððe on oðres ȝeðunȝenes witan, syxtiȝ

6, 3. scill. ȝebete hê 7 oðer syxtiȝ ȝesylle he to wite. Gyf ðonne on ȝafolȝylden huse oððe on ȝebures ȝefeohte, hundtwelftiȝ scill. to wite ȝesylle 7 ðæm ȝebures syx

6, 4. scill. 7 ðeah hit sy on middan felda ȝefohtan, hund-

6, 5. twelftiȝ scill. to wite sy aȝyfen; ȝyf ðonne on ȝebeorscipe hi ȝeciden 7 oðer heora mid ȝeþyldê hît forbere, ȝesylle se oðer .XXX. scill. to wite.

7. Gyf hwâ staliȝe swa his wif nyte 7 his bearn,

7, 1. ȝesylle syxti scill. to wite; ȝyf he ðonne stalie on ȝewitnysse ealles his hiredes, ȝanȝen heo ealle on

7, 2. ðeowet; tynwintre cniht mæȝ beon þyfðe ȝewita.

8. Gyf hwa him rihtes bidde beforan hwylcum scirmen oððe oðrum deman 7 abiddan ne mæȝe, 7 him wed syllan nylle, ȝebete .XXX. scill. 7 binnon seofen niht ȝedo hine rihtes wyrðe.

9. Gyf hwa wrace dô ær ðon he him rihtes bidde, þæt he him onnime aȝyfe 7 forȝylde 7 bete .XXX. scill.

10. Gyf hwa binnan ðam ȝemærum ures rices reaflac 7 nydnæme dô, aȝyfe he ðone reaflac 7 ȝesylle syxti scill. to wite.

11. Gyf hwa his aȝene leodan bebicȝe ðeowne oððe friȝe, þeah he scyldiȝ sy, ofer sæ̂, forȝylde hine be his wêre.

12. Gyf ðeof sy ȝefonȝen, swylte he deaðe oððe his lif be his were mon alyse.

6, 2. on for in | ealder | huse oððe on oþres witan ȝeþunȝenan ȝefeohte, .LX. | oþer .LX. to wite, vac. ȝesylle he || **6, 3.** ȝafolȝildan | .CXX. | ȝebure | .VI. || **6, 4.** ȝefeohten on middan felda, ȝefeohten, first e above | .CXX. | aȝîfen || **6, 5.** ȝyf End of p. 28 in B | hy | .XXX. to wite, scll. on marg. | **7.** hit nyte, hit ab. | .LX. || **7, 1.** ȝewitnesse | hyredes | ȝân- | hy || **7, 2.** .X. wintra | beon above || **8.** ryhtes | vac. oðrum | 7 him ryht abiddan | wedd, last d above | nelle | ȝebete above .XXX. | binnan | .VII. | nihtum | ȝedô || **9.** dô | ær he, vac. ðon | ryhtes | aȝife | forȝilde | ȝebete || **10.** reaflac 7 nydnæme binnan þam ȝemærum ures rices ȝedo | aȝife | after aȝyfe eras. in B | .LX. || **11.** aȝenne | leod above | ȝebycȝe | friȝne, 7 before ofer, sende after sæ̂ new in B, 7 ofer sæ̂ ȝesylle H | forȝilde | 7 wið ȝodd deoplice bete on marg. B, also Lamb || **12.** ȝefanȝen | vac. mon ||

114

.LVII.

13. Gif hwa beforan biscepe his ӡewitnesse 7 his wed
13, 1. aleoӡe, ӡebete mid .CXX. scill.; ðeofas we hatað oð
.VII. men, from .VII. hloð oð .XXXV., siððan bið here.

.LVIII.

14. Se ðe hloþe betyӡen sie, ӡeswicne se hine be .CXX.
hida oððe swa bete.

.LVIIII.

15. Se ðe hereteama betyӡen sie, he hine be his
15, 1. werӡilde âliese oððe be his were ӡeswicne; se að
15, 2. sceal bion healf be huslӡenӡum; þeof siððan he bið
on cyninӡes bende, nah he þa swicne.

.LX.

16. Se ðe ðeof ofslihð, se mot ӡecyðan mid aðe þæt
he hine synniӡne ofsloӡe, nalles ða ӡeӡildan.

.LXI.

17. Se ðe forstolen flæsc findeð 7 ӡedyrneð, ӡif he
dear, he mot mid aðe ӡecyðan þæt he hit aӡe; se
ðe hit ofspyrèð, he ah ðæt meldfeoh.

.LXII.

18. Cierlisc mon ӡif he ôft betyӡen wære, ӡif he æt
siðestan sie ӡefonӡen, slea mon hond oððe fot.

.LXIII.

19. Cyninӡes ӡeneat ӡif his wer bið twelf hund scill., he
mot swerian for syxtiӡ hida, ӡif he bið huslӡenӡea.

.LXIIII.

20. Gif feorcund mon oððe fremde butan weӡe ӡeond
wudu ӡonӡe 7 ne hrieme ne horn blawe, for ðeof he
bið to profianne oððe to sleanne oððe to âliesanne.

.LXV.

21. Gif mon ðonne þæs ôfslæӡenan weres bidde, he
mot ӡecyþan þæt he hine for ðeof ofsloӡe, nalles þæs

---

13. biscope | hundtwelftiӡum ‖ **13, 1.** with 14 as .LVIII., so also in
H | hatað .VII. men, vac. oð ‖ **14.** he for se ‖ **15.** teame | betiӡen | were-
ӡilde ‖ **15, 1.** byon ‖ **15, 2.** with 16 as .LX., so also in H | kininӡes |
swycne ‖ **16.** ofslehð | he for se | ӡeceþan mid aþe | þa (for þam?) ӡe-
ӡildanum ‖ **17.** ӡederneð | ofspereð ‖ **18.** Cirlisc | betwyӡen ‖ **19.** sweriӡen |
sixtiӡ | huslӡenӡa | 19 ends with p. 95 in E ‖ **20.** forcund | buton | hrime |
lesanne ‖ **21.** ðeofðe for ðeof | ofslæӡenan ‖

13. Gyf hwâ beforan bisceope his ʒewitnysse 7 his
13, 1. wed aleoʒe, ʒebete mid hundtwelftiʒ scill.; þeofas we
hatað oð seofen men, from seofon hloð, oð fif an-
ðrittiʒ here.

14. Se ðe hloðe betoʒen sy, ʒeclensie se hine be hundtwelftiʒum hida oððe swa ʒebete.

15. Se ðe hereteama betoʒen sy, hine be his werʒylde
15, 1. alyse, oððe be his were ʒeclænsie; se að sceal beon
15, 2. half be huslʒenʒum; þeof syððan he bið on cyninʒes
bendum, nah he ða ʒeswicne.

16. Se ðe ðeof ofslihð, se mot ʒecyþan mid aðe þæt
he hine scyldiʒ ofslôʒe, nalles ða ʒyldan.

17. Se ðe forstolen flæsc findeð 7 ʒedyrneð, ʒyf he
dear, he mot mid aþe ʒecyðan þæt he hit âʒe; se þe
hit ofspyrað, he ah þæt meldfeoh.

18. Cyrlisc mon ʒyf he oft betoʒen wære, ʒyf he æt
siþestan sy ʒefanʒen, slêa mân hand oððe fôt of.

19. Cyninʒes ʒeneat ʒyf his wer bið twelf hund scill.,
he mot swerian for sixti hîda, ʒyf he bið huslʒenʒa.

20. Gyf feorcuman man oððe fremde butan weʒe ʒe
on wudu ʒonde 7 ne ryme ne horn blawe, for ðeof
he bið to profianne oððe to alysenne.

21. Gyf man ðonne ðæs ofslæʒenan weres bidde, he
mot ʒecyþan þæt he hine for þeof ofsloʒe, nalæs ðæs

---

13. biscope | his above ʒewitnesse | wedd | ʒebete End of p. 29 in
B | 13,1. with 14 as .LVIII., so also in Bu | þeofas, Ð new over
þ, B | seo erased bef. seofen B | fram seofon mannum hloð oþ
.XXXV. | 7 syððan, after fif anðrîttiʒ, new B, siððan bið here H || 14.
ʒeswicne for ʒeclensie | .CXX. | oððe bete swa || 15. hereteame |
before hine new he above eras. B, he hine H | wereʒilde | þam new over
his B, were from H | ʒeswicne for ʒeclænsie || 15, 1. half new above
B, healf H || 15, 2. with 16 as .LX., so also in Bu | þeof, Ð new over
þ, B || 16. synniʒne for scyldiʒ | nallæs ða ʒeʒildan || 17. ʒedirneð |
ofspyreð | 18. Ciorlisc | man | of, t added new B, oft H | siðmestan,
m above | sî | hand of oððe fot || 19. .CXX. | swerizan | .LX. || 20.
feorcund | ʒeond for ʒe on | ʒonde, d made new into ʒ, B, ʒanʒe H |
hryme | profianne oððe to sleanne oþþe | alysanne, a above | alysenne End
of p. 30 in B || 21. nallæs | ofslaʒenan | ʒeʒildan ||

21, 1. ofsleʒenan ʒeʒildan ne his hlaford. Ʒif he hit ðonne
dierneð 7 weorðeð ymb lonʒ yppe, ðonne rymeð he
ðam deadan to ðam aðe þæt hine moton his mæʒas
unsynʒian.

.LXVI.

22.   Gif ðin ʒeneat stalie 7 losie ðe, ʒif ðu hæbbe
byrʒean, mana þone þæs anʒyldes;   ʒif he næbbe,
ʒyld ðu þæt anʒylde 7 ne sie him no ðy ðinʒodre.

.LXVII.

23.   Gif mon elðeodiʒne ôfslea, se cyninʒ ah twædne
23, 1. dæl weres, þriddan dæl sunu oððe mæʒas.   Ʒif he
23, 2. ðonne mæʒleas sie, healf kyninʒe, healf se ʒesið.   Ʒif
hit ðonne abbod sie oððe abbodesse, dælen on þa
23, 3. ilcan wisan wið þone kyninʒ;   wealhʒafolʒelda .CXX.
scill., his sunu .C., ðeowne .LX., somhwelcne fifteʒum,
weales hyd twelfum.

.LXVIII.

24.   Gif witeðeow enʒliscmon hine forstalie, hô hine
24, 1. mon 7 ne ʒylde his hlaforde;   ʒif hine mon ofslêa,
ne ʒylde hine mon his mæʒum, ʒif hie hine on .XII.
24, 2. monðum ne âliesden;   wealh ʒif he hafað .V. hida,
he við syxhynde.

.LXVIIII.

25.   Gif ciepemon uppe on folce ceapie, do þæt beforan
25, 1. ʒewitnessum;   ʒif ðiefefioh mon æt ciepan befo 7
he hit næbbe beforan ʒodum weotum ʒeceapod, ʒecyðe
hit be wite þæt he ne ʒewita ne ʒestala nære oððe
ʒielde to wite .VI. 7 .XXX. scill.

.LXX.

26.   To fundes cildes fostre, ðy forman ʒeare ʒeselle
.VI. scill., ðy æfterran .XII., ðy driddan .XXX., siððan
be his wlite.

21, 1. vac. ðonne | dirneð | wierðeð | remeð | þæm | þæm (aðe) | mæʒes |
unsinʒian ‖   22. habbe | berʒan | manna | anʒeldes | ʒeld | anʒelde ‖   23.
kininʒ | mæʒes End of Bu fragm. (cf. App. B.) ‖   25 and 25, 1. i in ʒewit-
nessum, e in beforan and e in þæt he, all at end of lines, dim ‖   25, 1.
.XXX. scill. ends p. 96 in E ‖

Continuation of Variants from p. 117.
for ne wîte | ʒilde | .VI. ‖   26. ðu, new y stroke B, ðy H | .VI. | 7 ðy
æfteran ʒeare .XII. | 7 þy | .XX. | 7 siððan ‖

21, 1. ofslæʒenan ʒyldan, ne his hlaford; ʒyf he hit þonne
dyrneð 7 weorðeð emb lonʒ yppe, ðonne rymeð he
ðam deadan to ðam aðe þæt hine moton maʒos
unsynʒian.

22.   Gyf ðin ʒeneat stalie 7 losiʒe ðe, ʒyf ðu hæbbe
borʒas, mana ðone ðæs anʒyldas; ʒyf he næbbe, ʒyld
ðu þæt anʒylde 7 ne sy him na þe ʒeðinʒodre.

23.   Gyf mon ælþeodiʒne mon ofslea, se cynʒ ah
twezen dælas þæs weres, ðriddan dæl sunu oððe maʒas;
23, 1. ʒyf he ðonne mæʒleas sy, half cyninʒ, half se
23, 2. ʒesið. Gyf hit ðonne abbud sy oððe abbudisse, dælon
23, 3. on ða ilcan wisan wið ðonne cyninʒ. Wealhʒafol-
ʒylda hundtwelftiʒ scill., his sunu hund, ðeow sextiʒ
scill. Somhwylcne mid fiftiʒ, weales hid mid twelfum.

24.   Gyf witeðeow enʒliscmon hine forstalie, hô hine
24, 1. mon 7 ne ʒylde his hlaforde. Gyf hine mon ofslea,
ne ʒylde hine man his maʒum, ʒyf hy hine on twelf
24, 2. monðum ne alysdon. Wealh ʒyf he · hæfð fif hida,
he bið syxhynde.

25.   Gyf cepeman uppe on folce ceapiʒe, do þæt beforan
25, 1. ʒewitnysse. Gyf ðeof mon feoh æt cyp men befô 7
he hit næbbe beforan ʒodum witum ʒeceapod, ʒecyðe
hit be wîte þæt he ne wîte ne ʒestala nære oððe
ʒylde to wite syx 7 .XXX. scill.

26.   To fundenes cyldes fostre, ðu forman ʒeare, ʒesylle
syx scill., ðu æftran twelf, ðu þriddan .XXX., syððan
be his wlite.

21, 1. dirneð | wurð | ymbe, e above | lanʒe | his before maʒos and
a above o new B, his maʒas unscyldiʒne ʒedôn H || 22. staliʒe |
byrʒean, e ab. | anʒyldes | ʒild | ʒeðinʒrode || 23. man first | cyninʒ |
dælas þæs weres, as þæs ab. || 23, 1. mæʒleas, a ab. | healf | cyninʒe | healf ||
23, 2. ðone bef. cyninʒ || 23, 3. .CXX. | red above eras. after hund, so
ne after ðeow B, .C. þeowne .LX. H | eras. aft. sextiʒ B || 24. ænʒliscman |
hô | man || 24, 2. byþ | hinde | syxhynde End of p. 31 in B || 25. ceap-
man || uppe above | dô | beforan ʒewitnesse, foran ʒe above || 25, 1. ðeof
erased, before feoh forstolen supplied new on marg., men new above
eras. B, ꝥif man forstolen feoh æt ceap men befô, ap above H | na ʒewita

.LXXI.

27.   Se ðe dearnenʒa bearn ʒestrieneð 7 ʒehileð, nah se his deaðes wer, ac his hlaford 7 se cyninʒ.

.LXXII.

28.   Se ðeof ʒefehð ah .X. scill., 7 se cyninʒ ðone ðeof,

28, 1. 7 þa mæʒas him swerian aðas unfæhða; ʒif he ðonne oðierne 7 oriʒe weorðe, þonne bið he wites scyldiʒ;

28, 2.   ʒif he onsacan wille, do he ðæt be ðam fêo 7 be ðam wite.

.LXXIII.

29.   Ʒif mon sweordes onlæne oðres esne 7 he losie, ʒielde he hine ðriddan dæle; ʒif mon spere selle, healfne; ʒif he horses onlæne, ealne he hine ʒylde.

.LXXIIII.

30.   Gif mon cierliscne monnan flieman feorme teo, be his aʒnum were ʒeladiʒe he hine; ʒif he ne mæʒe, ʒielde hine his aʒne were 7 se ʒesiðmon swa be his were.

.LXXV.

31.   Gif mon wîf ʒebyccʒe 7 sio ʒyft forð ne cume, aʒife þæt feoh 7 forʒielde 7 ʒebete þam byrʒean swa his borʒbryce sie.

.LXXVI.

32.   Gif wilisc mon hæbbe hide londes, his wer bið .CXX. scill.; ʒif he þonne healfes hæbbe, .LXXX. scill.; ʒif he næniʒ hæbbe, .LX. scillinʒa.

.LXXVII.

33.   Cyninʒes horswealh, se ðe him mæʒe ʒeærendian, ðæs werʒield bið .CC. scill.

.LXXVIII.

34.   Se ðe on ðære fore wære þæt mon monnan ofsloʒe, ʒetriewe hine ðæs sleʒes 7 ða fore ʒebete be

34, 1. ðæs ofsleʒenan werʒielde; ʒif his werʒield sie .CC. scill., ʒebete mid .L. scill. 7 ðy ilcan ryhte do man be ðam deorborenran.

34, 1. ðy ilcan End of p. 97 in E ‖

Continuation of Variants from p. 119.

n added B, man H | eras. bef. ofsloʒe | ʒetwywie, new r above B, ʒetriwe H | sleʒes 7 þa fore | ofslæʒnan | werʒylde, old l above r B, were H ‖ **34, 1.** his, s over eras. B | werʒild | .CC. | .L. | ylcan | ryhte | dô | man, new n ab. B ‖

27.   Se ðe dearnunᵹa bearn ᵹestreonað 7 ᵹeheleð, nah se his deaðes wêr, ac his hlaford 7 se cynᵹ.

28.   Se ðe ðeof ᵹefehð, he ah tyn scill., 7 se cyninᵹ ðone ðeof 7 ða maᵹas him swerian aðas unfæðða;

28, 1. ᵹif he ðonne oðerna 7 oriᵹe weorðe, ðonne bið he

28. 2. wites scyldiᵹ; ᵹyf he ætsacan wylle, do he *þæt* be ðam feo 7 be ðam wite.

29.   Gyf mon sweordes onlæne oðru*m* esne 7 hit losiᵹe, be ðriddan dæle he hit ᵹylde. Gyf mon spere sylle, healfne; ᵹyf mon hors onlæne, ealne he hine ᵹylde.

30.   Gyf man cyrliscne mannan flyman feormienne têo, be his aᵹenon were ᵹeladiᵹe hine; ᵹyf he ne mæᵹe, ᵹylde he hine be his aᵹenu*m* were 7 se ᵹesiþmon eac swâ be his were.

31.   Gyf mon wif bycᵹe 7 seo ᵹyft forð ne cume, aᵹyfe *þæt* feoh 7 forᵹylde 7 ᵹebête ðam byrᵹean swa his borhbryce sy.

32.   Gyf wylisc man hæbbe hide landes, his wer bið hundtwelftiᵹ scill.; ᵹyf he ðonne healfe hæbbe, hundeahtati scill.; ᵹyf he næbbe nan land, sixti scill.

33.   Cyninᵹes horswealh, se ðe him mæᵹ ᵹeerendian, ðæs werᵹyld bið twa hund scill.

34.   Se ðe on ðere fore wære ðær mon mon ofsloᵹe, ᵹetwywie hine ðæs slæᵹes oððe fore ᵹebete be þæs

34, 1. ofslæᵹenan werᵹylde; ᵹyf his werᵹyld sy twa hund scill., ᵹebete mid fiftiᵹ scill. 7 ða ilcan rihte dô man be ðam deorborenran.

---

27. ᵹestryn-ð | cyninᵹ ‖   28. .X. | unfehþa ‖   28, 1. oðerna, ao new above B, oþyrne H | orriᵹe, first r above ‖   28, 2. onsacan | wille | dô | were ab. and for feo ‖   29. man | oþres | êsne | 7 he | ᵹilde he hine ðriddan dæle | man | healfne dæl hine ᵹilde, dæl above | man | horses | læne | ᵹilde ‖   30. cierliscne | mannan, an erased B, man H | feormienne, nᵹe new above enne B, feormie H | 7 hine man teo | aᵹenum | ᵹeladie | he new above B, he hine H | ᵹilde | he above | be above | aᵹenan, n ab. | ᵹesiðman | eac above | were End of p. 32 in B ‖   31. man | ᵹift | aᵹife | forᵹilde | byrᵹean, attempt to make o over y, on marg. borᵹan new B ‖   32. wilisc | .CXX. | healfes | .LXXX. | næniᵹ næbbe, .LX. scillinᵹa ‖   33. ᵹeærndi-an | ðes wereᵹild is .CC. hund scll., eᵹild above ‖   34. þe above | þære | fôre | ðæt for ðær | man | mon (second), o into a and

120

.LXXVIIII.

35. Se ðe ðeof slihð, he mot aðe ᵹecyðan *þæt* he hine
flondne for ðeof sloᵹe, 7 þæs deadan mæᵹas him
swerian unceases âð; ᵹif he hit þon*ne* dierne 7 sie eft
35, 1. yppe, þonne forᵹielde he hine. Ʒif mon to þam men
feoh ᵹeteme ðe his ǽr oðswaren hæfde 7 eft oðswerian
wille, oðsweriᵹe be ðam wite 7 be ðæs feos weorðe;
ᵹif he oðswerian nylle, ᵹebete þone mænan að twybote.

.LXXX.

36. Se ðe ðeof ᵹefehð oððe him mon ᵹefonᵹenne aᵹifð
7 he hine þon*ne* âlæte oððe þa ðiefðe ᵹedierne, for-
36, 1. ᵹielde þone þeof his were; ᵹif he ealdormon sie,
ðolie his scire buton him kyninᵹ arian wille.

.LXXXI.

37. Se cirlisca mon se ðe oft betyᵹen wære ðiefðe 7
þon*ne* æt siðestan synniᵹne ᵹefô in ceape oððe elles
æt openre scylde, slea him mon hond ôf oððe fôt.

.LXXXII.

38. Gyf ceorl 7 his wif bearn hæbben ᵹemæne 7 fere
se ceorl forð, hæbbe sio modor hire bearn 7 fede;
aᵹife hire mon .VI. scill. to fostre, cu on sumera, oxan
on wintra; healden þa mæᵹas þone fru*m*stol oð ðæt
hit ᵹewintred sie.

.LXX*XIII*.

39. Gif hwa fare unâliefed fram his hlaforde oððe on
oðre scire hine bestele 7 hine mon ᵹeahsiᵹe, fare þǽr
he ǽr wæs 7 ᵹeselle his hlaforde .LX. scill.

.LXXXIIII.

40. Ceorles worðiᵹ sceal beon wintres 7 sumeres betyned; ᵹif he bið untyned 7 recð his neahᵹebures ceap
in on his aᵹen ᵹeat, nah he æt þam ceape nan wuht,
adrife hine ut 7 ðolie æfwerdlan.

---

38. if in aᵹife dim, | um in frum lost in a hole | ed sie dim ‖ **39.**
ððe in oððe and (next it) LXX dim, XIII gone, below it e of ᵹeahsiᵹe
gone, below this all but L of LXXXIIII dim ‖ **40.** ed ᵹif and aᵹen
dim | ut, clearer, ends p. 98 in E ‖

Continuation of Variants from p. 121.
worðiᵹ | wyntres | receþ | neahᵹebures ceap on his aᵹen ᵹeat in | ceape ab. |
nanwuht | hit for hine | æfwyrdlan ‖

35. Se ðe ðeof slihþ, he mot mid aðe ʒecyðan þæt
he hine fleondne for ðeof sloʒe, 7 ðes deadan maʒas
him swerian unceases að. Gyf he hit ðonne dyrne 7

35, 1. sy eft yppe, ðonne forʒylde he hine; ʒyf mon to
ðæm men feoh ʒetême þe his ætsworen hæfde 7 eft
ætswerian wylle, sweriʒe be ðam wite 7 be ðæs feos
wyrðe; ʒyf he ætswerian nylle, ʒebete ðone mænan
að twyʒbote.

36. Se ðe ðeof ʒefehð oððe him mon ʒefonʒene aʒyfð
7 he hine ðonne alæte oððe ða þyfþe ʒedyrne, forʒylde

36, 1. ðone ðeof be his were. Gyf he ealdorman sy, ðolie
his scire, buton him cyninʒ arian wylle.

37. Se ceorlisce man se ðe oft betoʒen were ðyfðe
7 ðonne æt siþestan synninʒne ʒefô in ceace oððe elles
æt openre scylde, slea him mon handa of oððe fot.

38. Gyf ceorl 7 his wîf bearn hæbben ʒemæne 7 fære
se ceorl forð, hæbbe seo modor hire bearn 7 fede;
aʒyfe hire man syx scill. to fostre, cû on sumera, oxan
on wintran; healdan ða maʒas ðone frumstol, oð þæt
hit ʒewintrod sy.

39. Gyf hwâ fare unalyfede fram his laforde, oððe
on oðre scire hine bestele 7 hine man ʒeacsiʒe, fare
ðær he ær wæs 7 ʒylde his laforde syxtiʒ scill.

40. Ceorles worði sceal beon wintres 7 sumeres betyned:
ʒyf he bið untyned 7 recð his nehhebures ceap in on
his aʒen ʒeat, nah he æt ðam ceape nan riht, adrife

35. mot aþe, vac. mid | fleonde | ðæs | unceastes | âð | forʒilde ‖ 35, 1.
man | ær oþsworen | oðswerian | wille | oþswerie for sweriʒe | ʒif he þonne oþ-
sweri-an nylle | twybote ‖ 36. fehð | mon End of p. 33 in B | ʒefanʒenne |
aʒifð | ða, a ab. | ʒedirne | forʒilde ‖ 36, 1. ealderman | poliʒe | butan |
se cyninʒ | wille ‖ 37. ciorlisca ¦ man þe | wære | þifðe | siðestan cyrre |
synniʒne | man ʒefô | in ceace oþþe scylde elles | man hand oððe fot, vac.
of ‖ 38. ciorl | 7 se ciorl forðfære | moder | 7 above aʒife | man hire | .VI.
| cû | wintra | healden | ʒewintred ‖ 39. unalyfed | hlaforde | ʒeaxie |
þær above he | wæs ær | ʒesylle for ʒylde | hlaforde | .LX. ‖ 40. Ciorles |

.LXXXV.

41.   Borʒes mon môt oðsacan, ʒif he wât *þæt* he ryht deð.

.LXXXVI.

42.   Gif ceorlas ʒærstun hæbben ʒemænne oððe oþer ʒedâlland to tynanne 7 hæbben sume ʒetyned hiora dæl, sume næbben, 7 etten hiora ʒemænan æceras oððe ʒærs, ʒân þa þon*ne* þe ðæt ʒeat aʒan 7 ʒebete þam oðrum þe hiora dæl ʒetynedne hæbben þone æwerdlan þe ðær ʒedon sie, abidden him æt þam ceape swylc

42, 1. ryht swylce hit kyn sie; ʒif þon*ne* hryðera hwelc sie þe heʒas brece 7 ʒa in ʒehwær 7 se hit nolde ʒehealdan se hit aʒe oððe ne mæʒe, nime se hit on his æcere mete 7 ôfslea 7 nime se aʒenfriʒea his fel 7 flæsc 7 þolie þæs oðres.

.LXXXVII.

43.   Ðonne mon beam on wuda forbærne 7 weorðe yppe on þone ðe hit dyde, ʒielde he fulwite, ʒeselle

43, 1. .LX. scill., forþam þe fŷr bið þeof; ʒif mon afelle on wuda welmoneʒa treowa 7 wyrð eft undierne, forʒielde .III. treowu ælc mid .XXX. scill.; ne ðearf he hiora mâ ʒeldan, wære hiora swa fela swa hiora wære, forþon sio æ̂sc bið melda, nalles ðeof.

.LXXXVIII.

44.   Gif mon þon*ne* aceorfe an treow þæt mæʒe .XXX. swina underʒestandan 7 wyrð undierne, ʒeselle .LX.

44, 1. scill.; ʒafolhwitel sceal bion æt hiwisce .VI. pæninʒa weorð.

.LXXXVI*III*.

45.   Burʒbryce mon sceal betan .CXX. scill. kyninʒes 7 biscepes þær his rice bið, ealdormonnes .LXXX. scill., cyninʒes ðeʒnes .LX. scill., ʒesiðcundes monnes landhæbbendes .XXXV., 7 bi ðon ansacan.

43, 1. LXXXVIII, III not in Ms.

o above | forðon | æx || **44.** man | .XXX. | wyrð | undirne | .LX. || **44, 1.** — hwitel End of p. 35 in B — | sceal beon æt hiwisce, a ab. | .VI. | peninʒa | wyrð || **45.** sceal, a above | mid .CXX. | Cininʒes, attempt to change C to c, B | biscopes | Ealder | .LXXX. | ðeʒnes | .LX. | .XXXV. | bið ofsacan, new am to make bi ðam B, byþ on ansacan H ||

41.   hine ut 7 ðolie ðone æfwyrlan. *Borꞡes* mon mot ætsacan, ꞡyf he wat *þæt* he riht deð.

42.   Gyf ceorlas habban ꞡærstun ꞡemæne oþþe oðer
ꞡedalland to tynanne 7 hæbben sume ꞡetyned heora
dæl, sume næbben, 7 etten heora ꞡemænan æceras oððe
ꞡærs, ꞡan ða ðonne þe *þæt* ꞡeat aꞡon 7 ꞡebeten ðæm
oðrum ðe heora dæl ꞡetynedne hæbben ðone æfwyrdlan,
ðe ꞡær ꞡedon sy, abiddon heom æt ðam ceape swylc

42, 1. riht swylce hit cyn sy.   Gyf ðonne hryðera hwylc
sy ðe heꞡas brece 7 ꞡa in ꞡehwær· 7 se hit nolde
ꞡehealdan se hit aꞡe oððe ne mæꞡe, nime se ðe hit
on his æcere ꞡemete 7 ofslea 7 nime se aꞡenfriꞡa his
flæsc 7 ðolie ðæs oðres.

43.   Ðonne mon beam on wuda forbærne 7 wyrðe yppe
on ðone ðe hit dýde, ꞡylde he fulwite, ꞡesylle syxtig

43, 1. scill., forðam ðe fyr bið ðeof.   Gyf mon afylle on
wuda *well* maneꞡa treowe 7 wurð *þæt* eft undyrne,
forꞡylde ðreo treowa ælc mid ðrittiꞡ scill; ne ðearf he
heora ma ꞡyldan, wære heora swa feola swa heora
wære, forðan seo eax bið melda, nalæs ðeof.

44.   Gyf mon ðonne aceorfe an treow *þæt* mæꞡe ðrittiꞡ
swina understandan 7 wurð undyrne, ꞡesylle syxtiꞡ

44, 1. scill.   Gafolhwitel æt hiwisce sceal beon syx peneꞡa
wurð.

45.   Burhbryce man sceal betan hundtwelftiꞡ scill.
Cyninꞡes 7 bisceopes, ðær his rice bið. Ealdormannes
hundeahtatiꞡ scill. Cyninꞡes ðeꞡnas syxti scill. Gesið-
cundes mannes landhæbbendes fif 7 .XXX. scill. 7 bið
ofsacan.

<hr/>

41. Second diff. in chapters from EH (cf. XXXV) | orꞡes, *B* new above,
B, Borꞡes H | man | — deð End of p. 34 in B — || **42.** ciorlas | ꞡærstûn
habban | al. ꞡedal land above to tyn-nanne | nabben | ꞡân | ðam | heora,
o above | betyned- | habben | ðonne, first n above | ꞡedôn | aft. sy new 7
ab. B | abidden | heom, o ab. | swylc cynn sy, vac. hit || **42,1.** hriðera, e ab. |
ꞡehwilc | ðæt for ðe | ꞡa ꞡehwær in | ꞡehealden, ꞡe ab. | se þe hit, þe ab. | flæcs |
ðoliꞡe || **43.** man | wurðe | ꞡilde | fulwite, second l new and small B, fullwite,
second l ab. H | .LX. || **43, 1.** well new over eras. B, welmaniꞡe H | treowa
wyrð eft, vac. þæt | forꞡilde | .XXX. | he nan mâ ꞡildan | heora, feola, heora,

.XC.

46. Ðonne mon monnan betyhð *þæt* he ceap forstele
oððe forstolenne ȝefeormie, *þonne* sceal he be .LX. hida

46, 1. onsacan þære þiefðe, ȝif he aðwyrðe bið; ȝif ðonne
enȝlisc onstal ȝa forð, onsace *þonne* be twyfealdum;
ȝif hit ðon*ne* bið wilisc onstal, ne bið se að na ðy

46, 2. mara; ælc mon mot onsacan frymþe 7 werfæhðe,
ȝif he mæȝ oððe dear.

.XCI.

47. Gif mon forstolenne ceap befehð, ne mot hine mon
tieman to ðeowum men.

.XCII.

48. Gif hwelc mon bið witeðeow niwan ȝeðeowad 7
hine mon betyhð *þæt* he hæbbe ǽr ȝeðiefed ær hine
mon ȝeðeowode, *þonne* ah se teond ane swinȝellan
æt him; bedrife hine to swinȝum be his ceape.

.XCIII.

49. Gif mon on his mæstenne unaliefed swîn ȝemete,

49, 1. ȝenime *þonne* .VI. scill. weorð wed; ȝif hie *þonne*
þær næren oftor *þonne* æne, ȝeselle scill. se aȝenfriȝea
7 ȝecyðe *þæt* hie þær oftor ne comen be þæs ceapes

49, 2. weorðe; ȝif hi ðær tuwa wæren, ȝeselle tweȝen .scill.;

49, 3. ȝif mon nime æfesne on swynum, æt þryfinȝ*rum*
þæt ðridde, æt twyfinȝrum *þæt* feorðe, æt þymelum
þæt fifte.

.XCIIII.

50. Gif ȝesiðcund mon þinȝað wið cyninȝ oððe wið
kyninȝes ealdormonnan for his inhiwan oððe wið his
hlaford for ðeowe oððe for friȝe, nah he þær nane
witerædenne, se ȝesið, forðon he hi*m* nolde ær yfles
ȝestieran æt ham.

.XCV.

51. Gif ȝesiðcund mon landaȝende forsitte fierd, ȝeselle
.CXX. scill. 7 ðolie his landes, unlandaȝende .LX. scill.,
cierlisc .XXX. scill. to fierdwite.

---

46. oððe for End of p. 99 in E |

---

first e in yfeles ab. ‖ **51.** mann, second n ab. | .CXX. | þoliȝe | Landaȝende .LX.
scillinȝa | Ccorlisc, o ab. | .XXX., vac. scill. | wite, ferd new ab. B, fyrdwite H ‖

46. Ðonne mon mon betyhð þæt he ceap forstæle oððe forstolene ʒefeormie, ðonne sceal he be syxti hîda

46, 1. ætsacan ðære ðeofðe, ʒyf he andwyrde bið. Gyf ðonne enʒlisc mon stalað, ʒa forð ætsace be twyfealdum; ʒyf hit ðonne biþ wylisc onstal, ne bið se að na ðe mare;

46, 2. ælc man mot ætsacan fyrmðe 7 werfæhðe, ʒyf he mæʒe oððe dêar.

47. Gyf mon forstolene ceap befehð, ne mot hîne mon tymon to ðeowan men.

48. Gyf hwylc mon bið witeðeow niwan ʒeþeowad 7 hine mon betyh þæt he hæbbe ær ʒeðeofad ær hine mon ʒeðeowade, ðonne ah se teond ane swinʒelan æt hîm; bedrife hine to swinʒlum be his ceape.

49. Gyf mon on his mæstené unalufed swin ʒemete,

49, 1. ʒenime ðonne syx scill. wurð wed. Gyf hi ðonne ðær næron oftor ðonne âne, ʒesylle scillinʒ se aʒenfriʒa 7 ʒecyðe þæt hi ðær oftor ne comon be ðæs

49, 2. ceapes wyrðe. Gyf hi ðær tuwa wæron, ʒesylle tweʒen

49, 3. scill; ʒyf mon nime æbesne on swinum, æt ðryfinʒrum þæt ðridde, æt twyfinʒrum þæt feorðe, æt ðumelum þæt fifte.

50. Gyf ʒesiðcund mon ðinʒað wið cynʒ oððe wið cynʒes ealdormannum for his inhiwan, oððe wið his hlaford for ðeowe oððe for friʒe, nah he ðar nane witeræddene, se ʒesiþ, forðon he nolde him ær yfeles ʒestyran æt ham.

51. Gyf se siðcunde man landaʒende fyrde forsitte, ʒesylle hundtwelftiʒ scill 7 ðolie his landes, unlandaʒende syxti scill., ceorlisc ðrittiʒ scill. to wite.

46. man | mon, ann above new, B, mon- H | forstolenne | ʒefeormiʒe | sceal, a above | .LX. | ðyíðe | aðwyrðe || 46, 1. enʒlisc onstal ʒa forð, onsace ðonne | biþ wylisc new above B, biþ wilisc H | onstâl | að mare, vac. na ðe || 46, 2. onsacan | mæʒʒ, second ʒ above | dear, new r added B, dearr H || 47. man | forstolenne | tyman | menn || 48. hwylc above man | man | betyhð | swinʒlum, l above BH || 49. man | unalyfed | .VI. | weorð | wedd || 49,1. ænne new ab. scillinʒ B | — friʒa 7 ʒe End of p. 36 in B — | hy | næron for ne comon || 49,2. twiʒa | .II. || 49,3. man | ab. ðryfinʒrum new spic B | ðridde, ð uncrossed B | ðumelum, new y stroke B, ðymelum H || 50. man | cyninʒ | wiþ his ealderman | innhiwum | friʒe, ʒe ab. | þær | nan | witerædene | forþon ðe he him nolde ær yfeles ʒestryran æt ham,

126

.XCVI.

52. Se ðe diernum ᵹeðinᵹum betyᵹen sie, ᵹeswicne hine be .CXX. hida þara ᵹeðinᵹea, oððe .CXX. scill. ᵹeselle.

.XCVII.

53. Gif mon forstolenne man befo æt oþrum 7 sie sio hand oðcwolen sio hine sealde þam men þe hine mon ætbefenᵹ, tieme þonne þone mon to þæs deadan byrᵹelse swa oðer fioh swa hit sie, 7 cyðe on þam aðe be .LX. hida þæt sio deade hond hine him sealde; þonne hæfð he þæt wite afylled mid þy aðe, aᵹife

53, 1. þam aᵹendfrio þone monnan; ᵹif he þonne wite hwa ðæs deadan ierfe hæbbe, tieme þonne to þam ierfe 7 bidde ða hond þe þæt ierfe hafað þæt he him ᵹedô þone ceap unbeceasne oþþe ᵹecyðe þæt se deada næfre þæt ierfe ahte.

.XCVIII.

54. Se þe bið werfæhðe betoᵹen 7 he onsacan wille þæs sleᵹes mid aðe þonne sceal bion on þære hyndenne an kyninᵹæde be .XXX. hida, swa be ᵹesiðcundum

54, 1. men swa be cierliscum, swa hwæþer swa hit sie; ᵹif hine mon ᵹilt, þonne mot he ᵹesellan on þara hyndenna ᵹehwelcere monnan 7 byrnan 7 sweord on þæt werᵹild,

54, 2. ᵹif he ðyrfe; witeðeowne monnan wyliscne mon sceal bedrifan be .XII. hidum swa ðeowne to swinᵹum, enᵹliscne be feower 7 .XXX. hida.

.XCVIIII.

55. Ewo bið mid hire ᵹiunᵹe sceape scill. weorð oþ þæt .XII. niht ofer eastran.

.C.

56. Gif mon hwelcne ceap ᵹebyᵹð 7 he ðonne onfinde him hwelc unhælo on binnan .XXX. nihta, þonne weorpe

---

52. hine be .CXX. End of p. 100 in E || 53, 1. unbeceasne, un dim || 54. æde, first part of æ dim || 54, 1. sweord dim || 55. Ewo, E dim || 56. Ends with p. 101 in E, dim on lower left hand corner ||

Continuation of Variants from p. 127.

hwylce unhælo | .XXX. | he ðone ceap to handa, ceap ab. | þam syllend new above to handa B | sweriᵹe | facen ||

52.   Se ðe dyrnum ʒeðinʒðum betoʒen sy, ʒeclænsie he hine be hundtwelftiʒum hîda ðara ðinʒa oððe hundtwelftiʒ scill. ʒesylle.

53.   Gyf man forstolenne man befo æt oðrum, 7 sy seo hand acwolon ðe hine sealde ðam men ðe hine mon ætbefenʒ, tyme ðonne ðone man to ðæs deadan byrʒenne, swa oðer feoh swa hweðer swa hit sy, 7 cyðe on ðem aðe be feortiʒ hîda þæt seo deade hand hine him sealde; ðonne hæfð he þæt wite afylled mid

53, 1. ðu aðe, aʒyfe ðam aʒendfrêo ðone man.   Gyf he ðonne wite hwâ ðæs deadan yrfe hæbbe, tyme ðonne to ðam yrfe 7 bidde ða hônd þe þæt yrfe hafað þæt he him ʒedô ðone ceap unbesacene, oððe ʒecyðe þæt se deade næfre þæt yrfe ahte.

54.   Se ðe bið werfæhðe betoʒen 7 he ætsacan wylle ðæs slæʒes mid aðe, ðonne sceal beon on ðære hyndene an cyninʒæðe be ðrittiʒ hîda, swa be ʒesiþcundum

54, 1. men swa be ceorliscum, swa hweðer swa hît su.   Gyf hine mon ʒylt, ðonne mot he ʒesyllan on ðæra hyndenna ʒehwylcre monnan 7 byrnan 7 sweord on þæt werʒyld,

54, 2. ʒyf he ðurfe.   Witeðeowne monnan wyliscne man sceal bedrifan be twelf hyndum swa ðeowne to swincum, enʒliscne be seo wær 7 ðrittiʒ hida.

55.   Eowu bið mid hire ʒeonʒe sceape scill. weorð oð þæt feowertyne niht ofer easton.

56.   Gyf mon hwelcne ceap ʒebyʒeð 7 he ðonne afinde him hwylcne unhæle on binnon ðrittiʒ nihta ðonne

---

ʒeðinʒum | ʒeladie hine, vac. he | .CXX. | ʒeþinʒa | .CXX. ‖ **53.** befô | oþcwolen | hine æt befenʒ, vac. mon | þone man above | to þære byrʒenne ðæs deadan mannes | þæm | .LX. | wîte | ðu, last stroke erased B, ðy H | 7 above aʒife | aʒen-friʒe | aʒendfrêo End of p. 37 in B ‖ **53, 1.** þanne | hand | hafeþ | ʒedô | deada ‖ **54.** wer, new r put in marg. B | onsacan | wille | sleʒes | .XXX. | cierliscum | hwæðer | su, new y stroke B, sy H ‖ **54, 1.** man above ʒylt | ân for on | hyndenna, first n above | ʒehwylcere, first e ab. | monna | werʒild ‖ **54, 2.** man | wiliscne | .XII. hidum | swincum, l above c new B, swinʒ-um H | be .XXXIIII. hida H, (seo wær st. feower B) ‖ **55.** Eowu, new e ab. u B | mid new ab. hire B | ʒeonʒan | .XIIII. nyht | easton, new r ab. B, eastran H ‖ **56.** man | hwylcne | him on

128

þone ceap to honda oððe swerie þæt he him nan facn
on nyste þa he hine him sealde.

.CI.

57.   Gif ceorl ceap forstilð 7 bireð in to his ærne 7
befehð þærinne mon, þon*ne* bið se his dæl synniʒ
butan þa*m* wife anu*m*, forðon hio sceal hire ealdore
hieran; ʒif hio dear mid aðe ʒecyðan þæt hio þæs
forstolenan ne onbite, nime hire ðriddan sceat.

.CII.

58.   Oxan horn bið .X. pæninʒa weorð.

.CIII.

59.   Cuu horn bið tweʒea pæninʒa, oxan tæʒl bið .scill.
weorð, cus bið fifa; oxan eaʒe bið .V. *pæninʒa* weorð,
59, 1. cus bið scill. weorþ; mon sceal simle to bereʒafole
aʒifan æt anu*m* wyrhtan .VI. wæʒa.

.CIII.

60.   Se ceorl se ðe hæfð oðres ʒeoht abyrod, ʒif he
hæbbe ealle on foðre to aʒifanne, ʒesceawiʒe mon,
aʒife ealle; ʒif he næbbe, aʒife healf on fodre, healf
on oþru*m* ceape.

.CV.

61.   Ciricsceat mon sceal aʒifan to þa*m* healme 7 to
þam heorðe þe se mon on bið to middum wintra.

.CVI.

62.   Þon*ne* mon bið tyhtlan betyʒen 7 hine mon be-
drifeð to ceape, nah þon*ne* self nane wiht to ʒesellanne
beforan ceape, þon*ne* ʒæð oðer mon seleð his ceap
fore, swa he þon*ne* ʒeþinʒian mæʒe on ða rædenne
þe he him ʒa to honda oð ðæt he his ceap him ʒeinnian
mæʒe; þon*ne* betyhð hine mon eft oþre siðe 7 bedrifð

---

59. first bið above line, but old ||

Continuation of Variants from p. 129.

mon | midde || **62.** man | nah þonne ...... beforan ceace on margin in H | nane |
ʒesyllanne | seleð, second e ab. | ræde-ne | vac. him before ʒeinni-an |
— ʒeinnian End of p. 39 in B — | mon ab. eft | bedrife þ,last e above | forh new
before nylle, old forh erased B, forð nele forstandan se þe, þe ab. H |
ceap ær | hine | þonne ab. | þoliʒe | þonne above | vac. se | he above him ||

weorpe ðone ceap to handa oððe swerie þæt he him
nan faen on nyste ða he hine him sealde.

57.   Gyf ceorl ceap forstylð 7 bereð into his ærne 7
befehþ ðær inne, ðonne biþ his dæl synniჳ butan ðam
wife anum, forðan heo sceol hire ealdre hyran; ჳyf heo
dear mid aðe ჳecyðan þæt heo ðæs forstolenan ne onbite,
nime hire ðæne ðriddan dæl ðære æhta.

58.   Oxan horn bið feowertyne peniჳa wurð.

59.   Cu horn tweჳea peniჳa wurð. Oxan tæჳl bið .IIII.
peoneჳa wurð. Cu tæჳl bið fif peneჳa wurð. Oxan
59, 1. eaჳe bið fif peoneჳa wurð. Cu bið scill. weorð; mon
sceal symble to bereჳafole aჳyfan æt anum wyrhtan
syx weჳa.

60.   Se ceorl se ðe hæfð oðres oxan ahyred, ჳyf he
hæbbe ealle on foðre to aჳyfanne, ჳesceawiჳe mon,
aჳyfe ealle; ჳyf he næbbe, aჳyfe healf on foðre, healf
on oðrum ceape.

61.   Cyricsceat man sceal aჳyfan to þam halme 7 to
ðam heorðe ðe se man on bið to middan wintra.

62.   Ðonne mon bið tyhtlan betoჳen 7 hine mon be-
drifeð to ceace, nah ðonne sylf nan wiht to syllanne
beforan ceace, ðonne ჳæð oðer man sylað his ceap
fore, swa he ðonne ჳeðinჳian mæჳe on ða ræddene ðe
he him ჳa to handa oð þæt he his ceap him ჳeinnian
mæჳe; ðonne betyhð hine mon eft oðre siðe 7 bedrifþ

---

57. ciorl | forsteleþ | byrð | huse, above it al. ærne | mann bef. befehþ,
hitt after, new B, hit man ðær inne befehð H | — ðær in End of p. 38
in B — | biþ bef. his dæl, scyldiჳ above synniჳ new B, bið his dæl
scyldiჳ H | ðon | sceal | hlaforde for ealdre | new h above eo B, heo H | hire
ðriddan ჳescead‖ **58.** teon | peniჳa, prob. orig. so, now penn, last stroke new
B, peninჳa H | weorð ‖ **59.** Each capital begins a line in B, making
appar. five chapters, not so H | Cû | bið .V. | peninჳa | weorð | before
peoneჳa .IIII. over erasure new B, scill. H | weorð | Cû bið .V. peniჳa |
.V. | peninჳa | weorð | Cû | eaჳe above cu new B ‖ **59, 1.** mon, large M
new B | simle | aჳyfen | .VI. pund wæჳa ‖ **60.** ciorl | vac. se | hæfð, ð old
over h B, hæbbe H | ჳeoht, e ab, for oxan | vac. aჳyfe ealle | aჳife ‖ **61.**
sceal new above aჳyfan B, sceal H | halme, l over eras. B, healme H |

to ceape: ᵹif hine forð nele forstandan se ðe him ær
ceap foresealde 7 he hine þonne forfehð, þoliᵹe þonne
his ceapes se ðe he him ær foresealde.

.CVII.

63.   Gif ᵹesiðcund mon fare, þonne mot he habban
his ᵹerefan mid him 7 his smið 7 his cildfestran.

.CVIII.

64.   Se ðe hæfð .XX. hida, se sceal tæcnan .XII. hida
ᵹesettes landes þonne he faran wille.

.CVIIII.

65.   Se ðe hæfð .X. hida, se sceal tæcnan .VI. hida
ᵹesettes landes.

.CX.

66.   Se ðe hæbbe þreora hida, tæcne oþres healfes.

.CXI.

67.   Gif mon ᵹeþinᵹað ᵹyrde landes oþþe mare to ræde-
ᵹafole 7 ᵹeereð, ᵹif se hlaford him wile þæt land
aræran to weorce 7 to ᵹafole, ne þearf he him onfôn,
ᵹif he him nan botl ne selð, 7 þolie þara æcra.

.CXII.

68.   Ᵹif mon ᵹesiðcundne monnan adrife, fordrife þy
botle, næs þære setene.

.CXIII.

69.   Sceap sceal ᵹonᵹan mid his fliese oð midne sumor
oððe ᵹilde þæt flies mid twam pæninᵹum.

.CXIIII.

70.   Æt twyhyndum were mon sceal sellan to monbote
.XXX. scill., æt .VI. hyndum .LXXX. scill., æt .XII.-
70, 1. hyndum .CXX. scill.; æt .X. hidum to fostre .X. fata
hunies, .CCC. hlafa, .XII. ambra wilisc ealað, .XXX.
hluttres, tu eald hriðeru oððe .X. weðeras, .X. ᵹees,
.XX. henna, .X. cesas, amber fulne buteran, .V. leaxas,
.XX. pundwæᵹa foðres 7 hundteontiᵹ æla.

---

64. Ends with p. 102 in E ‖ **66.** begins third Ot. fragm. (cf. App. A),
from which foll. variants: **67.** Ᵹif, i above y | londes ‖ **69.** þæt flys ‖
70. syx hyndum ‖ **70, 1.** wilisces ‖

to ceace: Gyf he hine nylle forstandan forh se ðe him ær ceap foresealde 7 he him ðonne forfehð, ðolie ðonne his ceapes se ðe he him ær foresealde.

63. Gyf ʒesiðcund man fare, ðonne mot he habban his ʒerefan mid him 7 his smið 7 his cildfestran.

64. Se ðe hæfð twentiʒ hida, se sceal tǽcan twelf hîda ʒesettes landes, ðonne he faran wylle.

65. Se ðe hæfð tyn hida, se sceal tæcan syx hida ʒesettes landes.

66. Se ðe hæbbe ðreo hida, tæce oðres healfes.

67. Gyf mon ʒeðinʒað ʒyrde landes oððe mare to rædeʒafole 7 ʒeerað, ʒyf se hlaford him wyle þæt land aræran to weorce 7 to ʒafole, ne ðearf he him onfon, ʒyf he him nan botl ne sylþ, 7 ðolie ðara acera.

68. Gyf mon ʒesiðcundne monnan adrife, fordrife ðy botle, næs ðære setene.

69. Sceap sceal ʒonʒan mid his flyse oð midne sumor oððe ʒylde þæt fleos mid twam peneʒum.

70. Æt twyhundum were man sceal syllan to monbote .XXX. scill., 7 æt syxhyndum hundeahtatiʒ scill., æt
70, 1. twelfhyndum hundtwelftiʒ. Æt tyn hidum to fostre tyn fata hunies, ðreo hund hlâfa, twelf ambra wylisces ealoð, ðrittiʒ hlutres, twa ealda ryðeru oððe tyn weðeras, 7 *tyn ʒees 7 twenti henna 7 tyn cysas*, amber fulne buteran, fif leaxas, twentiʒ pund weʒa fodres 7 hundteontiʒ ǽla.

---

64. .XX. | tæcnan, first n ab. | .XII. | wille || **65.** .X. hida landes | tæcnan, first n ab. | .VI. || **66.** .III. hida landes | tæcne, n ab. | oðres healfes hides ʒesettes || **67.** man ʒyrde landes ʒeþinʒeð | ʒeereð | wile | slihð for sylþ | 7 þoliʒe his æcera || **68.** mann || **69.** ʒilde | flys | .II. || **70.** hundum, y stroke new B, hyndum H | manbote | .LXXX. | .XII. | — twelf hyn End of p. 40 in B — | .CXX. || **70,1.** .X. | .X. fata huniʒes | .CCC. hlafa, fa ab. | .XII. ambres, s ab. | wilisces, es ab. | .XXX. hluttres, first t ab. | .II. ealde, last e ab. | hryþeru | .X. weþeras | Insertion new on marg. B | .X. ʒês 7 .XX. | .X. | buteran, e ab. | .V. | .XX. | pund ab. wæʒa | .C. ||

.CXV.

71. Ȝif mon sie wertyhtlan betoȝen 7 he hit þonne ȝeondette beforan aðe 7 onsace ǽr, bide mon mid þære witerædenne oð ðæt se wer ȝeȝolden sie.

.CXVI.

72. Gif mon werȝild ðeof ȝefehð 7 he losiȝe ðy dæȝe þam monnum ðe hine ȝefoð, þeah hine mon ȝefô ymb niht, nah him mon mare æt ðonne fulwite.

.CXVII.

73. Gif hit bið nihteald þiefð, ȝebeten þa þone ȝylt þe hine ȝefenȝon swa hie ȝeþinȝian mæȝen wið cyninȝ 7 his ȝerefan.

.CXVIII.

74. Gif ðeowwealh enȝliscne monnan ofslihð, þonne sceal se ðe hine ah weorpan hine to honda hlaforde
74, 1. 7 mæȝum oððe .LX. scill. ȝesellan wið his feore; ȝif he þonne þone ceap nelle foreȝesellan, þonne mot hine se hlaford ȝefreoȝean, ȝielden siððan his mæȝas þone wer, ȝif he mæȝburȝ hæbbe freo, ȝif he næbbe, heden
74, 2. his þa ȝefan; ne þearf se friȝe mid þam þeowan mæȝȝieldan, buton he him wille fæhðe ôfaceapian, ne se þeowa mid þy friȝean.

.CXVIIII.

75. Gif mon ceap befehþ forstolenne 7 sio hond tiemð þonne, sio hine mon ætbefehþ, to oþrum men, ȝif se mon hine þonne onfon ne wille 7 sæȝþ þæt he him næfre þæt ne sealde ac sealde oþer, þonne mot se ȝecyðan, se ðe hit tiemþ to þære honda, þæt he him nan oðer ne sealde buton þæt ilce.

.CXX.

76. Gif hwa oðres ȝodsunu slea oððe his ȝodfæder, sie sio mæȝbot 7 sio manbot ȝelîc; weaxe sio bot be ðam were swa ilce swa sio manbot deð þe þam hlaforde

---

74. mæȝum End of p. 103 in E || 75. forstollenne | hond tymð ||

Continuation of Variants from p. 133.
ab. se, eras. after ȝe and cyþan on marg. B, þonne mot se ȝecyðan H | tymð, t made out of c B | þære || 76. weaxe, W new out of w B ||

71. Gyf mon sy wertyhlan betoʒen 7 he hit ðonne
ʒeandette beforan aðe 7 onsace ær, abide mon mid
ðære witerædenne oð þæt se wer ʒeʒolden sy.

72. Gyf mon werʒyld ðeof ʒefehð 7 he losie ðu dæʒe
ðam mannum ðe hine ʒefoð, ðeah hine man ʒefô ymbe
niht, nah him mon mare æt ðonon fulwite.

73. Gyf hit bið nihteald ðyfð, ʒebeten ða ðone ʒylt
ðe hine ʒefenʒon swa hiʒ ʒeðinʒian maʒon wið cyninʒe
7 his ʒerefan.

74. Gyf ðeowwealh enʒliscne man ofslihð, ðonne sceal
se ðe hine ah weorpan hine to handa hlaforde 7 maʒum
74, 1. oððe syxtiʒ scill. ʒesyllan wið his feore.   Gyf he
ðonne ceap nelle foresyllan, þonne mot hine se hlaford
ʒefreoʒan, ʒyldan syððan his maʒas ðone wer.   Gyf
he mæʒborh hæbbe freo, ʒyf he næbbe, heden his ða
74, 2. ʒefan; ne ðearf se friʒêa mid ðam ðeowan men
ʒyldan, buton he him sylle fæhðe ofaceapian, ne se
ðeowa mid ðam friʒean.

75. Gyf mon ceap befehþ forstolene 7 seo hand tymð,
ðonne seo hine mon ætbefehð ðe to oðrum men, ʒyf se
mon hine onfon nylle 7 sæʒð þæt he him næfre þæt
ne sealde, ac sealde oðer, ðonne mot se ʒecyþan, se
ðe hit tymð to ðara handa, þæt he him nan oðer ne
sealde buton þæt ilce.

76. Gyf hwa oðres ʒodsunu slêa oððe his ʒodfæder,
sy seo mæʒbot 7 sêo manbot ʒelic; weaxe seo bot be
ðam were swa ilce swa seo manbot deð þe ðam

71. abide man | ræde-ne || 72. werʒildþeof | losi-e | ðu, new y stroke
B, ðy H | monnum | ʒefô | ymb | nyht | man | ðonne for ðonon || 73. nyht |
hy ʒeþinʒian | cyninʒ || 74. man, second new n above B, man H | þe above
hine | hine ab. after weorpan | .LX. || 74, 1. þone ceap | nylle | foreʒesyllan |
þonne, onne new at end of line B, þonne H | ʒildon | siððan | mæʒburh | his
ðonne ða ʒefan || 74, 2. — mid ðam End of p. 41 in B — | þeowan mæʒʒyldan
butan | wille for sylle | ofaceapian, first a ab. || 75. man | æt befehð to
oðrum men, vac. ðe | man hine þonne | þæs ceapes ab. after nylle | mot

76, 1. sceal; ᵹif hit þonne kyninᵹes ᵹodsunu sie, bete be
76, 2. his were þam cyninᵹe swa ilce swa þære mæᵹþe. Ȝif
he þonne on þone ᵹeonbyrde þe hine sloᵹ, þonne ætfealle sio bôt þæm ᵹodfæder swa ilce swa þæt wite
þam hlaforde deð; ᵹif hit biscep sunu sie, sie be
healfum þam.

76, 2. ætfealle Ot, æ fealle E | second sie above, but old E ||

76, 1. hlaforde sceal. Gyf hit ðonne kyninȝes ȝodsunu sy,
bete be his were ðam cinȝe swa *ilce* swa ðære mæȝðe.

76, 2. Gyf he ðonne on ðone ȝeonbyrde ðe hine sloh,
ðonne ætfealle seo bot þam ȝodfǽdere, swa *ilce* swa
þæt wite ðam hlaforde deð; ȝyf hit bisceop sunu sy,
sy be healfum ðem.

76, 1. Gif hit þonne sy cyninȝes ȝodsunu, þonne above | cyninȝe | *ilce,*
prob. orig. so, new same over eras. B, same H ǁ **76, 2.** ðæm ȝodfæder | ilce,
see note on 76, 1, B, same H | biscop | sunu, down stroke erased below first
u B | þam seo bote ǁ In B follows: We cwedon be ðam blaserum etc.
In H, as CXXI, the same, after which there is a space of two lines ǁ

APPENDICES.

APPENDIX A. MS. OT.

I. Be þon þ. mon ne scyle oþru. deman buton swa he *wille þ. him* mon deme.

*II. Be aþu*m 7 be weddum.

*III. Be circ*ena socnum.

*IIII. Be b*orh bryce.

*V. Be hl*aford searwe.

VI. Be circena friðe.

*VII. Be circ*an stale.

VIII. Be þon þe mon on cyninᵹes healle feohte.

*VIIII. Be n*unnan hæmede.

*X. Be b*earn eacnum wife ofsleᵹenum.

*XI. Be t*welf hyndes monnes wife forleᵹenu*m.*

*XII. Be c*irilscre fæmnan onfenᵹe.

*XIII. Be n*udu bærnette.

*XIIII. Be d*umbra monna dædum.

XV. Be þam monnum þe beforan bisceopu. *feohta*ð.

XVI. Be nunnena onfenᵹe.

XVII. Be þa. monnu. þe hiora wæpen to monslyhte *læna*ð.

XVIII. Be þa. þe munecum heora feoh buton lea*fe befæsta*ð.

XVIIII. Be preosta ᵹefeohte.

XX. Be eofetes andetlan.

XXI. Be hundes slyte.

XXII. Be nietena misdædum.

XXIII. Be ceorles mennenes nied*h*æmede.

XXIIII. Be twyhindum men æt hloð *slyhte.*

*XXV. Be s*yx hyndum *men.*

*XXVI. Be t*welf hy*ndum men.*

Italics for parts wanting in Ot and supplied from E. Abbrev. forms retained, but with period after word instead of line over last letter as in Ms. Ot. prefers þ to ð, espec. initial. For description of Ms. see pp. 12, 19, 25.

XVII. hiora, hi above the line, but old.

APPENDICES.

FIRST FRAGMENT. (FOL. 49.)

XXVII. Be unȝewintredes monnes wif ned hæmde.

XXVIII. Be swa ȝerades *monnes* sleȝe.

XXVIIII. Be folcleasunȝe ȝewyrhtum.

XXX. Be ȝod borȝum.

XXXI. Be ciepe monnu*m*.

XXXII. Be cyrlisc*es monnes* byndellan.

XXXIII. Be speres ȝemel*e*asnesse.

XXXIIII. Be bold ȝe*t*ale.   [ȝefeohte.

XXXV. Be þon þe mo*n* beforan ealdormen *on* ȝemote

XXXVI. Be cierlisces monnes fletȝefeohte.

XXXVII. Be boclondum.

XXXVIII. Be fæhþe.

XXXVIIII. Be mœsse daȝa freolse.

XL. Be heafod wunde.

XLI. Be feax wunde.

XLII. Be earsleȝe.

XLIII. Be monnes eaȝwunde 7 oðöerra missen*licra lima.*

XLIIII. Be ines domum.

XLV. Be ȝodes þeowa reȝole.

XLVI. Be ci*l*dum.

XLVII. Be sunnan dæȝes weorcum.

XLVIII. Be ciric sceattum.

XLVIIII. Be ciric soc*num.*

L. Be ȝefeohtum.

LI. Be stale.

LII. Be ryhtes bene.

LIII. Be þam wrecendan ær he him ryhtes bidde.

138

hundniʒontiʒ *scill.* oþres bisceopes 7 ealdorm*onnes*
.LX. scill. twelf*hy*ndes monnes .XXX. scill. syx*hyndes*

40, 1. .XV. scill. ceorles edorbryce .*V. sc*ill. Ʒif þisses hw*æt*
ʒelimpe þenden fyrd *ute sie oþþ*e in lencten fæst*en*

40, 2. hit sie twybo*te.* *ʒif mon in lenct*enne hali*ʒ ryht in*
folce butan leafe *alecʒʒe ʒebete mid .CXX. scill.*

41. Se mon se þe bo*cland* hæbbe 7 him his .XXXVII.
mæʒas *læfden þonne setton we þæt he hit ne moste*
sellan of his mæʒburʒe ʒif *þær* bi*ð ʒenrit* oð*ð*e
ʒewitnes *þæt hit* þara manna *forbod* wære *þe hit*
on fruman ʒest*r*yndon 7 þara *þe hit him* seald*on þ. he*
swa ne mote 7 *þǽt* þonne on cyninʒ*es* 7 on bisceop*es*
ʒewitnesse ʒerecce befor*an his mæʒum.*

42. Eac we beoda*ð se mon se þe his ʒefan* .XXXVI*II.*
hamsittendne wite þ*æt he ne f*eohte ær þam he *him*

42, 1. *ryhtes b*idde. Ʒyf he mæʒnes hæbbe þ. he his *ʒefan*
beride 7 inne besitte ʒehe*alde* hine .*VII. niht inne*
7 *h*ine on ne feohte ʒif he inne *ʒeþolian wille* 7 *þon*
ne ymb .VII. niht ʒif he wille o*n hand ʒan* 7 *wæpenu*
*sell*an ʒehealde hine .XXX. *nihta ʒesundne* 7 *hine*

42, 2. *his* maʒum ʒebodie 7 hi*s friondum ʒif he cirican*
þonn*e* ʒeierne sie *þonne be þære cirican are swa we*

42, 3. *ær* bufan cwædon. Ʒyf *he þonne þæs mæʒenes ne hæbbe*
þ*æt* he hine inn*e besitte ride to þam ealdormen*
bidde hine ful*tumes ʒif he him fultuman ne*

42, 4. *wille ride to cyninʒe ær he feohte.* *Eac swelce*
ʒif mon becume on his ʒefan 7 *he hine ær ham*

---

40. hundniʒontiʒ, d above, but old. ‖ **42, 2.** sie, i above.

SECOND FRAGMENT. (FOL. 50.)

*fæst*ne ne wite. ჳif he wille h*is* *wæ*pen sellan hine
mon ჳehealde .XXX. nihta 7 hine *his* freondum
ჳecyþe. ჳyf he *ne wille* his wæpenu sellan þonne
mot he feohtan on hine. ჳif *he wille* on hond ჳan
7 *his wæpenu sellan* 7 *hwa ofer þæt on* him feohte
ჳielde *swa wer* swa wunde *swa he* ჳewyrce 7 wite

42, 5. 7 *hæbbe his mæჳ* forworh*t.* *Eac we* cwæðað þ. mon
*mote mid his h*laforde *feohtan orwiჳe* ჳif mon *on*
þone hlaforde fiohte swa mot se hlaford mid þy men

42, 6. *feohtan. æfter þære* ilcan wisan *mon mot feohtan*
mid his ჳeborene mæჳe. ჳif hine *mon* on woh on
*feohteð buton wið his h*laforde *þæt we* ne lyfað

42, 7. 7 *mon mot feohtan* orwiჳe ჳif he ჳemeteð o*þerne*
æt his ænum wife betynedum durum oþþe *un*
der anre reon *oþþe æt* his dehter æ*wum borenre*
oþþe æt his sweo*ter* borenre oþþe æt *his medder*
þe *wære to* æwum wife forჳyfen his fæ*der.*

43. *Eallum* frioum monnum þas daჳas *sien .XXXVIIII.*
*forჳy*fene butan þeowum monn*um* 7 *esne wyrhtan*
.XII. daჳas on ჳehhol 7 *þone dæჳ þe crist þone*
deofol oferswiþde 7 scs. *ჳreჳorius ჳemynd dæჳ*
7 .*VII.* daჳas to eastro*n* 7 .*VII. ofer* 7 *an dæჳ æt*
sce. petres tide 7 *sce.* pau*les* 7 *on hærfeste þa ful*
lan wican ær sca. *marian mæssan* 7 *æt eallra*
haliჳra weorþunჳe *anne dæჳ* 7 .*IIII. wodnes*
daჳas on .IIII. ymbren wicum þeowum monnum
eallum sien forჳifen þam þe him leofost sie

42, 7. sweoster borenre, cannot have been æwum bor., no room for
æwum; this clause is found above the line in E, and on the margin of
H, which latter, with Lamb, has æwum ‖ **43.** oferswiþde, d above.

140

APPENDIX A. MS. OT.

ʒesettes landes.   *.CX.*

66.   Se þe hæbbe þreora hida *tæcne oþres healfes. .CXI.*

67.   Ʒyf mon *ʒeþinʒað* ʒyrde londes *oþþe mare to ræde*
ʒafole 7 *ʒeereð* ʒif se hlaford him *wile þæt land aræ*
ran to weorce 7 *to* ʒafole ne þearf *he him onfon ʒif*
he him nan botl ne selð 7 *þolie þara æcra. .CXII.*

68.   Ʒif mon *ʒesiðcundne monnan adrife fordrife þy*
botle næs þære setene.   *.CXIII.*

69.   Sceap *sceal ʒonʒan mid his fliese oð midne sumor*
oþþe *ʒilde þæt flys mid twam pæninʒum. .CXIIII.*

70.   *Æt twyhyndum* were *mon sceal sellan to mon bote*
.XXX. scill. æt syx *hyndum .LXXX. scill. æt .XII.*

70, 1. *hyndum .CXX. scill. æt .X. hidum to* fostre *.X. fata*
hunies .CCC. hlafa .XII. ambra *wilisces* eala\ð
.XXX. hluttres tu eald hriþeru oþþe *.X.* weðeras
*.X. ʒees .XX. henn*a *.X.* cesas amber fulne *buteran*
.V. leaxas .XX. pundwæʒa fodres 7 hund *teontiʒ*
æla.   .CXV.

71.   *Ʒif mon sie wertyhtlan* betoʒen 7 *he hit þonne*
ʒeondette beforan aðe 7 *onsace ær bide mon mid*
þære wite rædenne oð ðæt se wer ʒeʒolden sie.

72.   *Ʒif mon werʒild þeof ʒefehþ* 7 *he losiʒe .CXVI.*
ðy dæʒe þam monnum þe hine *ʒefoð þeah*
hine mon ʒefo ymb niht nah him mon mare
æt þonne fulwite.   *.CXVII.*

73.   *Ʒif hit bið nihteald þiefð ʒebeten þa þone ʒylt*
þe hine ʒefenʒon swa hie ʒeþinʒian mæʒen

---

67. Ʒyf, i above y. || **70, 1.** fodres perhaps foðres || ll of scill,
end of 70, is last of the part reset as fol. 52, fostre and all below is
from 53 || This page most charred and blackened of all: the little that
can be deciphered costs great labour.

THIRD FRAGMENT. (FOL. 52—53.)

wið cyning 7 his ʒerefan. .CXVII*l*.
74. *Ʒif þeow wealh enʒlis*cne monnan ofslihð þonne
     sceal se þe hine ah weorpan hine to honda hlaforde
74, 1. *7 mæʒum oþþe* .LX. scill. ʒesellan wið his feore. ʒif he
     þonne þone ceap nelle foreʒesel*lan* þonne mot
     *hine se hlaford ʒefreoʒean ʒield*en siþþan his mæʒ
     *as þone wer ʒif he mæʒburʒ h*æbbe freo ʒif he
74, 2. *næbbe heden his þa ʒefan ne* þearf se friʒe mid
     *þam þeowan mæʒʒieldan buto*n he him wille fæhþe
     ofaceapian ne se þeowa mid þy friʒean. .CXIX.
75. *Ʒif mon ceap* befehþ *forsto*llenne 7 *sio* hond tymþ
     *þonne s*io hine mon æt befehð to oþrum men *ʒif*
     *se m*òn hine *þon. onfon ne* wille 7 sæʒþ þ. *he him næfre*
     þ. ne sealde *ac* sealde oþer þonne mot *se ʒecyðan*
     se þe hit tiemþ to þære honda *þ. he him nan oþer ne*
     sealde buton þ. ilce.   .CXX.
76. Ʒif hwa oþres ʒodsunu slea *oþþe his ʒodfæder sie*
     sio mæʒbot 7 sio manbot ʒe*lic weaxe sio* bot
     be þam were swa ilce swa sio *manbot deð þe þam*
76, 1. *h*laforde sceal. *ʒif hit þonne kyninʒes ʒodsunu*
     sie bete be his were *þam cyninʒe swa ilce swa þære*
76, 2. *mæʒþe. ʒif he þonne on þone ʒeonb*yrde *þe hine*
     sloʒ þon. ætfealle sio bot þæm ʒodfæder *swa*
     ilce swa þ. *wite þa*m hlaforde *deð ʒif hit biscep*
     sunu sie sie be healfum þam.

What remains of this page is quite legible, the fire having at-
tacked the other side more directly. All in 74, also llenne, ð to oþr,
wille 7 sæʒþ, onne mot, belongs to the upper fragment (52); Ʒif, þ be,
and all below, to the lower (53).

142

APPENDIX B.   MS. BU.

æfter *þam wære aw*endende þas ure domas.

1. Ærest we *beb*eodaþ þte ᵹodes .XLV.
ðeowas h*i*ora ryht reᵹol on ryht heal
den. æfter þæ. we bebeodað þte ealles fol
ces æw 7 domas þus sien ᵹehealdenne .XLVI.

2. *C*ild binnan .XXX. nyhtu. sie ᵹefullod. ᵹif hit
swa ne sie .XXX. scill. ᵹebete. Ᵹif hit ðon.
sie dead buton fulwihte ᵹebete he hit
mid eallu. þæm þe he aᵹe. .XLVII.

3. Ᵹif þeowmon werce on sunnan dæᵹ be his
hlafordes hæse sie he freoh 7 se hlaford

3, 1. ᵹes*elle* .*XXX.* scill. *to wite.* ᵹif þon. se þeowa
butan his ᵹewitnysse wyrce þolie his

3, 2. hyd*e.* ᵹif ðon. se friᵹea þy dæᵹe wyrce
buton hlafordes hæse þolie his freotes .XLVIII.

4. Ciric sceattas sien aᵹifene be Sce. mar
tines mæssan. Ᵹif hwa þ. ne ᵹelæste sie he
scildiᵹ .LX. scill. 7 be .XII. fealdu. aᵹife
ðone ciric sceat.   .XLVIIII.

5. Ᵹif hwa sie deaþes scyldiᵹ 7 cirican ᵹeær
ne habbe his feorh 7 bete swa him

5, 1. ryht wisie. Ᵹif hwa his hyde forwer
ce 7 cirican ᵹeirne sie hi. sio swinᵹel
le forᵹifen.   .L.

6. Ᵹif hwa ᵹefeohte on kininᵹes huse sie he

Italics for the parts wanting and supplied from E. Abbrev. retained
with period after the abbrev. inst. of mark over last letter, as in Ms. Note
that from upper right-hand corner of second page and from upper left-
hand corner of third most is gone; on the double leaf these are contiguous.
For information concerning Ms. see pp. 13, 20, 26.

143

FIRST LEAF.

scyldiȝ ealles *his ierfes* 7 *sie on cyninȝes dome*

6, 1. hwæþer he lif habbe *þe næbbe. 3if hwa on mynst*er ȝefeohte *hund twelftiȝ scill ȝe*

6, 2. bete. *3if hwa on ealdormonnes huse* oð ðe on oðres ȝeþunȝenes *witan ȝefeohte .LX.* scll. ȝebete 7 oðer .LX. *scill ȝeselle to wite.*

6, 3. 3if mon on ȝafolȝildan *huse* oððe on ȝebu res ȝefeohte .CXX. scill. *to wite ȝeselle*

6, 4. 7 þam bure .VI. scill. 7 *þeah hit sie on mid* dan felda ȝefeohtan .CXX. *scill. to wite sie*

6, 5. *aȝifen. 3if ðonne* bið on ȝebeor*scipe ȝeciden* 7 *oðer hiora mid* ȝeðylde *hit forbere ȝeselle* se oðer *.XXX. scill. to wite.*   *.LI.*

7. 3if hwa sta*lie swa his wif nyte* 7 *his bearn ȝe*

7, 1. selle .LX. scill. *to wite. ȝif he ðonne stalie on ȝe* witnysse eallæs his hired*es ȝonȝen hie*

7, 2. ealle on ðeowot .X. wintre *cniht mæȝ* beon þeofðe ȝewitæ.   *.LII.*

8. 3if hwa hine ryhtes bidde b*eforan hwelcum* scirmen oððe oðru. dema*n* 7 a*biddan ne* mæȝe 7 hi. wed sellan nelle ȝebete mid .XXX. scill. 7 binnan .VII. nyhtu. ȝedo hine ryh tes weorðe.   *.LIII.*

9. 3if hwa wræce do ær ðon he hi. ryhtes bidde þ. he hi. onnime aȝife 7 forȝylde 7 ȝebete

---

7, 2. ȝewitæ or ȝewitte.

144

APPENDIX B. MS. BU.

mid .XXX. scill. .LIIII.

10. *Ȝif hwa binnan þam ȝemæru.* ures rices
reaflac 7 niednæme do aȝife he þone
*reaflac 7 ȝeselle .LX. sci*ll. to wite. .LV.

11. *Ȝif hwa his aȝenne* ȝeleod bebycȝe þeow
ne oððe friȝne þeah he scildiȝ sie ofer
sæ forȝielde hine his were. .LVI.

12. *Ȝif þeof sie* ȝefonȝen swelte he deaðe oððe
his lif be his were monna liese .LVII.

13. *Ȝif hwa beforan biscope his* ȝewitnesse
7 his wed aleoȝe ȝebete mid hund twelf
tiȝum scill. .LVIII.

13, 1. Þeofas we hatað .VII. men. from .VII. hloð

14. oð .XXXV. siððan bið here. se ðe hloðe be
tyȝen sie ȝeswicne he hine be .CXX. hida
oððe swa bete. .LVIIII.

15. Se ðe here teame betiȝen sie he hine
be his wereȝilde aliese oððe be his

15, 1. were ȝeswicne. se að sceal byon healf be
huslȝenȝum. .LX.

15, 2. Þeof sið þan he bið on kininȝes bende

16. nah he þa swycne. Se ðe þeof ofslehð
he mot ȝeceþan mit aþe þ. he hine syn
niȝne ofsloȝe nalles þa ȝeȝildanum.

17. Se þe forstolen flæsc findeð .LXI.

---

12. liese or læse.

SECOND LEAF.

7 ӡederneð ӡif he dear he mot mid aðe ӡecyðan
þæt he hit aӡe, se ðe hit ofspereð he *ah þ. meld*
feoh.   .LXII.

18.   Cirlisc mon ӡif he oft betwyӡen wære *ӡif*
he æt siþestan sie ӡefonӡen slea mon h*ond*
oððe fot.   .LXIII.

19.   Cyninӡes ӡeneat ӡif his wer biþ twelf hun*d*
scill. he mot sweriӡen for sixtiӡ hida *ӡif*
he bið huslӡenӡa.   .LXIIII.

20.   Ӡif forcund mon oððe fremde buton weӡe
ӡeond wudu ӡonӡe 7 ne hrime ne horn *blawe*
for ðeof he bið to profianne oððe to slean
ne oððe to lesanne.   .LXV.

21.   Ӡif mon ðon. þæs ofslæӡenan weres bidde
he mot ӡecyþan þæt he hine for ðeofðe
ofsloӡe nalles þæs ofslæӡenan ӡeӡildan

21, 1.   ne his hlaford. ӡif he hit dirneð 7 wierðeð
ymb lonӡ yppe þon. remeð he þæm deadan
to þæm aðe þ. hine moton his mæӡes unsinӡian.

22.   Ӡif þin ӡeneat stalie 7 losie ðe ӡif .LXVI.
þu habbe berӡan manna ðone þæs anӡeldes.
ӡif he næbbe ӡeld ðu þ. anӡelde 7 ne sie him
no ðy ðinӡodre.   .LXVII.

23.   Ӡif mon elþeodiӡne ofslea se kininӡ ah twæd
ne dæl weres ðriddan dæl sunu oððe mæӡes.

APPENDIX C. BOTH TEXTS OF

MS. B, p. Ðis is ðæt friðð ðæt ælfred cyninc 7 ᵹyðrum cyninᵹ
83, l. 15. 7 ealles anᵹelcynnes witan 7 eal seo ðeod ðe on east
ænᵹlum beoð ealle ᵹecweden habbað 7 mid aðum ᵹe-
feostnod for hy sylfe 7 for heora ᵹinᵹran, ᵹe for
ᵹeborene ᵹe for unᵹeborene, ðe ᵹodes miltse recce oððe
1.   ure.   Ærest ymb ure landᵹemæra : up on temese, 7
ðonne up on liᵹan, 7 andlanᵹ liᵹan oð hire æwylm,
ðonne on ᵹerihte to bedan forda, ðonne up on usan oð
*P. 84. 2. wætlinᵹa stræt.   *Ðæt is ðonne, ᵹif man ofslæᵹen
weorðe, ealle we lætað efen dyrne enᵹliscne 7 deniscne,
to .VIII. healf mearcum asodenes ᵹoldes, buton ðam
ceorle ðe on ᵹafollande sit 7 heora liesenᵹum, ða syndan
3.   eac efen dyre æᵹðer to .CC. scill.; 7 ᵹif man cyninᵹes
ðeᵹn beteo manslihtes, ᵹif he hine ladian dyrre, do he
þæt mid .XII. cininᵹes ðeᵹnum; ᵹif ma ðone man betyhð ðe bið læssa maᵹa ðone se cyninᵹes ðeᵹn, ladiᵹe
he hine mid .XI. his ᵹelicena 7 mid anum cyninᵹes
ðæᵹne; 7 swa æᵹehwilcre spræce ðe mare sy ðone
.IIII. mancussas; 7 ᵹyf he ne dyrre, ᵹylde hit ðryᵹylde
4.   swa hit man ᵹewyrðe. 7 þæt ælc man wite his ᵹetyman
5.   be mannum 7 be horsum 7 be oxum.   7 ealle we
cwædon on ða dæᵹe ðe mon ða aðas swor þæt ne
ðeowe ne freo ne moton in ðone here faran butan leafe
ne heora nan ðe ma to us; ᵹif ðonne ᵹebyriᵹe þæt for
neode heora hwylc wið ure biᵹe habban wille oððe we
wið heora mid yrfe 7 mid æhtum, ðæt is to ðafianne
on ða wisan þæt man ᵹislas sylle friðe to wedde 7
to swutulunᵹe þæt man wite ðæt man clæne bæc hæbbe.

Variants of Lamb. trom Text I: fryþe | cyninᵹ | eastenᵹlum | ᵹe-
fæstnod | hi || **2.** Headed Be ofslæᵹenan mannes were | ofslaᵹen | butan |
ðæm | lysinᵹum | syndon || **3.** Headed Be ðeᵹnum ðe betoᵹene synd |
mon | manslihtes beteo | dô | cyninᵹes | st. ma ðone man, mon ðonne
ðeᵹn | ðeᵹne for ðæᵹne | æᵹhwylcre | ðonne | ᵹif | dyrne | ᵹyld | ðry-
ᵹyld | mon || **4.** Headed Be ᵹetymum | And, vac. þæt || **5.** ðæm st. ða | nân |
hwylce | hæbban | mon | fryþe | vac. to wedde 7 | swutelunᵹe | mon | mon |
clæn | marg. al. flæsc || On both Mss. all the names of the places are
scribbled on the margin.

TREATY BETWEEN ÆLFRED AND GUTHRUM.

P. 6. Ðis is þæt frið ðæt ælfred cynʒ 7 ʒuðrum cinʒ 7 ealles
anʒelcynnes witan 7 eal sêo ðeod ðe on eastenʒlum
beoð, 7 ʒesworen habbað ʒe for hy sylfe ʒe
for heora ofspryʒ.

1. Ærest ymbe heora landʒemæra: andlanʒ temese
þonne up on liʒean, andlanʒ liʒean oð hire æwylm,
ðanon on ʒerihta to beda forda, þanon upon on usan
2. oð wætlinʒa strǣt. 7 hi cwædon, ʒyf mon ofslæʒen
wurðe, eal we letað efen dyrne enʒliscne 7 denisce, þæt
is to .VIII. healf marcum asodenes ʒoldes, buton ðam
ceorle ðe on ʒafollande sit, 7 hêora lysynʒon. . . . . .
3. 7 ʒyf man cynʒes ðeʒen beteo manslihtas
7 he hine ladian durre, do hê þæt mid .XII. cynʒes
þeʒnas 7 ʒyf mon ðone man betyhð þe bið læssa
maʒa, ladie hîne .XI. his ʒelicena, 7 anum cyninʒes
ðeʒene.

5. 7 ealle hiʒ ʒecwædon ða man þa aðas swor þæt
naðor ne we on ðone hêre faran buton leafe, ne heora
non ða ma to us, buton man trywan 7 betwynan
ʒyslas sylle, friðe to wedde 7 to swutelunʒe þæt man
mid rihte fare, ʒyf þæt ʒeneodiʒe, þæt ure æniʒ to
oðrum fæce mid yrfe and mid æhtum.

Above Text II, red Alfredes Laʒa Cyninʒes. Above swor new cweþ,
making ʒecweþen prob., on marg. new 7 mid aþum ʒefæstnod | ofspryn
underlined and to ʒ inʒran added new ‖ 2. 7 hi cwædon, on marg. þæt
is þonne | lysynʒon, eras. here, on which þa sy ndoneac efendyre new;
æʒþer twa hund scyll. follows above and on marg.‖ 5. ða ma, e new
above a of ða ‖

See for information p. 16. and Schmid, Einl. XXXVIII — XXXIX.
Text I is the original form.

www.ingramcontent.com/pod-product-compliance
Lightning Source LLC
Chambersburg PA
CBHW021539260326
41914CB00001B/83